A PROVEN MANAGEMENT MANUAL

THE TRUTH OF THE MATTER

CONTENTS

CHAPTER TWO   p. 24

ONSITE WORK ON BUSINESS CHALLENGES

CHAPTER THREE

> A COLLATION OF THE PRINCIPLES USED TO RESOLVE
> THE ONSITE BUSINESS CHALLENGES

> THREE STARTING REQUIREMENTS THAT ENABLE
> AN ORGANISATION TO FURTHER DEVELOP ITS MANAGING HABITS

INTRODUCTION

I have spent the past thirty seven years supporting managers in seven organisations across six industries (oil, drinks, agricultural chemicals, dairy foods, packaging, and education), in their efforts to resolve novel or previously intractable problems – such as setting up a more effective and different type of multinational, turning around failing corporations, achieving the change from crisis to proactive business management in an originally loss making organisation and radically improving production standards to levels that are factors ahead of industry best standards, etc.

This manual enables the line manager to study and re-apply the managing principles derived solely from the above successful operational work. Efforts also had to be made to simultaneously improve how the organisation performed as a whole. Principles from this wider activity are also detailed to allow the reader to appropriately re-apply them.

The unusual fact that these principles derive solely from successful experience has given them three distinct features:

- firstly, they have had to accurately take account of every fundamental issue at the root of the operational problems. They therefore bypass the artificial boundaries and missed interactions unavoidably built into any management theory, and the modular analysis / training of management concerns

- secondly, they have provided a secure way of replicating successful business results across different organisations and industries. They have been thoroughly and repeatedly tested in every detail in the most demanding of business challenges in the various industries. Targeted commercial results were always exceeded, and better than industry-best standards achieved in the majority of cases

- thirdly, the scope and depth of work needed to solve the operational challenges produced the much sought-after 'cultural change' across the organisation, which conventional management theory and modular training has difficulty in reliably achieving

The manual also summarises tried and tested guidelines for re-applying these principles to different organisations and industries. The reader can then take account of these in forming his/her own judgement on how to improve their own situation.

CHAPTER ONE

CURRENT MANAGEMENT 'METHODS'
DO NOT PERFORM WELL ENOUGH

PRINCIPLES DERIVED SOLELY FROM EXPERIENCE
PRODUCE FAR BETTER RESULTS

NATURE OF THIS WORK

As an ex line manager, I have had the privilege of supporting managers in six industries (oil, drinks, agricultural chemicals, dairy foods, packaging and education) and seven organisations to successfully tackle a range of challenges. Over the last thirty seven years' work they have included:

- turning around consistently failing corporations

- creating a fundamentally different and more effective multinational

- moving loss making organisations to sustainable profit by achieving the change from crisis to business management

- radically uprating the performance of production functions to a step change beyond industry best standards

- moving a national subsidiary company within a multinational out of its 'performance doldrums'

- retrieving the start up and commissioning of new production facilities whose scale and technology were a step change up from the rest of the world's competition

etc.

These challenges and others described later had previously proved to be intractable or were novel to the management teams concerned. The work involved every single function of an organisation, and reached into every aspect of its business. Case histories are detailed in Chapter Two. Managing principles were progressively analysed from each operational problem and successfully retested in challenges within subsequent different organisations and industries. They are consequently thoroughly battle-hardened in every detail, and repeatedly proven in the most difficult of situations. They have always delivered better than targeted results throughout the many years of testing, and in most cases significantly better than industry-best standards were achieved.

The most direct way of illustrating this work is to describe a part of the challenges faced within one of the organisations. The problems confronting managers are outlined, together with their responses and the results they achieved.

TYPICAL EXAMPLE   **AN OPERATIONS DIRECTOR IMPROVES THE PERFORMANCE**
OF HIS WHOLE AREA

o   **A more effective, less busy picture of how to run the business starts to form.**

I was once asked by an ambitious, hard working new Operations Director of a recently formed multinational food company how I would recognise his success in twelve months' time.

'It's going to be really simple,' I said. 'I'm going to be standing in your office, as I'm doing now, and your desk will be clear of everything on it except for maybe two documents – generally only one. You will be relaxed and enjoying yourself, because there will long periods in the working day when you will not be under any time pressure – or any other pressure. There will be no back to back meetings, no queue at the door, no backed up phone calls and messages to deal with, and no simmering emergencies that you personally need to get involved with. You will be the one manager in your part of the organisation with the maximum time to just think, or go and visit some part of the operation, and observe what is happening. You will be starting and ending each day at the normal business times, and not be working at weekends. You will be taking leisurely lunch breaks. I will be able to just drop into your office, at any time, and you will always be able to immediately spend time with me. You will feel no pressure in taking time out to have a leisurely but penetrative discussion.' He was speechless, then laughed and said, ' I'm far too busy to lead that sort of life '.

'Yes, I can certainly see that is true,' I replied, 'as things stand now. But am I right in understanding that the company's plans over the next year indicate that this operation has somehow to substantially improve its capacity at a reduced cost? You're already working much longer hours than any of your managers – and they're all working the very hardest that they know how to. What do you think? Can that improvement come from continuing to do much as you're doing now?' He thought for quite a while, and said that he couldn't see that happening. I agreed.

o **The Director and his men work hard at working differently.**

He worked hard over the next year to develop his daily managing habits by applying the principles described in Chapter Three. He diligently helped his senior managers to do the same. He encouraged and supported their efforts to enable each of their management lines to carry out similar work on their own particular habits. All this happened within the tackling of the normal daily business. There was no special 'change programme', no special 'additional activity', no 'specially designed diagnostic tools', no 'special task forces', and no 'new jargon to describe everything with'. No new management band wagon rolled into town. They just concentrated on managing the usual daily business problems differently. This is not to say that they didn't find it difficult. Much sustained effort was spent. Changing long standing managing habits 'on the job' has always proved to be no mean feat. However, line managers clearly understood the principles that they had to re-apply in their own style to achieve this change within their teams. They used proven guidelines distilled from others' successful re-application of this work which are detailed in Chapter Four.

One day I popped in unannounced. He had his feet on the desk – a clear desk, with just his diary on it, and an agenda for a meeting scheduled in two days' time. We chatted for around an hour about a complex issue, had an early lunch, and he went back to do some thinking about a strategic issue in one of the overseas operations. There wasn't an emergency – he just thought it might be prudent to do the thinking ahead of time. He didn't even think that what had just happened between us was worthy of note. It was just the way life was for him–now. It was only when I met him and his wife for dinner that night that she reminded him very forcibly of the total change he had wrought in his working life – and in the lives of the teams that worked for him. She had heard chapter and verse from their wives.

o **The challenge is effectiveness – not activity.**
The prize is commercial success.
The reward is improving the quality of people's lives.

It is tempting to live a life filled in every moment with pressured activity, a continuously overloaded time schedule, involvement in many more activities than the ones already over crowding the diary, as proof that 'I'm doing an important job, important things are happening, I'm giving the business value for money with all this frenetic activity'.

In all the instances where I have seen these managing habits, the improvement in productivity and effectiveness that is possible is truly startling. The consequent commercial prizes have proved beyond what was previously imagined as possible.

The reward in improving the quality of people's lives has been fundamental. People who worked for this Operations Director said that they used to come to work very early. They saw each day as one in which they would work their hardest and longest. They would usually be unhappy and dissatisfied with what was achieved. 'Now', they said, 'we look forward to coming into work. There's a smile on our faces. We know that whatever we tackle, the strong chance is 'we're going to win'. There isn't much we can't do successfully.' Commercially, that indeed turned out to be the case for this Director and his teams. They became the hub of a growing and successful multinational food company operating in the EEC, and a key player in securing a sustained and rapidly growing bottom line.

He said to me after some time, 'I now realise that it isn't the amount I do that counts. It's what I achieve, and the way it's achieved.'

- ○ **TWO EXAMPLE ISSUES THAT WERE WORKED AT EFFECTIVELY**

Of course, there was a great deal beneath the surface of this example, which explained how such a fundamental and sustainable development was achieved. To give the reader a more detailed grasp of the direction of this work, a flavour of two of the issues tackled is briefly outlined below.

- ▪ **The processes that would produce the desired targets were continuously focused on. The targets themselves were regarded as just one consequence of those processes.**

  The Operations Director – I shall name him Jack to preserve his anonymity – had previously followed the convention of putting tremendous pressure on the delivery of targets. His different managing habit was to put sustained and continuous pressure on whatever were the fundamental processes that would produce the desired numerical indices. These always proved to be intangible.

  For example, he would always press his managers to unearth exactly what would produce a targeted sales performance to a given major customer. In a typical instance, some additional feature was particularly desired in the relevant product range. He would press further, and as an example, find that the key bottleneck in installing that feature was the availability of certain production plant for new product testing. He would press even further, and get his managers to grasp that in the particular instance the process of agreeing priorities between manufacturing and product development would control how soon that equipment could be used for testing new products. He would then be sure that he had his managers focused on one of the root intangible processes that was particularly crucial to producing the targeted sales performance. He subsequently ensured that he was regularly updated on that issue of priorities from both product development and production managers. He would not even mention the 'end result' of the original desired target, except to regularly and privately check on its progress.

  His teams therefore developed the skill of identifying and focussing on the intangible processes at the root of desired targets. The basis and reasoning for such a way of managing are explained in detail in Chapter Three. Suffice it to say at this point that it always achieved the desired targets, radically altered how business was transacted, and stimulated far more initiatives within the business. It also had the effect of substantially eroding an original culture of 'blaming and avoidance' that is a common feature of target focussed organisations, and instead, nourished people's desire to cooperate.

- **The 'no go' area of Engineering Maintenance was reclaimed for the business.**

  Jack fundamentally restructured the engineering function that maintained the equipment in all his factories.

  He started with a virulently unionised, staggeringly expensive, deeply entrenched workforce, who demonstrated outstanding creativity in inventing restrictive practices. These led to maximum manning and overtime levels, and minimum work output of the poorest quality. Problems had to be repeatedly reworked. His previous managing habit was the convention of regarding and treating these men as one group. Countless weeks and months and much resented energy were consequently spent negotiating with the unions – to no good effect.

  His different strategy was to manage the same men individually, and form them into small line managed teams (i.e. a maximum of around six people). These operated to the same principles as all his other managed teams. The productivity and quality dramatically rose, and permanently sustained their new levels. The costs were consistently minimised, manning levels fell to less than industry minimums, and all restrictive practices totally and permanently disappeared. There was no industrial unrest in installing these developments. The detailed principles that led to these changes are also explained in detail in Chapter Three.

BACKGROUND CONTEXT

To understand how such effective, wide-ranging methods have evolved, and exactly what caused their unusual success, I need to explain what prompted the search for these principles. The truth of the matter needs to be said about the common trends within in our organisations today. Some of those trends are significant strengths; some are less helpful. As an ex manager who's spent his life working alongside other managers, I have tried, like all my colleagues, to use those strengths to grapple with the less helpful trends. That effort eventually persuaded me to seek out better ways of tackling difficulties and improving how total organisations worked. I became convinced that those methods could only be derived from sustained problem solving to tackle live operational challenges in a variety of industries. Particular characteristics of those methods are briefly summarised below (p.20).

You will then be clear what initially stimulated this work to commence and have a picture of the direction it took. This is intended to put you in an informed position to decide whether you will take any further interest in this manual.

Should you decide to venture further into this material, you will also better understand the nature of what you will be exploring.

THE BAD NEWS

- **OUR CURRENT MANAGEMENT 'METHODS' DO NOT PERFORM WELL ENOUGH**

Organisations find the present conditions difficult. They will get far more difficult.

Today's world poses tough challenges for our organisations. Market conditions demand reliable efficiency, increasing flexibility, and sustained innovation, all delivered in very testing financial circumstances. Those enterprises that do not master these challenges and their many associated problems languish at the bottom of their market places, or disappear at increasing speed. All the major trends and predictions for market conditions, financial, regulatory and environmental factors say that tomorrow's world will inexorably raise the bar significantly on all those challenges. Our organisations will have no choice but to find ways to operate at even better standards, at even higher reliability levels, and deliver more striking numerical results in even tighter financial circumstances. The inevitable continued emergence of the East Asian economies alone will ensure that this pressure is exerted. This and other clear market trends show that organisations failing to find those ways of coping with the rising bar will disappear at even quicker speeds.

Our current norms for organisational efficiency have significant shortcomings.

Of course it is risky to generalise. However, supporting the intense work by managers to solve large scale operational problems across the six industries concerned discloses a consistent and vulnerable picture. There was a natural wide variation in the operation of the seven organisations involved in those industries. Reported information from other organisations' operations also exampled that variation. Nevertheless, it became very clear over the period that our management population experienced certain underlying trends in their work places.

On the positive side, we:

- can demonstrate the ability to fundamentally improve how our organisations respond to large challenges. The commercial results are excellent when this happens. It is a beacon of hope, and unfortunately is very much the exception

- have a wealth of talented, hard working managers who genuinely want to make a key difference to how business is done. They have demonstrated the tenacity to keep doing their best despite the worst excesses of their organisations

- possess a depth of technical talent across our many industries that is also highly innovative.

On the negative side, we:

- **obsess about new management theory/fashion.**

  We have a tendency to roll a series of 'new management band wagons' through the doors of the organisation.

This stems from seeking out the latest management theory/guru and 'getting religion'. It is not the fault of the theories that management teams become fundamentalist believers in their thinking. A lot of the theories have interesting, creative, and thought-provoking ideas to offer. They are capable of usefully prompting managers' own independent re-examination of their problems, and re-thinking how they might tackle them. Unfortunately, the trend is to become a 'slave' to such theories and not their 'master'. We choose to be mesmerised by the physical trappings of the new theory and insist on everyone applying them with totalitarian uniformity. Only 'the new diagrammatic diagnostic tool(s)' should be used, all problems at all presentations will have to be described in 'the new terminology/jargon', 'the new change programme' will be rigidly applied across all departments and ahead of any other priority, all managers will attend all 'the newly created task force activities that will operate a fixed formulaic way of tackling affairs dictated by the theory', only 'the new type of structure invented by the theory' will be rigidly installed across the organisation, etc. And so the new band wagon comes to town.

Prudent, hard working, independently minded, effective managers realise that they still have a business to deliver, and that they will be roundly condemned if they fail to do so. They also know that significant 'political skin' will have been invested in the new band wagon by some influential people. They have therefore dutifully learned to sing all the new band wagon songs with the best of them. Much grinding of teeth has followed as they realise that their work load has doubled. They have to continue completing all their existing duties to deliver the business as well as engage with all the extra activities and work devised by the band wagon.

Eventually – and it could take a very long time – one possibility has been that people start to notice that the solutions being implemented continually fail to deliver consistent, sustainable, quality commercial results. Gradual disenchantment follows and the stage is set for the next step.

The search for the new theory.

It has often been met with the same infatuated zeal as the last one. Another new band wagon comes to town, complete with the different merchandising devised by the theory's inventors. The hard working, effective, now long suffering managers try and get used to the repeated doubling of their work load. They realise that whatever happens, they still have to continue performing their normal activities that deliver their business. They have mortgages to pay and families to look after. They are obliged to undertake the band wagon inspired activities and take part in what they regard as a cyclic charade during which their organisation is operating at a vulnerably low standard.

Management by blindly following any theory – no matter how creative and ground-breaking – has abrogated the central managing obligation to independently think, analyse and implement our own solutions to our problems. It has fostered a dependency on outside influences – not a healthy, robust, enquiring independence. It has contributed unhelpfully to how our organisations work.

- **see management issues as self-contained, separated 'modules'.**
  Inevitably, we are driven to repeatedly 'solve' the same management problems.

Our ingrained habit is to view and market each management issue as a separate, stand alone module.

The market place overflows with 'leadership', 'motivation', 'teamwork', 'strategy', 'time management', and 'decision making' modules, amongst many others. Each module offers an analysis of its chosen issue, which has some useful and relevant things that the ordinary manager can apply. I have been trained through some of them and am grateful for that initial help. Having said that, the everyday reality facing each line manager is that the problems he faces are the direct result of a combination of particular management issues. In addition, those problems are inescapably influenced by the inherent interactions between those issues. They have never been, nor can ever be, self-contained. A brief pause for an example may be useful.

A typical instance was that a persistent product quality problem resulted from:

- the way in which a production team had been led

- its method of decision taking

- and the way it generated its operating procedures

Equally, the problem was as deeply influenced by the interactions that inescapably exist between these managing issues of leadership, decision taking, and generating procedures. This situation could only be sustainably improved when those interactions were thoroughly understood and taken account of within the plans to correct matters. Each management issue has only been competently analysed in the light of its inevitable interactions and interdependence with other management issues.

Applying the stand alone conventional modular analysis for any of these issues ignores this key reality, and provides solutions that cannot strike at the very roots of the difficulty. Managers relying on such solutions are then faced with the problem returning in different guises. They feel 'the ground hog day' experience starting to haunt their problem solving efforts.

- **isolate strategy from both the core daily business, and the commitment and creativity of our working managers.**

The convention is that strategy – throughout its many meanings – is something that results from a piece of work solely happening at the senior level. It is a handed-down piece of thinking created from issues only one level in the organisation has selected as its priorities. It is a tablet of stone. Two key effects have followed.

- Firstly, the statements in that strategy reflect the senior team's view of issues that concern them. Quite properly, that view will be the broadest in scope, and be stated in the most generalised form compared to any other level. The detailed application of these broad generalised statements to all the key daily business issues facing the other levels cannot reasonably be spelt out in such a document. One of two options has then occurred.

  - Managers have needed to interpret the implications of the strategy for the actual business issues they grapple with. On the rare occasions this has happened, it has been equally rare to see an interchange with the senior team to check if that interpretation was consistent with the original strategic thinking.

  - Alternatively, in the majority of cases, managers have regarded the strategy statements as self-evidently correct, and so generalised as to only provide 'motherhood and apple pie' truisms. These cannot of their nature offer help in making the more detailed business choices facing them. Such strategies have then been consigned to live in drawers – in the dark – and only get paraded for the politically correct bits of high profile presentations. They become substantially isolated from the daily business carried out at all operational levels in the organisation.

- Secondly, as the concerns and thinking of every other level in the organisation are excluded from this type of strategy, this tablet of stone eliminates at a stroke their ability to contribute supportively to this work by the senior team. Any commitment and creativity that others throughout the enterprise are capable of offering to such a challenge is denied the business. Indeed, this type of strategy and its way of formulation has been interpreted as meaning 'they (i.e. the senior team) are not interested in our experience', and 'we (i.e. the senior team) will decide on our own what we're all going to be committed to'. All managers except those at the senior level are disenfranchised from a pivotal decision making process. As a result we nurture conformity and not commitment and creativity. The business is the significant loser.

These three trends are a small selection from a large range, each of which has significant negative effects on businesses, people and organisations. Chapter Three deals with the replacement of all these trends, and the description of proven positive alternatives.

Looking at these weaknesses from the perspective of our strengths, the underlying way in which we operate our organisations is not as secure as it could be. It is not surprising that a lot of our organisations struggle with today's challenges. It makes tomorrow's challenges and the inevitable raising of the bar unnecessarily risky.

We need to tip the balance in our favour.

THE GOOD NEWS

● **PRINCIPLES SOLELY DERIVED FROM EXPERIENCE PRODUCE FAR BETTER RESULTS**

Line management experience points the way to start the search.

With a starting discipline in chemical engineering, I worked for eleven years as a line manager within an American oil multinational. I was lucky enough to witness many examples of managers who dealt effectively with a wide range of difficult problems and challenges. I still draw benefit from their fine example.

Nonetheless, I grew absolutely convinced that the above balance of strengths and weaknesses applied to the majority of organisations. I experienced that the ordinary working manager such as myself needed different and better tools to tackle complex operational problems. I saw that organisations needed similar quality tools to securely advance their operation as a whole and hence grow their businesses.

I realised that such answers could not come from any theory with its inbuilt artificial boundaries and assumptions. Initial involvement in working on operational problems sufficiently complex to affect the running of a whole organisation indicated a clear, unique, yet daunting route forwards.

> *'Fundamentally solve a large range of operational problems in different organisations and industries, and produce sustainable results.*
>
> *Analyse their success for principles that could be continuously retested in the solution of subsequent new operational problems.*
>
> *Continue repeating this 'learning and discovery from testing' until the range of proven principles unearthed from successful practice covered every aspect of the challenges facing managers and organisations.*
>
> *Collate the results, so that other managers could re-apply the principles in their own fashion to suit their problems and organisations.'*

I was simultaneously excited and daunted by the sheer scale of the challenge. I checked all the major consultancies and the management literature. There was no one out there attempting this. They were all concerned with piecemeal theories, pre-set proprietary packages, and modules. I tried ignoring the whole idea for a while. It all seemed too risky, and just too 'big'. However, I was continually and inexorably drawn back to the unyielding logic that underpinned such a quest. With both excitement and the greatest trepidation, I left the safe shores of full time employment with the oil multinational, and set out on an entirely uncertain journey. It very much felt like stepping off the planet, and leaving life as I had known it. Friends and family voiced understandable and strong concerns; where was the next meal coming from?, what was the long term future?, who else was doing this?, where were the managers whom I would need to work with and who understood what I was trying to do?, what reputable consultancy agreed with my idea?, had they tried it, and had it succeeded?, and what was I offering other managers and industries that was as easy to understand as the theories and modules which they already bought? I could only smile wryly, agree with their fears, and hope fervently that Providence would look after an apparent fool – but a convinced fool.

THE JOURNEY

That was thirty seven years ago.

The journey has been a white knuckle ride, challenged at every turn by the intractable or novel problems offered by every organisation I was invited into. It has been packed with the drama of the vivid personalities whose lives depended on and revolved around the successful solution of those problems. It has had its fair share of tension as the highest stakes of commercial survival and reputation were played for. Most of all it has had the elixir of fun – the very best fun: that of sustained success with hard working talented colleagues. By great good fortune and the determined stamina of those colleagues, all the operational problems yielded both successful sustainable commercial results, and the crock of principles I thought might exist. I can only say a deep thank you to all those managers who asked me for help with operational problems that they had previously wrestled with unsuccessfully. The fact that they then derived and implemented their own successful plans to solve those problems – aided by whatever support I could give them to help focus the principles they needed to apply in their own way – deserves my yet deeper thanks and my respect.

This is the management manual collating the results of the thirty seven year long 'exploration by testing' – including some early work done within the oil multinational.

● OUTLINE CHARACTERISTICS OF THE RESULTS

Business results

The numerical and other tangible results achieved have been better than industry-best standards. These have often been exceeded by significant margins: factors of 1.5 to 2 have been commonly reached. These are results that people are initially taken aback by and find hard to believe. As they talk to previous clients and hear the detail of their results, they become intrigued as to how they were made to come about – and remain sustainable.

Some of the key characteristics of the principles derived solely from experience.

This is a snapshot of some of the key features of those principles:

- As they emerged solely from successful problem solving, the exact manner in which they shape the characteristics of all our challenges becomes clear.

o Analysing the solution of actual operational problems shows that each relevant principle intimately interacts with the rest. Only such a work based analysis can disclose a full picture of this interdependence.

No imagined theory can possibly provide that understanding. In fairness, none has attempted to do so. By definition, the modular view of management issues does not recognise that such interactions exist.

Building them into the plans to solve problems has been the test as to whether the analysis disclosing them was accurate. Subsequent results have had to be sustainable, quantitative, and of high quality to validate that analysis. The fact that those results have unfailingly been delivered into a wide range of businesses/organisations/industries over a protracted period cannot be a happenstance.

o Every improvement to management habits to solve operational difficulties has been completely focused on what routinely happens to accomplish the everyday business. It has been led by the relevant line managers. They alone have developed the quality of the work they lead their subordinates to do within the daily problems. There are no externally inspired 'change programmes/new jargon/new diagnostic tools/new task forces', etc. that have been allowed to distract from the central obligation of carrying out that regular work more competently. The entire attention centres on gradually and relentlessly changing the habits to accomplish that duty – led only by those whose normal job it is to deliver it. This development work has only happened by integrating it both within the daily business and the leadership of each line manager.

o Strategy emerges as one of the key processes that can powerfully bind the whole organisation together. It has only achieved that when it has been meticulously led to involve every level in the organisation. That leadership has ensured that each level contributes its judgements on the directions it can take to best benefit the business at its level. The process also ensures that all the contributions across the different levels mutually support one another. The result is a continuum of strategy statements covering every key concern at each level. This has unleashed unusual and cohesive horsepower right across the organisation at its full range of commercial concerns. The strategy has become a living way of doing daily business. A key basis for sustainably improving the enterprise's performance has been put into position.

o The three factors that emerge as the cornerstones determining how the organisation operates as a whole are its structure, its procedures, and its man management areas. An example is the above described creation of a strategy using principles from the man management area. That work usefully specifies how to generate commitment and creativity in setting and agreeing aspirations for the business.

Each of these factors has a rich wealth of practical principles to offer. Identifying them from live problem solving has proved that each of the three factors themselves also intimately interacts with the other two. This has meant that systematically developing how the whole organisation works has demanded that those interactions are accurately understood and taken account of.

A practical example of this feature may help at this point.

An astute CEO realised that installing his new devolved structure would first require different procedures.

The new CEO of a troubled dairy foods company clearly saw the need to rescue his organisation by rapidly altering its moribund structure. He realised the pressing commercial necessity to install multidisciplinary teams responsible for delivering designated businesses within the enterprise.

Recognising that all his accounting and financial systems were totally centralised – the inheritance from a previously disastrous functionalised structure – he wisely saw that the first priority was to commence the work of setting up financial and accounting systems that solely served each designated business. Only when this procedural activity was well progressed, did he turn his attention to the core of the structural job of commissioning the new multidisciplinary teams.

He was richly rewarded for this systematic development by the new teams 'lifting off' at speed and playing a pivotal role in turning around the entire enterprise.

All the principles so far uncovered within these three cornerstone factors are recalled in Chapter Three.

●   **KEY FEATURES OF THE DEVELOPMENT WORK THAT UNCOVERED THE PRINCIPLES**

This has been a long sustained 'exploration by testing'.

Senior managers in various organisations have asked for help in tackling previously intractable or novel problems. The priority need was to support them to solve those difficulties, so that their businesses could rapidly and securely grow. The bonus has been to gradually uncover the principles underpinning that success, and have the chance to continuously retest them in the most challenging circumstances – in yet further operational problems in different organisations and industries.

This inevitably means that I have not 'invented' anything 'new' that is 'mine'. I realise that all I have done is be privileged enough to uncover what has always been there. It just may not have been clearly focused, or deliberately and systematically applied. It has, however, always been there for anyone to explore should they wish to do so.

I do not claim any of this work as 'my creation'. I would like to do so, as it has been remarkably successful – indeed 100% successful for forty years. However, the reality is that such success comes from the inescapable truth that the principles are inbuilt into the fabric of getting things done effectively in ways that nourish all the people doing the work. They are, and always have been, just a natural and inextricable part of doing things well.

This development work can therefore have no 'copyright' or exclusiveness to one person – certainly not to me. Instead it is open to all to pursue in their own chosen fashion.

The underlying reason for this manual is to invite you to consider taking the same journey to explore these principles that so excited and daunted me thirty seven years ago. Hopefully with the experience captured in this manual at your elbow, you will be less daunted, and can be more adventurous in however you choose to journey.

I wish you exciting and rewarding times.

Most of all, I wish you at least some of the fun I had.

CHAPTER TWO

ONSITE WORK ON BUSINESS CHALLENGES

A detailed account of tackling business challenges and difficulties

across different organisations and industries

INTENT AND FORMAT

This chapter was exciting to live through. Working through the various business difficulties was challenging to the point where success seemed on many occasions to be highly unlikely. However, it was also exhilarating, full of high drama, intense emotions and lots of laughter. Fortunately all the work also turned out to be highly successful and deeply rewarding.

Analysing the solution of these onsite difficulties has gradually disclosed the principles that form the basis for this work. This chapter sets out to share with the reader the detail of the operational challenges that drove the emergence of those principles. The second intention is that the reader can then refer back to this 'raw data' as he sifts through the full set of principles collated in Chapter Three.

The work is described in the following format:

The context of the challenge, and the perceived problem

- A statement of the client's business and needs prior to commencing the development work

What happened - Sequence/selection of events in the work

What the effects were - Some of the key results

What was learned - Highlights from the key lessons learned from the work

For the sake of simplicity the rest of this book refers to managers as 'he' – most of the people I have worked with have been men, though the women I have met have been exceptionally talented and been recognised as such. Clients who have implemented this work have also significantly increased the proportion of female managers beyond industry norms by paying rigorous attention to selection information – not gender. Please therefore take my stated 'he' to represent 'he/she' and 'his' to represent 'his/her', without any inference on diversity.

BUSINESS CHALLENGE ONE

MULTINATIONAL OIL COMPANY :   A SUCCESSFUL AFFILIATE COMPANY REPEATEDLY UNDER PERFORMS ON A KEY TARGET

CONTEXT OF THE CHALLENGE, AND THE PERCEIVED PROBLEM

The Scandinavian company affiliated to one of the largest American oil majors had a well deserved reputation as a competent and well run organisation. Its refining operation consistently performed well on the wide range of performance criteria set for such facilities. As a consequence it attracted significant and repeated investment from the American parent company. It was also understood that should any affiliate company consistently fail to meet their criteria, then the Americans would not hesitate to permanently shut down its operation. In the past they had swiftly closed down extremely large refining facilities that had repeatedly not met certain criteria. It was therefore vital to the Scandinavians that they sustained their pattern of consistently meeting their measures of success.

Worryingly, their performance against one specific target started to deteriorate. It was one that gave a particular measure of the entire operation's efficiency. With the very significant rise in the price of oil, any poor performance against this criterion meant the potential loss of large sums of revenue. Not unsurprisingly, strong attention was focused on correcting the situation. Unfortunately, internal task forces and changes in policy brought no improvement in results. The performance against the criterion continued to be unacceptable and erratic. The pressure rose higher to solve the problem, as the threat to reputation and inward investment loomed larger on the horizon.

I was still working full time for the multinational at the time, and was sent on assignment to the Scandinavian operation to help resolve this problem.

This was the seminal piece of work to which some of the early development principles were first applied. It was to play a key role in later convincing me to start off on the long journey to discovering what the rest of the principles were. That work would be as an independent consultant, partnering the efforts of fellow managers trying to solve problems in their organisations. However, at this stage, I was still an employee of this multinational, and directly responsible as an ordinary manager for this piece of work. It is therefore written from the memory of my own feelings. Consequently, this recall is somewhat personal in a way that the rest of the case studies in this chapter are not. The reader can make his own allowances for elements that are clearly and strongly subjective.

WHAT HAPPENED

The worst of starts

The work had a threatening and unpromising beginning: none of the relevant departments within the company were keen to discuss with me the detail of what was occurring. Past file notes about the problem were in Norwegian. The person who had written them and had previously analysed the problem had recently left the company. The numerical tables and graphs that he had appended to his work made little sense to me. Two weeks were allocated to finding an answer. Experience had shown that several man months were needed to analyse the performance against a target as complex as this one, and reach secure conclusions. The arrangements and resources for this assignment seemed so inappropriate that I began to suspect it was a political manoeuvre to ensure my failure. The Scandinavian operation could then be seen to be vindicated: 'Well, we tried our very best – even that guy from the UK who'd tackled this sort of thing before couldn't find anything wrong'. Indeed, I couldn't at the time see any way to succeed and began to picture ways of accepting defeat. I felt I was trapped in the deepest of pits, and turned to the only thing that had never failed me: certain principles that I had used in the past, without having the remotest idea what solution they might bring. I only knew that when I had previously followed them they had always succeeded. There were two principles in particular that had proved vital in handling other emergencies and 'tight corners'. They were the unlikely combination of:

- Rigorously reviewing progress every hour on the hour with absolutely no exception, and no interruption. The reviewing had to be done in a pattern and at a standard later described in the Man Management Section in Chapter Three.

- A minute examination of the meaning of the information to hand had to be a disciplined part of each review. Any action plans to probe those meanings would need to be quickly formed and immediately carried out.

The story started to unfold

During the first review, I pondered over every piece of information I had about the Scandinavian operation and probed them for meaning. I came across one that I knew to be a fact: the Scandinavian company had an outstanding reputation for operational excellence amongst its working crews. They were all recruited from the Scandinavian merchant navy. These men had a proven track record of meticulous procedural efficiency and reliability in complex refining operations. The departments within the company might not be keen to talk to me about what they regarded as a failure, but maybe the operating crews would. It seemed to me worth visiting the various shifts of operators – particularly the night shifts – and finding out what they knew of the operational problem the company had with the particular performance criterion. Their reputation said they were likely to know something.

It was like hitting the jackpot. They mostly spoke excellent English, or were keen to have what they wanted to say translated there and then. As was the habit with seamen – particularly the officer grade – they each carried a ubiquitous little black note book. They kept meticulous notes in these books of the detail of all the operations they had been part of. They were all aware of the problem with the particular performance index, were starved of being consulted about basic problems with the operation, and were fiercely enthusiastic to explain what they thought the causes were. They had copious data to validate their individual views. I was immediately given numerous leads as to the complex mixture of causes for the problem with the index. At a stroke, the access to diligently collated operational information, backed by the crews' surging enthusiasm to be involved in what they regarded as 'their operation', had totally transformed the situation. It had suddenly turned from one of certain defeat to one of possible success. Not yet probable, but certainly possible.

I instantly started to investigate the implications behind the data they had collated. My efforts were strongly aided and actively supported by the different crews as they cooperated with one another to help smooth any difficulties I had in accessing further data, or probing what it may mean. Their generosity in helping with this part of the work shortened the time to analyse the difficulties to such an extent that meeting the original deadline of two weeks became a possibility. That analysis was supported by more first-hand operational data than I was used to seeing before or since in the tackling of any complex problem. I consequently became completely certain of the answer it indicated. To double-check the conclusions, I submitted all the data to the UK office for a sophisticated statistical analysis. The answer by return telex confirmed that the conclusions were soundly based. A solution was at hand. Success was no longer just a possibility – it had become a probability.

Using a proven but unconventional principle gains commitment to the solution

I was only too aware of the senior management team's reputation, and its likely response to the solution I intended to propose. I judged that they would be resistant, and be concerned about what us easterners (I am ethnically Chinese) call 'loss of face'. I had experience of another unusual principle that gave the best chance of dealing with that difficulty. The problem was that I only had one day left of the original two weeks deadline, and to action that principle would require an entirely different and additional piece of work to be completed. Nonetheless, I judged that it was absolutely necessary. I would just have to complete as much of the work as I could in the remaining time. The principle concerned is described in detail in Chapter Three. It is summarised as: 'Always ensure that people see their weaknesses in the perspective of their strengths. Never encourage them to examine their weaknesses first, or see them in the perspective of other weaknesses'.

The Scandinavians were well known for the professionalism with which they scheduled the running of different types of crude oil through their refining facilities. They were experts at it. In the remaining day I talked with the departments – they were now keen to discuss what they knew was a success in their operation – and deduced some of the principles behind the effective practices they used for scheduling crude oil. There were lots of them. Amongst them were the very principles they were not applying to the performance criterion at which they were failing.

So late was I in completing this additional piece of work that the final presentation to the senior team the next day was being typed as I was presenting each previous page. I hadn't even seen what the finished presentation looked like before presenting it. I can remember a feeling of uncomfortable uncertainty as I discovered what was actually typed on each page as it was handed to me. The senior team clearly did not think much of this unprofessional arrangement. They were initially taken aback when I explained that I didn't want to present the work done on the problem performance index; I wanted instead to talk about their well deserved reputation for crude oil scheduling, and what caused it. I started to recount what I knew they already knew: the detailed analysis of the successful operational practices that underpinned their crude oil scheduling. For each practice I explained the principle from which I thought it derived. These managers were bright; they would not have got to their positions without being so. I had only got about a half-way through the analysis when the CEO stopped me and said, 'It's obvious. We don't apply these successful, proven principles to our problems with the performance index you came to examine. I take it that is your conclusion?' I agreed. He thanked me for the work, asked that I leave the analyses of crude scheduling and the problem performance index on the table, and asked his senior team to stay behind. They were to immediately find their own ways of taking the principles that worked so well for them on their crude oil scheduling, and apply them to the troublesome performance index. Unsurprisingly, they proved to be highly successful. Their sustained performance on that efficiency index became the best one world-wide for that multinational.

A bitter sweet and revealing epilogue

Two years later the Americans called a worldwide conference of all the people involved with that overall efficiency index. It included all the relevant operational managers responsible for that index across the world. The price of oil had surged even further upwards, and poor performance at the index would cost the organisation serious and embarrassing amounts of money. The Americans had data that said that each affiliate's performance over the two years either left significant work to be done, or left an awful lot to be desired. Each affiliate was made to present their performance and what they were going to do about it. It was not a pretty sight, and made for uncomfortable listening.

There was only one exception: the Scandinavians presented just one overhead showing a single graph. It displayed the path of the index month-on-month through the last two years. With this index, the lower its value, the better the operation was performing. The graph plummeted down at the start of the two year period to levels well below target level. It stayed there for eighteen months. In month 19 there was a small spike upwards that took the index close to the target level for one month. In month 20, the graph returned downwards to its previous very low level, where it remained for the rest of the period. The presenter gave the only two sentence presentation I have ever heard. He stood up and said, 'At this spike in month 19, we lost sight of one of the principles that had made us successful for eighteen months. We reviewed our operation, and returned to using this principle by month 20'. He sat down to total silence. The Americans called for the next affiliate to present their analysis and plans – which turned out to be the expected poor performance with assurances that things would get better. No reference was ever made to the Scandinavian performance, or what it meant, or indeed the meaning of the two sentence presentation made by their representative. It all remained a matter of no interest.

WHAT THE EFFECTS WERE

It seemed to me that there were three sets of different effects: those that involved the Scandinavians and their operation, those that affected the Multinational, and finally there were those that affected me.

The Scandinavians and their operation

Subsequent to my time with them, it was abundantly clear that they totally owned the improvements made to how their organisation dealt with the particular efficiency index. This was an inevitable consequence of them grasping the connection between their successful crude oil operation and their faltering performance on the index. They understood that they were successful in one because they operated certain principles that they had failed to use in the other. They were also living proof of the principle of always examining failures/weaknesses in the light of analysed successes.

This level of ownership was capable of driving a world-beating performance sustained over a significant period of time. It could not be a happenstance.

Similarly, that ownership put them in total control when the 'spike' upwards occurred on month 19. They were so confident of their ability to manage the problem that they didn't even bother contacting or informing me. A truly independent relationship existed between us. That is the ultimate sign of effective development work: independence, not dependence.

The Multinational

As far as I could observe, the work had not the slightest effect on the wider organisation, nor had they the smallest interest in it. The fact that only one affiliated company was offering the single success story prompted not the tiniest flicker of attention. Neither the 'centre' in America nor any of the other affiliates thought it worthy of any enquiry.

The effect on me

The experience of being totally lost and having not a single notion as to how to solve a complex problem in an inadequate amount of time, with no apparent cooperation or access to operational information, lives with me to this day. I found it a truly scary experience. I was without hope.

Turning to the principles I knew of at the time was simply an act of last resort, because there was nowhere else to turn. I learned again that one doesn't need the vestige of a solution at the beginning of tackling a problem to eventually succeed. One needed only to apply the appropriate principles with whatever rigour one is capable of, and hope it was enough to weather the situation. The principles themselves would be powerful enough to handle the problem if I could but apply them appropriately.

It persuaded me that if the few principles I was aware of at the time could produce a world-beating performance starting from one of the darkest of places I have ever been in, then the journey to discover other possible principles would be well worth making. I saw it as a difficult, lengthy and risky journey, but one that was daily becoming a more and more irresistible adventure to set out on.

WHAT WAS LEARNED

Some specific lessons emerged from this work:

- In a crisis, time spent probing the meaning of the information you know can save the day.

- Listening carefully to the first hand operational information at the levels that actually live with the problem concerned gives unrivalled access to irrefutable facts. Solutions can then become soundly based, and are fire proof in later examinations.

- Gathering information about a challenge, and probing it to understand the implications, is arguably the most critical step within complex problem solving and decision making. It is the hinge step on which the door to the solution will swing open. Without this hinge, the door won't open (see later section in Chapter Three on Decision Making steps). Too often under the pressure of the business the temptation is to make the mistake of immediately focusing on possible solutions. That is like banging on a number of locked doors at random, in the hope that one of them might fortuitously open.

- Taking account of information offered by people who work directly with it has the most profound effect on their motivation to help. It is a basic way of paying them respect. As a natural consequence, there is very little they won't do to help.

- The factual, detailed analysis of people's strengths is the most powerful basis to enable them to examine weaknesses and failures. It produces a surge in confidence, and an un-defensive appetite to deal with whatever difficulties confront them. It produces an enduring firm determination to maintain a tight grip on future performance. It produces an intense ownership of whatever problems subsequently arise.

This felt like a difficult and precarious event and I felt fortunate to learn valuable lessons from its outcome. These practices that provided success were clearly reliable tools in the kit bag of managing habits that I was keen to fill.

BUSINESS CHALLENGE TWO

MULTINATIONAL DRINKS COMPANY : ONE NATIONAL OPERATION PERSISTENTLY OVERRUNS ITS

MAINTENENCE BUDGET

CONTEXT OF THE CHALLENGE, AND THE PERCEIVED PROBLEM

A maintenance budget goes out of control

An international drinks company distributed ales and beer throughout a national territory, using its own fleet of trucks operating out of four distribution centres. Over the previous three years, the maintenance budget for the transport fleet was overspent by around mid-year, and further monies had had to be made available to maintain the operation. By year end, the enlarged budget was also consistently and significantly overspent. The company was embarrassed and irritated by these repeated failures. No effort was spared to try and correct a situation that was judged to be out of control. Internal task forces, changes in maintenance policy, and external management consultants were all options that were tried to no effect.

The Distribution Manager decided to tackle the problem himself using the development principles of this work

Feeling that he was fighting a losing battle, the National Distribution Manager – Alan (not his real name) – decided to ask me to help. I would support his efforts to tackle the problem using the development methods and principles described within this work. Answering to him were the four Regional Distribution Managers covering the entire country, and the National Engineering Maintenance Manager. Answering to the Engineering manager were various technical engineers sited at each distribution centre. Each centre had its own distribution-focused staff.

WHAT HAPPENED

The operational group agreed the scope of the problems together

Alan, his four local Distribution Managers, and the National Engineering Maintenance Manager, spent eight working days together spread out over some two months, agreeing what they jointly saw as:

- **the key issues**
  facing the maintenance operation, including those producing the budget overruns

They then worked through the following areas to resolve those issues. Together they devised:

- **an appropriate maintenance policy (i.e. a statement of aspirations)**
  that they could pursue in their everyday business

- **appropriate procedures**
  for a redesigned maintenance operation

- **appropriate initial targets**

- **a way of agreeing their maintenance standards**

- **a way of monitoring any changes they agreed to make**,
  and thereby adjusting them

Deep-rooted, firmly held, and long-standing differing views were aired during the work on these six areas. The discipline of meticulously recording verbatim all views and information before they were discussed proved to be a vital basis for success. Recounting the outline of the work:

- **The key issues**
  facing the maintenance operation, including those producing the budget overruns.

  Those causing strong concern were:

  o **The engineering staff were highly committed engineers and felt deeply that nothing short of a 'Rolls Royce' standard was appropriate** .

    The fact that such a standard should apply was a matter of professional pride amongst these engineers. They also strongly felt that the transportation fleet needed to be seen as 'perfection on the road'. Their absolute conviction was that it was the right and proper image for what they saw as an illustrious multinational organisation.

    The other distribution staff throughout the four national centres had quite different views about the appropriate criteria that the fleet should meet. Their major concern centred on the security of delivery to customers, and the costs of maintenance work.

    This difference of opinion had caused much heated division, and unresolved debate.

  o **A significant amount of maintenance work was carried out by contractors at the different distribution centres**.

    A lot of disquiet was felt at the centres over what they saw as the low level of control over the costs and quality of work done by the contractors.

  o **No connection existed between the existing maintenance policy and the reality** of how the operational decisions were taken on a daily basis at the various centres. No one disagreed with the statements in the policy – they were seen as valid generalisations that had little specific applicability to everyday decisions.

   o **The systems and procedures for planning/monitoring were not consistent** between distribution centres and the national head office.

These issues were resolved by tackling the following areas together.

- **Devising an appropriate maintenance policy (i.e. a statement of aspirations)**
  that they could pursue in their everyday business

  The norm in the company had been for policies to be created at the most senior levels, and handed down to operational levels such as the Regional Distribution Centre Managers. In this instance, it was seen as a novel departure for any sort of policy formulation to be undertaken by an operational group. This particular group created a new maintenance policy that:

   o **captured their common agreement as to the aspirations** they would all pursue for each of the above key issues of concern

   o **was simultaneously consistent with the broader, more generalised statements** in the existing maintenance policy previously generated at more senior levels

  Much effort was spent in those eight days on taking each aspiration agreed in the new policy and exploring its operational implications. Managers needed to be absolutely certain that what they were personally signing up to would indeed help tackle each of the previously identified key issues of concern.

  Much effort was also put into revisiting and appropriately amending the new policy's statements as each subsequent phase of the work was completed. This confirmed exactly how every piece of the subsequent work/thinking tied up with the new policy, and the important need to appropriately alter either or both as the need arose. It ensured that the operational maintenance policy stayed relevant to changing circumstances.

- **Devising appropriate procedures**
  for the new maintenance operation

  Having got an agreed 'first pass' at their new policy statements, the managers turned their attention to every procedure operated at the local distribution level and the national head office. These sanctioned, planned and monitored the completion and quality of maintenance work. Each procedure was scrutinised in the light of the new policy, and appropriate amendments were made.

  This would sometimes mean either significant changes or whole-sale removal of existing practices. Equally important was the group's initial testing of the new/modified procedures. They selected typical operational difficulties with which they were totally familiar, and jointly checked that the modified procedures would indeed tackle those sample difficulties appropriately. Useful changes were made as a result. Occasionally, changes in authority and accountability for specific activities within the procedures were also agreed. The whole group set up times for subsequent reviews when it took stock of how the new changes were working. It thence agreed any modifications it decided to retest. As expected, these later reviews disclosed important changes that proved commercially effective. This ensured the new procedures stayed relevant to the operation, and that the people delivering them both owned and controlled them.

- **Devising appropriate initial targets**

The stakes were high in setting, agreeing and delivering these targets.

The team realised that it needed some short range measurable/tangible targets that would give them confidence they were making progress. It is important to restate that this was the first time in the company's long history that operational managers had taken any part in forming policy. They consequently felt a strong need to reassure themselves that:

  o their policy was indeed tackling the real problems

  o undeniable improvements were being achieved in those problem areas

This was **their** policy, and the outcome would clearly be seen to be their sole responsibility. Intense ownership and an understandable concern to 'get it right' were keenly felt. Failure would be a very public affair, and they were justifiably sure that fingers would be pointed. The very least they expected from such an outcome was that the company would cease allowing operational staff to be involved in formulating future policy. They were candidly sure that significant 'career blight' was a pragmatic probability. Consequently, the very long standing and deep differences of view amongst the team, about such issues as 'standards' (referred to above on p.32), needed to be thoroughly resolved.

- **Devising a way of agreeing their maintenance standards**

They had created clear, commonly agreed policy statements about the reliability of the transportation fleet, the impact on deliveries to the customer, and the effect on the reputation of the company. Starting with this common basis, the team deliberately searched for consequent common ground amongst their widely differing views on standards. They relied heavily on the principles recalled in the section 'Managing Ideas', Chapter Three, Issue 3 – 2.12, p174.

Much thought led them to agree that there were critical areas of maintenance whose poor completion would severely disrupt delivery patterns. All could agree that such areas did indeed need to be kept at 'Rolls Royce' standard. This would be consistent with their policy statements on customer satisfaction, and securing the long term health of the business.

Much more thought led them to categorise the different types of other maintenance problems that would potentially have less severe effects on the business. Referring back to their agreed policy on customer service and satisfaction, they agreed a scale of differing standards of maintenance for these different categories of problems. These standards were appropriately less demanding than the 'Rolls Royce' ones agreed for the previous critical maintenance.

An agreed solution to the previously insoluble and emotion-laden issue of targets was at hand. The effect on the team was to unite it more closely, and significantly energise it to deliver its targets.

- **Devising a way of monitoring any changes they agreed to make,**
  and thereby adjusting them.

The team realised that their new maintenance operation would directly affect the business, their working lives and those of their subordinates. They needed no encouragement to set up procedures to regularly monitor the progress of their changes amongst themselves. Meetings were arranged to review the status of their work using the disciplines described in the section 'Responding to Success and Failure' – detailed in Chapter Three, Issue 3 – 2.8, p.137. Those disciplines led them to be cohesive in their view of matters, and encouraged improvements to how they did things. Importantly, it provided the appropriate chance to check financial and operational progress against the short term targets, reset them if needed, and set longer term ones.

These arrangements provided a tight control of what was occurring, and gave Alan the much needed confidence that his venture into this work would be successful. He had certainly risked his reputation in seeking outside help – a route his company disapproved of as a matter of habit.

SOME KEY EFFECTS

At the end of the first six months of the modified operation, accounts were presented to the head office of the entire organisation. Central Accounts decided that the amount of money saved was exceptional, and would not be included as such within the total group's accounts. Their advice was to spend the saved monies on investment. The distribution team decided to re-equip the four national distribution centres. Improvements continued to be made to the operation via the regular reviews held by the team, and significant savings versus ever tightening budgets continued for two more years.

WHAT WAS LEARNED

● **Decisions made at the point of maximum information are of higher quality.**

The decision to work together at the operational level had a key effect on the quality of decisions made. It enabled the maximum first-hand detailed information to be used in those decisions. These consequently closely reflected the reality of the situation 'on the ground'. They simultaneously commanded much more respect from the people who would have to regularly implement them. Formerly, analyses and decisions as to how to respond to the problem were taken at levels more remote from where that information was common currency.

● **Forming a common view of the problems as a basis for working together.**

The discipline of patiently 'listing and describing key issues of concern' was seen as a critical foundation step. The group did not discuss/consider differences of view or remedies until this step was completed. As described above, there were long standing strong disagreements amongst the team about how individuals saw these issues. They consequently found the discipline of working through the full diversity of views without debate emotionally difficult. It has always called for restraint and determination to listen completely to views that one has totally disagreed with in the past. Nonetheless, they were rewarded for their patience and persistence with their first comprehensive sight of the full extent of the issues involved.

By contrast, all previous discussions to try and remedy these problems had not been based on a shared basis of pooled information, and a resulting commonality of view. Instead, what they generated was a heated mix of individual concerns, strongly held solutions, suggestions about changes to policy, convictions about the need to change the structure, strong differences of opinion about particular individuals, etc. As is natural with such a mixture of firmly held opinions, inordinately long meetings became the norm, tempers frayed, divisions deepened and no progress was made.

● **Formulating a more specific policy at the operational level was a key basis for success.**

The unusual step of asking operational managers to create the policy automatically enabled information about their concerns to feature in their aspirations. They naturally saw the results as relevant to their needs and were strongly committed to implementing them within their day-to-day operations. This produced great cohesion amongst the staff at the four different regional distribution centres.

By contrast, previously derived policy statements were generated at a much more senior level, as idealised 'concepts'. These gave rise to 'motherhood and apple pie' statements, which whilst obviously true gave no guidance in handling daily difficulties in the business and thence help in improving operational cohesion.

- **Resolving fundamental differences on standards/targets became possible in the light of an agreed and relevant policy. It had previously proved impossible without it.**

  Using a shared view of the key issues facing the group allowed the team to successfully see their strong differences in opinion from that common position. The principle of exploring any difference from the basis of what is commonly shared has always proved an effective way of working. It has provided the widest possible constructive perspective from which to view those differences.

  Using the commonality of a shared policy to then deliberately seek out what was consistent between the differing opinions on standards was the key to resolving the problem. Of course, the natural temptation instead was to justify why one's own view of an issue was so much more relevant/appropriate than another's. The team had previously spent endless time proving that habit produced highly theatrical arguments, but no resolution. This time, using the disciplines described in 'Managing Ideas', p.174, Chapter Three, enabled them to work through to the consistencies between standards that had previously been fought over as inconsistent.

  It very much stands to their credit that despite their deep and differing feelings on the matter of standards, they had the determination to apply the principles of this work in a rigorous fashion. Their reward was a notable victory over an opponent who had defeated them time and again up to that point.

- **Having the operational group modify procedures ensured quality and commitment**

  The practice of using managers directly responsible for the daily operation of the maintenance effort to review/modify every procedure that controlled that effort had two significant effects:

  - **it became possible to jointly decide the aspirations each procedure was to pursue.** This ensured consistent action across different locations (i.e. regional distribution centres and the national head office). It was also key to cementing their joint commitment to the modified procedures.

  - **it became a simple matter for that group of managers to organise the subsequent repeated reviews** and modification of procedures. This enabled their work to remain relevant to changing business conditions.

- **Generating agreed interim targets both raised the game and aided cohesion.**

  Agreeing interim targets for the operation, which were regularly reviewed and updated by the group, had the effect of keeping it highly focused on its ambitions. Indeed, it helped to significantly raise the levels it aspired to. Its sustained performance over at least two further years, and the consequent significant monies saved, was a source of deep and lasting pride to the managers involved. It provided real operational proof of their independent capacity to sustain control of their business. They became a highly cohesive group.

It enabled these managers to be successful in a venture that was novel within their organisation, and whose failure would have damaged their careers.

BUSINESS CHALLENGE THREE

NATIONAL AGRICULTURAL CHEMICALS COMPANY : GETTING OUT OF THE PERFORMANCE DOLDRUMS

CONTEXT OF THE CHALLENGE AND THE PERCEIVED PROBLEM

The company marketed and distributed agricultural chemicals to the farming communities throughout a particular nation. The organisation was the affiliated subsidiary of a multinational chemicals company that manufactured, marketed, and distributed a very wide range of chemicals, and chemical based products. Both the parent company and its national subsidiary were bywords for conservatism, and had an ambivalent attitude to change.

The multinational had just promoted a senior manager from one of its other subsidiaries to become the new CEO of the national company. Most unusually, he was not of that conservative mould. He was clearly quite a different person from the rest of his colleagues, and was definitely his own man. He saw a company with undoubted potential, but whose entire performance was bureaucratic, non business focused, deeply attached to historical ways of doing things, and complacent about its long static bottom line. It was most usually compared to a gentleman's club that favoured the well-heeled intellectual.

He asked me to support his efforts to energise this company, and take its operation and bottom line performance into the later part of the twentieth century (as it was then), from its current position somewhere in the early 1900s.

WHAT HAPPENED

The new CEO, Paul (not his real name), decided that three areas deserved priority attention. He needed:

- **a competent Operations Director** to deal with the daily business of the company,

- **a business strategy that directly influenced daily decisions,** and

- **management lines that were business focused,** and capable of working in teams.

Explaining the outline of what occurred in each of these three issues:

- **A competent Operations Director**

Sometimes the brave make their own luck. On Paul's senior team was a disgruntled and deeply demotivated long serving manager who had given up any pretence of wanting to work. He was 'parked' in the job of 'Administrative Manager', and people were happy not to probe what exactly that meant. His reputation amongst staff was 'Give Bill something to do if you don't want it done'. He was a large, lugubrious, slow speaking, florid man who couldn't wait for his last two years to go by. He looked forward to his retirement at the end of that time, which he hoped would be full of holidays playing bridge.

Bill dutifully attended a residential week long management training course that Paul had chosen for the whole senior team to work through. It demanded that delegates try out all the elements described in the Man Management Section of Chapter Three. For whatever reasons, Bill suddenly decided that here was a different way of doing things that made sense to him, and that he was going to turn over a new leaf. He would embark on the strenuous path of developing his own managing habits within the daily business. It was an entirely unexpected turn of events, and was to prove a key starting point to a remarkable period.

He was absolutely resolute in his determination to tackle the daily business problems in the fashion that he glimpsed was possible on the week's training course. The transformation was rapid and took all his colleagues by total surprise. His reputation soon changed to 'if you want something done, give it to Bill'. Paul gave Bill the extremely challenging job of Operations Director. His sustained appetite for tackling the fundamental core issues at the root of long standing difficulties was both startling to see and a pleasure to witness. Key to this unexpected and spectacular turnaround was the absolute certainty in Bill's mind that Paul would always support him in difficult situations. Indeed, that always proved to be the case, especially when Bill was tackling the most long standing and intransigent of difficulties. He effectively resolved each and every one of them, gave no quarter, and thoroughly deserved the resounding commercial success he achieved.

- **A business strategy that directly influenced daily decisions.**

The fashion at the time was for strategies to be devised by senior teams alone – or even worse, with or by consultants. Associated with such work were mission statements created by the same means. Paul's experience was that these practices were politically acceptable to the multinational head office, because they were the convention of the time. However, he clearly saw that such strategies were totally divorced from how the everyday business operated. They were marooned in a place that no one ever visited, except in the empty rhetoric of politically correct presentations. Instead, he decided that he wanted a strategy that was firmly owned by every level in his organisation, and used continuously within the hurly-burly of the daily business. This did not occur anywhere else in that multinational.

Casual discussions between managers were generally socially focused, and certainly no practical business exchange ever referred to the organisation's strategy. Typically, Bill set an earthy and extremely pragmatic target for an effective strategy. He wanted every daily discussion that he chanced upon between his managers to be about the business issues that confronted them. He further wanted to hear them automatically and naturally refer to the new business strategy as an aid to help them in the decisions with which they were grappling.

It took a year of very hard and persistent work to both create such a strategy, and have it operating within the everyday fabric of the business. Bill's target was continuously met en route to achieving that. The detailed steps needed to create, understand, and use a strategy of this type are described in the Man Management Section of Chapter Three (Issue 3-2.9: p.144). However, the outline history of this part of Bill's work, supported by Paul, is summarised below.

- **Each level chooses its key concerns.**
  Managers throughout the organisation – including Paul and Bill – chose key issues of specific concern to them. Inevitably, the issues tended to be more widely focused and less tangible at the more senior levels. They tended to be more specific and tangible at other levels. Bill checked that the full range of issues selected across the levels covered the entire range of business concerns that he knew the organisation had to resolve.

- **Each level stated fundamental aspirations for their concerns.**
  These usefully clarified the direction they would take on each issue, and specified priorities if they were needed.

- **Each level's aspirations supported those of the level above.**
  This feature created a network of supportive strategy statements to which the whole organisation was committed.

- **Each level's strategy flexed appropriately as the business conditions changed.**
  The operational information about particular chosen issues naturally changed throughout the period. The managers affected would automatically be the first to become aware of such changes and were best placed to appropriately amend their section of the strategy. They were also able to alert colleague managers at different levels about their possible need to make similar changes. That enabled the whole strategy to flex with changing business conditions at any level.

These steps produced a mutually supportive continuum of strategy statements about issues of direct concern to every level in the organisation. Its key effect was to help managers help themselves to operate the business more coherently and cohesively. Despite its 'obviousness' and the simplicity of its concept, the experience has been that it has always taken considerable effort and time to implement within any organisation. Such a strategy demands an entirely different set of managing habits to the norm. It asks managers to think through in detail where any of their daily actions is taking the business in both the longer term and the wider perspective. The convention is to simply concentrate on getting an activity done in the time available. It therefore inexorably demands that managers learn to approach their every day work with quite different thinking habits. Bill's achievement in managing that development within the year compares extremely well to similar attempts in other organisations.

- **Management lines that were business focused, and capable of working in teams.**

  - ○ **The threat of industrial action provides the opportunity to kick-start the installation of the management lines.**

    The company's standard practice was to rely on various committees that spent their time on centrally run union negotiations to deliver annual agreements on pay structures. It was very much a process that ran outside the operation of the normal every day business. Very soon after Paul's arrival he was told that these negotiations had run into trouble, and that a staff strike was 'inevitable'. This had never happened in the company's history. Whilst such a strike would have been more a reflection of using centralised negotiations to deliver agreements on pay structures, it would have been a significant political 'black mark' on Paul's stewardship of the organisation.

    Paul immediately took the opportunity to use this crisis to commence establishing the normal line management habit of individual dialogues with all staff. These had been totally absent up to that point, and were not part of normal practice anywhere in the multinational. New standard guidelines were rigorously followed, i.e.:

    - **Those judged as 'strengths' amongst the teams were consulted first,** in a one-to-one dialogue.

    - **Individuals' concerns were sought and immediately taken into account.** An open and enquiring dialogue was started about the information that people had about the issue in hand. Specifically, people's concerns were sought and immediately taken into account in whatever way seemed sensible. The results of these efforts were fed back, and the dialogue continued until both people shared the same view of matters.

    - **Those judged to be 'marginals or weaknesses' amongst the teams were consulted** after the dialogues with the strengths had concluded. This second round of dialogues followed exactly the same pattern as the ones described above. Managers consequently became clear about where each person stood in relation to all the issues.

    - **Only then did management meet with union representatives** to inform them of the decisions that had been made.

    The strike was called off, and sensible arrangements made for pay that were mutually seen as equitable.

    This form of managing essentially focuses on taking account of people's individual concerns so as to reach a commonly shared conclusion. Its other focus is to use the dialogues with the strengths in the teams as the basis for agreed solutions. It is the very antithesis of management by negotiations. It demands that the management line discharges its continuous obligation to meet both the needs of individuals and the business.

    Bill set about using the success of averting the strike to cement this way of managing within the everyday pattern of how his management lines worked. He realised that the above one-to-one routine dialogues between manager and subordinate were the very backbone of the management line. It was these dialogues that ensured business challenges were always met and never became long standing problems. They were also the key means of developing the managing habits that subordinates used in tackling their daily work. It is not possible to overstate their contribution to commercial success.

Other related issues were tackled during the two year span of this development work. However, the above three focuses were the main directions into which the major energy was channelled.

SOME KEY EFFECTS

Taking each of the above three focuses in turn:

- **Having Bill in position enabled Paul to guide the installation of all the developments that the business needed.**

  Bill's commitment to tackling the core issues confronting him allowed Paul to support him in making the following major changes.

  o **Structural changes:**

  Key accountabilities were altered from traditional activities that didn't serve the needs of the business to ones that did.

  A typical example would be the traditional response of sales staff to difficulties with sales volumes. They would urgently increase activity with a random and changing selection of customers on the basis that the key was to increase any activity. In contrast Bill ensured the management lines continuously identified the developmental plans and direction being pursued by each customer. Consequently, sales staff continually knew the different support that each of their customers needed, and hence their different potential during times of low sales volumes.

  Similarly, Bill worked hard at getting sales managers to see clearly what accountabilities they alone could deliver to the business. The traditional role for such managers would have been a more active, busier looking version of their sales representatives. In contrast, Bill's desire was for his sales managers to both acutely know the overall state of their business and pursue proactive plans to improve it. This of course also meant a level and depth of contact with senior managers within the customer base that was not the normal practice.

  o **Procedural changes:**

  The historical focus amongst the sales and marketing staff was to be seen as continuously busy. Deeply understanding what was happening in their business, and responding appropriately was not a priority. This led to unacceptable levels of credit building up across the customer base. One senior manager was consequently prompted to remark tartly, 'Gentlemen, we are in the business of selling agricultural chemicals to the farming community. We are not in the business of running a bank.'

Bill's appetite for tackling long standing habits that did not serve the business led him to fundamentally alter this situation. On the surface of matters, people had to alter their well established procedures for sales and payment. Some of these were lamentable. Simple in concept though this appeared, it proved much harder in practice to effect these changes.

The core difficulty was deeper than first met the eye. People's view of the company, their job and their customers had to change. They regarded the enterprise and its customers as a privileged club where payment was almost regarded as an un-gentlemanly obsession. They saw their job as primarily providing high quality scientific expertise. Payment was seen as something 'tradesmen' worried about. They consequently paid it scant attention and had allowed customers to build up substantial debts.

Bill found that some of his men struggled to adhere to an appropriate mix of technical excellence and prudent commercialism. Much painful readjustment followed to get them to change their view of matters, and thereby alter their relationships with customers.

Bill showed his usual tenacity, and the procedures controlling the payment and debt position with customers became a well organised issue.

o **Man Management changes**

This was a company that prided itself on a long tradition of intellectualism, and with it came a high regard for articulate debate. People were very much judged on their capacity to excel at these interchanges. This grew the habit of fascinating discussions full of endless analyses – all of them learned and rooted in much education. More and more issues were always raised in addition to whatever was the original concern of the debate. Unfortunately for the business, this trend did not nurture the habit of creating incisive proposals as to what to do about any of the mounting number of issues being debated. In fact, an onlooker could be forgiven for thinking that the distinct rule of the game was not to come up with something as philistine as a proposal to do anything. This might stifle yet further interesting, stimulating and expansive debate.

Bill had recognised from his training week that he needed to tackle this culture of intellectual verbal gymnastics. He correctly started with his own performance at making proposals about matters of concern. He soon became known as someone determined to move things along. Likewise, people realised he would relentlessly but courteously insist on others making proposals for resolving issues. He would not allow them to consume his time indulging their habit for intellectual debate. Inexorably, Bill steered his key part of the organisation towards the daily managing habit of making proposals. Predictably, the operational part of the organisation that Bill now ran showed a much better performance at taking initiatives than it did before Bill's leadership.

- **Having a strategy embedded within the daily business decisions
  completely altered the company's capacity for cohesive, consistent problem solving**

The company's reputation amongst customers was that its products were technically of good quality, well researched chemically, and could be relied on to be effective on the farm. Equally, they also saw the staff's capacity to respond to problems as erratic, having no cohesive strategy, and occasionally as entirely inconsistent. This performance had its inevitable effect on business results, which was the situation that Paul and Bill inherited.

Creating an overall strategy that was used at every level in the organisation within the daily business decisions helped to totally transform this situation. It enabled managers to turn an erratic, inconsistent performance into one recognised for its cohesiveness and consistency. This too had its inevitable effects on the business's results.

- **Growing the line management discipline of regular one-to-one dialogues**
  enabled issues to be resolved and management habits to be developed

This was a fundamental and far reaching change to how every day business was transacted. The principles underpinning the operation of the management line were a cornerstone to the success of the whole organisation. They are fully described in the collation of principles detailed in Chapter Three. However, the particular experience within this company is summarised below.

The move away from committees handling various issues such as industrial relations problems to the daily one-to-one dialogues within the management line had the following pivotal effects:

- **Regular managing of issues**
  It moved the handling of matters away from crisis management to regular discussion and the immediate resolution of difficulties before problems could develop.

- **More sensitive and personal information was taken into account**
  The centre of attention changed from all the traditional public posturing and private manoeuvring so beloved by those whose vested interests lie in 'negotiation'. Instead, it allowed much more sensitive and personal reservations to be directly shared and rapidly taken into account. The privacy and trust of the one-to-one dialogues within the management line specifically nurtured that ability.

- **Managers allowed and obliged to manage**
  Custom and practice moved away from abrogating the core management responsibility for the welfare and well being of staff to 'offline groups'. It prevented the perverse habit of those groups imposing decisions on managers about the welfare and reward of their own staff. Instead, it allowed and obliged managers to fulfil their duty to directly manage what is one of their core responsibilities.

- **People treated as individuals – not as one group**
  Managers stopped treating people as 'one group'. In that situation, their interests inevitably became vulnerable to 'decisions ruled by the lowest common denominator that survived the negotiation process'. Instead, the management line dialogues consistently produced results that accurately

reflected the performance and views of each individual. They provided the basis for genuine motivation in future work. Standards were therefore set at the highest throughout a working group.

This combination of effects had a profound impact on the daily management of the company. In essence it allowed and demanded that line managers met their obligations to manage on a regular and appropriate basis.

The more fundamental inconsistencies between 'management by negotiations' and 'management via the line' are explored below in 'What Was Learned'.

The translation of these principles into the tackling of daily operational problems had equally far reaching effects:

- o **Managing operational problems, not responding to them**

  The habit of only surfacing issues when they had already become problems stopped. Instead, the regular operational one-to- one dialogues enabled progress to be steered and supported to ensure that proactive initiatives were pursued. Regular 'crises' that inevitably resulted from responding to problems instead of anticipating them ceased to occur.

- o **Developing subordinates' performances within the daily business**

  Operating the previous sink or swim strategy on subordinates' work ceased. Instead, managers became accountable for the processes that their subordinates used in tackling daily business. The key responsibility was to develop the managing habits that subordinates used within those processes to achieve results. This correct use of the management line had some very sharp teeth. The sharpest of these was the first and prime need for managers themselves to become skilful at those processes and habits.

The combination of these effects had a fundamental impact on how the daily business was transacted.

In essence, it obliged managers to pursue the development of their own managing habits as the only legitimate basis for leading the development of their subordinates' habits.

It demanded that they proactively develop the way business was tackled by their subordinates so as to ensure that their performance deliberately moved forward – instead of lurching unpredictably into difficulties.

WHAT WAS LEARNED

● **Personal style is packaging. Skill is content**

Bill's road to Damascus experience, and his consequent personal choice to engage with his own development, was a crucial spark that Paul was able to fan to ignite progress across the company. It was a startling demonstration of another principle that reoccurs throughout this work. As described, Bill's style was the very antithesis of the educated intellectualism and verbal sophistication so prized throughout the multinational. He was seen as slow, ponderous, pedestrian, and not given to too many words. The fact that this was merely the packaging in which came a quick, agile, penetrative, and very determined mind was to prove many people's undoing in consistently underestimating Bill's response to issues.

A key lesson was to distinguish style from actual skill and ability. Paul's decision to choose Bill for the pivotal job of Operations Director was crucial to the success that followed. Many more 'obvious' and 'intellectually more gifted' choices were open to Paul. He chose the apparently least attractive option in terms of style, but the one that had the skill range and determination to deliver high quality business results.

● **Supporting Bill's development of the operation, installing a strategy that lived in the business, and building the management line, struck at the very core of the company's performance bottlenecks**

   ○ **Making the appropriate choices about which issues to focus on was vital**

   It is all too simple to get lost in the plethora of issues that one might focus on in trying to turnaround the total performance of a company. This is especially true when, as was the case in this instance, the organisation had languished in the doldrums of poor managing habits for many years. It was critical to discern which priority issues would unlock the potential for high performance. Even more demanding was the determination to resolve them, no matter how unconventional the required path appeared. Paul demonstrated just such discernment, determination, and courage. The rewards of the commercial results for the company stand to his credit.

   ○ **The choice to manage via the 'line' and not negotiate is sadly uncommon – but highly effective**

   All three issues that Paul correctly chose to focus on had unconventional but effective solutions. Yet one solution stands out as being the most unconventional, and having the strongest vested interests opposing it. It is the issue of managing via the line and not via negotiations. The contrast between these two processes is stark. It is worth our while pausing to look more carefully at the detail and implications of this matter.

      ▪ **Negotiations are a competition in manipulation,**
      where what is sought is an acceptable balance of power embodied in a compromise acceptable to the competitors involved.

      In contrast, the essence of the management line one-to-one dialogue is a cooperation between manager and subordinate. It is aimed at coming to a mutual understanding on the full range of each person's individual concerns. The desire to achieve that mutuality has only been demonstrated when each person habitually works at whatever reservations the other person has raised. This needs to be especially true of the manager. This is not a manipulation by force/pressure, or partially disclosed information, which is the trademark of negotiations. This is the genuine attempt by two minds to openly work together at creating a commonality of view. There is no compromise to be reached in this way of managing: the process of work and sharing continues until that mutuality is generated.

- **Negotiations dangerously undermine the authority and power**
  of the very people we ask to deliver high quality business results

Negotiations subvert the authority of the management line to deal with the pivotal issue of recognition and reward. In contrast, the management line one-to-one dialogues confirm those managers as the authority empowered to decide that issue. Management by negotiations has always been inconsistent with a strong, competent, and respected management line. The loser has always been the business.

Common sense notwithstanding, I am sadly confident that the knee jerk response of most managers will be a reliance on 'management by negotiations'.
It's the less demanding, more immediately visible, conventionally supported, 'let someone else do the work / take the responsibility' option. I find it revealing that every time a client pursues 'management via the line', he achieves far better commercial results than 'management via negotiations' ever gave him previously. It would seem that there is strong comfort in conforming to the conventions of the time, and sticking with the 'negotiations option'. Doing what seems sensible and business effective appears mysteriously less attractive.

In addition the uncomfortable truth is that powerful vested interests whose livelihoods have grown to depend on all the rituals of negotiations continue to nourish the myth of their necessity (see Chapter Three, p.100 – p.104 for a full recall of a proven successful alternative).

● **Sustained success needs a focus on development, and continuous vigilance.**

Shortly after achieving the above sustained and demonstrable success, Paul decided to advance his career and personal development in a different company. The multinational replaced him with a manager whose entire view and priorities were inconsistent with every aspect of the above developmental achievements that Paul had delivered as business results. The new CEO firmly believed in tradition and convention as an end in itself. He consequently made haste to dismantle every part of the processes painstakingly developed by Paul and Bill. He achieved the inevitable result of rapidly returning the company to its previous moribund state. Bill's retirement date fortuitously coincided with the arrival of the new CEO, and he was spared the sad sight of his successful work being dismantled. Those who had proved their talent in aiding the company's turnaround and could leave also left. The comment made was, – 'it was like experiencing someone switching on the light in a previously pitch-black room – and then someone else switching it off again'.

There were two vital lessons to be absorbed from this event.

- ○ **The choice is political evolution or conscious development.**

  The first reality is that large organisations are especially vulnerable to the lottery of evolution by politics. They can on occasions appear to make inspired decisions that apparently penetrate to the heart of the matter. Promoting Paul to his first CEO position appeared to be such a decision. It wasn't. It was merely the throw of the political dice, demonstrating the balance of power within the multinational at that time. Like all managing situations wedded to the pursuit of power, that balance shifts back and forth with time. The promotion of the replacement CEO demonstrated a subsequent and different balance of power between the factions involved. It is an extremely common example of an organisation following the indeterminate and erratic switch-back progress of political evolution. Of course the real danger of pursuing 'management by political evolution' is the distinct possibility of extinction. Competency levels will inevitably cycle steeply downwards at times in such circumstances, and on occasions coincide with predatory moves by competitors. Indeed, huge though this multinational was, it did not survive. It suffered this precise fate and was sold to a competitor some years later.

  The short but consistent history of Paul's stewardship of the national affiliated company shows a quite different view of how to run an organisation. In essence, that process is not one of political evolution; it is one of conscious thought through development. That is the fundamental choice facing us within organisations: political evolution or conscious development. One offers the comfort of convention, while the other demands the courage to follow the less trodden, narrower path of consistently tackling the real issues facing the business.

- ○ **Continued success needs vigilance**.

  The second reality is that this work has shown that no success is self sustaining. The price for its continuation is vigilance. In this case, if the senior men involved in making key appointments have not the perception or inclination, or neither, to grasp what has occurred, then any and all successes that have been achieved are totally reversible. The harsh reality during this work was that every single day brought the need to engage heart and brain to breathe life into the processes that underpin success – just because it happened yesterday has not guaranteed in the smallest way that it will happen again today. Success has proved to have no auto pilot. Negligence in grasping this need for continuous vigilance has wrought havoc in organisations, especially when it has happened at the most senior level.

BUSINESS CHALLENGE FOUR

DAIRY FOODS COMPANY : THE JOURNEY FROM FAILING NATIONAL COMPANY TO SUCCESSFUL MULTINATIONAL

CONTEXT OF THE CHALLENGE, AND THE PERCEIVED PROBLEM

I graphically remember sitting in my then office one Sunday and unexpectedly receiving a call from Mike (not his real name) – someone I knew to be the CEO of a medium sized dairy cooperative. He and I had worked together on a number of residential management training courses of the sort that Bill had experienced. I knew that Mike knew the detail of the development work within the international drinks and the agricultural chemicals companies. He said he was in town and wanted to talk immediately. I was naturally intrigued. His news was that he had just been made CEO of a large dairy cooperative, which he assured me – as I knew absolutely nothing about the dairy industry or cooperatives – was inherently a sound business.

However, he admitted that it was currently in significant difficulties. It had made increasing losses over the last three years, the banks were on the point of recalling its loans, its shareholders were deserting it and joining other rival cooperatives, and the reputation of its management team amongst the farming community was odious. As one commentator wryly put it, 'There's nothing wrong with this company, except for its products and its people'. Mike wanted me to support his efforts to turnaround this ailing company. I remember my reply: I said that if he didn't mind the fact that I knew nothing about the dairy industry, had no working experience of cooperatives, had similarly no experience of the farming community, and had never worked in a rural environment, then I was relaxed about taking up the challenge. We agreed to venture forth together on what turned out to be the journey of a lifetime.

Every factor of the management of this company had been severely mishandled. All its products had long lost any market advantage they originally might have had. Product development had long since stopped. The staff were totally demoralised by the chaos around them. The financial institutions had justifiably lost faith in the management team's ability to find their way forwards. The farming community were so enraged with the previous management team's performance that they picketed the head office. A truly deep and comprehensive crisis surrounded the start of Mike's stewardship of the company.

WHAT HAPPENED

<u>**The immediate fires were put out – permanently**</u>

With the scale of crisis at hand, Mike needed to put in progress a coherent and consistent plan to accurately tackle all of the issues at speed. The fundamental approach to that plan was:

- **To first step back and widen the perspective in which the problems were viewed.**

  One of the most difficult and vital habits for clients to develop is to respond to crises by having the nerve and determination to take one step back. This conceptually simple but extremely difficult skill allows the crisis to be viewed in the widest possible perspective. Only by achieving this have they had any chance of clearly seeing all the issues to be tackled. Secondly, only then did they have any chance of viewing those issues in a balanced way, so as to decide strategies and priorities that would stand the test of time.

  Of course, the natural temptation is to be seized by the heat of the moment and the encircling situation, and knee-jerk the closest expedient action to hand, with the highest 'visibility'. It would have been understandable for Mike and his senior men to fold under the pressure and respond in that conventional fashion. They demonstrated the nerve to do otherwise.

  Their considered, wider perspective told them it was critical to:

  - **ensure consistent responses** to the financial institutions and the farming communities

  - **share with local farming communities the guidelines** that would control decisions to rationalise services provided to them. Unpopular decisions would be based on first agreeing what was needed to secure and grow the business. The convention of seeking compromises in the long grass of local politics was absolutely ruled out

  - **ensure those guidelines were consistent with those used in the longer term.**
    Hard and unpopular decisions would have to be taken in the short term, and one of the most challenging tasks was to accomplish this via principles that the organisation would hold fast to in the longer term. There would be no short term fixes that would return to haunt both the business and the local farming communities

  - **publically take time out to listen to people's concerns and views before decisions and action were taken.** Whilst action was going to be relentlessly taken at speed, there could be no short cut to the effort put into taking people's views into account

  - **then rapidly take unequivocal decisions and instantly communicate them.** Rural rumour machines have a track record of brewing up intense thunderstorms at great speed. The new team needed to show patience in listening but incisiveness in both taking decisions and communicating them

- **The plan.**

  Mike and his team met with the financial institutions, and were open and clear about the business strategy that would be pursued at the senior level. They took care to paint a consistent picture with the longer term direction they would take.

  Mike and his team spent the first two weeks holding open evening meetings with local farming communities. He presented his business strategy, and spent the rest of the time listening carefully to all their concerns.

  He explained to those communities exactly what policy would be followed in deciding the level of local services that the cooperative would provide for them. Inescapably, there would have to be rationalisations. Such changes had previously been an issue of intense politics, obsessive lobbying, and escalating discontent. The key to success in this instance was to openly share the exact business criteria by which decisions would be taken, before that happened.

  These decisions then took account of the concerns raised by those communities. Most importantly, this was supported by a willingness to subsequently explain the detailed business rationale behind each decision. However, changes were not made to any decision simply because it was not liked by one vested interest or another. This prevented the intense and endless politicking and lobbying that was the time-honoured tradition amongst farmer owned cooperatives.

  The time and effort spent visiting, talking with, and listening to the financial institutions and local farming communities were to prove vital. It enabled broken bridges to be mended, and created the basis for making difficult, unpopular, but effective changes in the future.

Subsequent changes were made throughout the operation, which were consistent

This is the story of the next ten years of intense developmental work on every conceivable aspect of the running of a company. It spans the rise of the company over three years to what was regarded as the most successful dairy cooperative in its country. The company won the accolade of a prestigious national prize awarded by the country's prime minister for achieving such a turnaround. It then covers its successful transition to an effective multinational. Recalling all the numerous events that made up this remarkable and sustained performance would consume all the space in this book. It would certainly bore the reader, and I suspect be much akin to 'let me show you a hundred and fifty more holiday photographs of our time in....'. You will doubtless be relieved to hear that I therefore intend to describe only a very few of the multitude of activities that filled those ten years.

To aid the reader, it is best to describe what happened separately within the three key factors of the organisation: its structure, procedures, and man management. Recalling the chronological sequence of initiatives would not easily give the reader a coherent picture of the strategy being pursued. Such a sequence had to take account of the business priorities at any one time and the developmental needs of the people concerned.

Consequently, I have described a small selection of the changes in the above three organisational factors, which helped deliver the commercial results achieved. For simplicity, the effects of each change are explained after its description.

A.   What happened structurally, and what were the effects?

The overall direction was :

> **One consistent set of developments pursued,**
> which both continuously prioritised **customer service**
> and automatically sustained a '**flat and lean**' organisation.

Six of the implemented developments are chosen to give a flavour for this sustained work, four of which are described below. The other two are attached in Appendix One, in order not to overburden this section, yet allow the reader access to sufficient information.

The key focus for all the developments was to build a structure whose actual shape and use of accountability would overtly prioritise customer service.

The second focus was to create a structure that was capable of rapid and extensive expansion, whilst continuously staying very 'flat' in minimising management levels and head count. It remained permanently 'lean' and was not vulnerable to debilitating changes in direction or periodic head count cuts.

1.   The fundamental direction of the structure changed to 'face the customer'

Business Units replaced a structure consisting of functional departments.

The original functional departments 'faced inwards'. They were primarily concerned with running their own separated, different functions, and whatever energy was left over from that focus was spent 'looking outwards' at the market place. On too many occasions that would amount to very little energy, or none at all.

The decision was made to change to a structure that 'faced the customer'. This demanded a Business Unit based organisation in which all operational groups were clustered around selected customer bases. People's prime concern and only job justification became the initiatives they could take to support the market place. There was neither energy left over for inwardly focused priorities nor any appetite for them.

This involved splitting the total business into component businesses that were sufficiently independent but often shared operational links. In the case of this organisation, the split was done on the basis of product groupings. Each such section was managed by a Business Unit Head, whose team consisted of the disciplines needed to service that part of the total business. He had total accountability for its operational and financial performance. Working alongside him were a group of Functional Heads (e.g. Finance, IT, Production, etc.)

who had two key duties that only functional experts could discharge. Firstly, they created and monitored the technical standards operated within the various business units. Secondly, they created, gained commitment to, and delivered the strategies the organisation implemented for the particular technical expertises that they headed. The senior team consisted of a selection of Business Unit Heads and Functional Heads, together with the CEO.

The effects

- **The needs of the business became the key focus.**

  The various multidisciplinary teams worked to business aspirations that they generated with their Business Unit Head. As a result, only the needs of the business were prioritised. Functional priorities had previously featured strongly within the organisation, and had often competed with/overshadowed overall business needs. That now ceased to happen.

- **Accountability became absolutely clear for all situations.**

  The Business Unit Head had full financial and operational accountability for the entirety of his business. This clarity enabled the one team of multidisciplinary experts, and its manager, to directly decide what would be done for any issue in that business. Both the quality and speed of decision making greatly improved.

- **The connection between Business Unit and Functional Heads benefited the business.**

  The combination of the Business Unit Head covering every operational and financial aspect of a business, and the Functional Heads covering every technical aspect, enabled every facet of each business to be accounted for. Both sets of managers clearly saw that each provided the other with a key element that allowed them to discharge their accountability for the total enterprise. Each needed the other for both to succeed. The basis was laid for a mutually beneficial partnership, which simultaneously controlled every aspect of a successful outcome for each business.

2. <u>**The exact shape and size of the structure was dictated by the need to grow the business**</u>

Having decided the above overall direction of the structure, as always, 'the devil was in the detail' of precisely how many people would be doing what jobs in which parts of the organisation. Clients have always found this type of restructuring difficult to think through systematically.

> **The key challenge was to think anew, and not be limited**
> **by the negative circumstances of the existing situation.**

Mike followed a conceptually simple though difficult process to define a detailed structure capable of giving him sustained growth in his business. The stages in his thinking were:

- **he first pictured the ideal way in which the needs of the business would be met.** Importantly he assumed he had to hand all the resources he needed

- **he then pictured the ideal structure** needed to deliver those needs in that fashion. Again, he assumed he had all the resources he needed

- **he then identified the immediate step to install that structure.** If he was forced to make interim steps, he made plans to progress to the ideal structure as quickly as possible

The effects

The significant advantages of rigorously following such a process were:

- **A sharp focus on the possibilities of the future became clear, unhindered by the difficulties of the past.**

  Senior managers attempting this process have always found it particularly difficult to specify the detail of the ideal operation, and its structure. Their problem stemmed from feeling restricted by the very real negatives that still surrounded them. Understandably, they felt constrained by them. It has always demanded significant discipline to hold these to one side, and especially difficult to do when it came to the particular issue of management expertise. They invariably experienced this to be in critically short supply. Consequently, it has seemed 'fanciful' to them at the time to imagine that they had access to all the resources they might need. Difficult though it is, the rewards for persisting with this process have always been significant and long lasting, i.e.:

  o it has laid a clear practical basis for **taking advantage of the possibilities** within the business

  o it has given the organisation **a path to break free of its past** pattern of unsuccessful managing habits

  o at the same time it has **used the positive possibilities to handle the difficulties**

  This last attribute has proved time and again to be the most important strategic advantage to gain. It has always produced the basic structural thinking that has provided the key to later success.

- **It changed anxiety and pessimism to fact based confidence and optimism.**

  A common emotional stance amongst senior managers faced with restructuring at the point of a crisis is one of anxiety and pessimism. They feel themselves to be beleaguered, 'on the back foot', and are only too well aware of the personal and business consequences of further failure. Their view as to what is possible has been heavily constrained by the recent crisis that in most cases still partially besets them. In contrast, the above process allows them to break free of that dark emotional landscape. It invites them to relook at the detail of their business opportunities through the lens of what is possible for them to do. The emotional landscape that they consequently create is the one they need to enable them to lead the organisation out of its difficulties. It is one of fact based confidence and optimism.

- **It produced changes that were based on business logic – not ones based on fear.**

This process does not produce the knee jerk 'one size fits all – across the board head count or overheads cut'. That is a doctrine driven by fear, and is a common feature of the above dark emotional landscape.

Instead, this process highlights that if the ideal way of meeting the business's needs is for the organisation to slim down a particular section of its structure, then it is the logic of meeting the business's needs that drives that change. Similarly, if the business's needs dictate that another part of the organisation's structure should increase its manning levels, then it is the business logic that drives that change. Similarly again, if the process indicates that the business's needs are best met if yet another part of the organisation stays exactly as it is, then that logic must drive that decision. It is a process strictly driven by the best way of factually meeting the business's needs.

- **It helped convince people that senior management had the nerve to succeed.**

Inevitably, people take particular note of how their senior managers respond when the going gets tough. It tells them accurately what sort of people they work for. It cuts through any fine sounding rhetoric that can be used to obscure what is occurring.

This process offers the senior team a chance to make a reasoned attempt to nourish the health of the business at times of difficulty. It shows their determination to increase its capacity to create wealth and job security. When the rationale for the changes has been shared with those who are affected, the result has always been the same. They have shown that they instantly understand the difference in outlook and courage between this process and the conventional 'across the board cuts'. The consequent positive effect on morale and motivation at times of difficulty has been truly significant, and sorely needed.

3. <u>Product development became integrated within the normal operations</u>

The organisation previously had the reputation of very occasionally being the first to conceive a new product idea. However, it had a 100% track record of either being the last amongst its competitors to reach the market with any idea, or in some cases not reaching it at all.

The new strategy was to embed the product development process within the everyday operation of the business, and give it the highest priority.

This meant that the Business Unit team became the product development team for its particular business. During that work it was headed by the Product Development Manager, who answered directly to the CEO.

The effects

- **The range of new products, their quality, and the 'time to market' took a step change upwards.**

  The times taken to get new products to market became consistently shorter than the competition. In some instances these times were so short that supermarket customers were told they were much longer in order to gain credibility. It was judged that they simply would not believe the times achieved.

- **Using the Business Unit team as the product development team gave immediate access to the full range of trends and ideas** throughout every part of the business's operation.

- **The different expertises represented in the Unit ensured that there were no delays anywhere in the development process.**

  They saw the development ideas as their own, and were deeply committed to speedily bringing them to market. They became intimately familiar with the technical, operational and business justification for each product. This meant that as the developmental phases for every product were progressed, the appropriate facilities were automatically prioritised by the relevant Business Unit member. No delays occurred throughout the development process. Equally, this also meant that very early debugging occurred on full scale production facilities.

- **The Business Unit naturally saw this activity as their future bottom line, and prioritised any required problem-solving.**

  The drive and commitment of each functional expert within the business unit to produce saleable products needed no encouragement. It was never a question of product development trying to persuade functional experts to 'divert' their time, energy, and resources to solving the many problems that arose during such work. On the contrary, Business Unit members saw it as their life line to help solve such problems as early and as rapidly as possible.

Those experienced with the conventional structures used for product development will know that the above four benefits are very elusive. They will note the marked absence of a separate 'Product Development Department' with all the paraphernalia of its bureaucracy, internecine struggles with other business functions, and consequent disadvantages to the enterprise.

The net result was to harness the ideas, total commitment and energy of the managers driving the business to what they viewed as 'their' product development. This produced a commercial advantage that was not equalled or bettered by the competition at any time during the organisation's life span.

It changed the company's reputation and standing from being derided as the most incompetent throughout its industry to being one of the most feared and respected in this activity.

4. A different type of multinational structure was created

- **Rethinking how the 'centre' and 'national teams' worked together.**

The company's remarkable turnaround from a basket case condition to a pre-eminent position in the industry, won it a prestigious national prize from the country's prime minister. I considered my support of the development of the organisation and its business to be satisfactorily completed. Mike agreed that the original business aims for the development work were more than met.

However, he decided that the company should now become a multinational, and asked for support to achieve this ambition.

I remember a pivotal discussion about 'what would be the core nature of the new multinational?', and hence whether my continued support was appropriate. All the multinationals I had observed had:

- o **centralised power over all key decisions**

- o **reserved the right to place senior managers from the centre** into selected local management positions

- o **reserved the right to directly change any locally made decision** to whatever the centre judged was appropriate

I asked Mike if this conventional and well established picture of a multinational was what he wanted. Fortunately his desire was to create something different, which was consistent with the successful national company he had so effectively re-fashioned from the ashes of the previous organisation. We agreed that the new multinational would:

- **delegate total accountability for all national business decisions** to the local management teams

- **have local managers manage** all local teams at all times

- **have the centre responsible for strategy and developmental processes, i.e. :**

  - the company-wide strategies that all nationally generated strategies would have to support

  - the developmental processes (to improve managing habits within the structural, procedural, and man management areas) to be used throughout the organisation

- **A cooperative of accountabilities.**

It seemed to me that here was an unusual and unique opportunity to create a fundamentally different type of multinational which would be significantly more effective.

Here was a chance to create a situation in which the centre and national companies pursued accountabilities that genuinely supported one another and simultaneously played to their different strengths.

National companies are positioned to have extensive local information. The centre is positioned to see a broader strategy and have a deeper expertise at the developmental processes common to all operations. This reality seemed to me to offer the possibility of creating a business focused cooperation of accountabilities. The fundamental aspiration was to significantly raise the levels of competence in the very large organisation, and eliminate its traditional frictions and inertia.

Having agreed this overall remit, we set out to create the new multinational. It took seven further years to accomplish the task of building a successful enterprise operating within the EEC and prove that the above guidelines were an effective engine for generating sustainable profit and growth. The conventional centralised multinational structure was no longer the only alternative. Neither was it the most competent one.

There were numerous examples of the above structural guidelines being actioned to enable the multinational to lay the basis for its success and growth. Some highlights were:

- **Lived examples of the above guidelines were needed**

    The guidelines were instantly understood.
    Skill at applying them had to be developed.

    The concept of decentralising power to the national teams to make all local decisions, whilst the centre ensured consistency on strategy and developmental processes, was totally new to those teams. Whilst people instantly understood the concept, managers in the local teams discovered they had not yet grown the skills to operate it. This has been the experience with every principle this work has uncovered. They have proved simple to understand intellectually – they are after all just common sense. However, it has never proved possible to apply any of the principles skilfully without considerable effort to develop the appropriate managing habits.

- **Training followed by a main focus on business practice**

    In addition to intensive training, managers needed the experience of living through a number of examples of the guidelines being actioned within the business. Only then did they start to develop operational skill at the managing habits for the new guidelines and absorb the real implications for them personally, and their business.

Critically, they needed full time local coaching support to achieve this.

The centre foresaw the need for that support and delegated a manager with the appropriate skills to provide it. Importantly, he did not have line management responsibility, and his assignment was strictly a temporary one. His specific success criterion was to continuously and rapidly increase the national teams' independence from any support – including his own. The national teams obviously realised that they were being given the real and highly unusual opportunity to grow their own development, and take their own business decisions.

However, they equally realised that the Multinational's senior team attached the highest priority to the work of their local coach. It would be prudent to take account of what this person had to contribute, and foolhardy to ignore it.

Below are three examples of the numerous changes made in the structural area of the multinational.

EXAMPLE 1   THE REMOVAL OF A DESPOTIC MANUFACTURING MANAGER

Local laws gave absolute responsibility for change to a legally protected 'Works Council'.

George (not his real name) was the Manufacturing Manager, and well known for his belief in an authoritarian 'command and control' style of managing. He was irretrievably wedded to this view of leadership, although it produced poor operational results within his function. European employment law empowered a works council with the legal right to approve all structural changes. The council consisted of legally elected representatives from across the employee groupings. Custom and practice was to simply stand aside, not interact with the 'Council', and accept whatever emerged out of it as a legally approved and protected process.

Local team apply principles of the Management Line, with support from the centre.

With the help and support of the coach, the national senior team set about systematically working with the Works Council on a one-to-one basis. They used the same principles that they applied within the management lines to reach a mutual view with individual council members as to what was beneficial for the business. Only after these one-to-one dialogues had successfully reached a mutually agreed and understood view was a council meeting called.

Manufacturing Manager interrupts Council meeting to protest.

George had 'got wind' of the process in hand and gate-crashed the Council meeting to protest at its inappropriateness. He insisted that he remain in his position. The council ordered his removal from the meeting, and remained focused on the commonly understood view of matters that they had individually worked through prior to the meeting. George was replaced by someone who had an appetite to work with his subordinates and take account of what they had to offer to the operation. The subsequent beneficial performance effects within manufacturing were plainly visible.

EXAMPLE 2   SUCCESSFULLY MANAGING A STRATEGIC THREAT FROM THE EEC

The EEC unilaterally decided to change the rules and threaten the bottom line.

The structure of the EEC's food subsidies policy was a key element in the existing financial balances that formed the national company's bottom line. The EEC was about to take a unilateral decision that took no account of how the industry functioned, and that threatened to seriously affect the company's financial performance. Such matters were deeply entrenched within the byzantine bureaucracy of the EEC's centre. It presented a daunting challenge to even identify the different factions involved in such a complex decision, let alone understand and influence how they interacted. The standard industry response was to rely on what lobbying system existed, or simply accept that the decision was too complex to affect.

The national company formed a specific working group of its own managers to directly influence the decision.

The local company decided they would take on the job themselves of influencing the decision. They set up a working group of their managers who made it their personal mission to gain the confidence and trust of all the relevant parties. Inevitably, this represented an enormous amount of accurately coordinated work in endless and countless meetings within the EEC. The team was diligent in using developmental principles carefully thought through with their coach. They focused their efforts entirely on one-to-one dialogues in which they took account of people's varied concerns, shared business information, and worked hard at finding ways of meeting mutual needs. Care was also taken to include data that gave the context of how the total industry worked. So widespread, accepted and trusted did this initiative become within the various working committees, that the EEC actually named it after the company. The effort was successful in getting the initial decision reconsidered and amended to reflect the realities facing the industry. The company's bottom line was consequently protected from serious and arbitrary damage.

EXAMPE 3   TRANSFERRING THE BUSINESS UNIT STRUCTURE INTO MANUFACTURING

**National companies operated the conventional 'top down',
'command and control', functionalised structure.**

The European companies were highly traditional in how they ran their manufacturing units. The Production Manager generally took all decisions, and all other levels lived lives of dutiful obedience. Of course this very much applied to operatives – regarded as the humblest and most basic form of life. Associated activities e.g. quality control, maintenance, ware-housing, technical support, etc. were all split into different groups. The performance of such a functionalised structure was inevitably poor. Problem anticipation did not exist, and any resolution was slow to glacial. Solutions endured poor to zero commitment. Similarly low levels of cooperation existed between the different functions, making organised cohesive responses to problems impossible to achieve. The effects were plain to see in all the numerical indices describing the manufacturing activity.

**Multidiscipline 'Plant Groups' were set up to problem-solve
the whole activity.**

The principles underpinning the Business Unit structure were transferred into the manufacturing activity. 'Plant Groups' were set up, which contained representatives from each relevant discipline. Manufacturing crews, maintenance, quality control, technical support, ware-housing, and procurement were all represented. Supervisors led the groups in a systematic working through of problems. They were prioritised against guide lines developed within the teams. The groups implemented their own agreed solutions and were supported where needed by appropriate resources via their leader's approval.

**Greatly improved performance,
but only after supervision changed their views of leadership.**

The appetite for tackling the operational problems amongst the functional representatives in the Plant Groups was determined and sustained. This was especially true of the operating crews who had never experienced any opportunity whatsoever to influence their working lives. It was to prove the basis for a step change in performance within manufacturing. It is interesting to note that the consistent difficulty in unlocking this repressed talent and desire to make a contribution was the supervisors' view of leadership.

Their initial conviction was that they should take all the decisions within the group. Old habits die hard. Much effort and support was needed to get them to first realise that this was not a business competent way of leading the groups. Considerably more effort and support was needed to get them to gradually learn to live a different way of leading their men. They had to make the challenging shift to being focused on the:

- o **processes** the groups were using to reach their decisions

- o **support** they needed in carrying out those processes

- **quality** of the final decision and its consistency with wider priorities

- **resources** needed to implement those decisions

To achieve such a development on an issue as emotive as a supervisor's view of authority has always proved difficult. It is a considerable testament to the people involved and the work done that it succeeded and achieved the desired business effects.

Absolute commitment from the centre was key.

It also succeeded because managers were in no doubt about the absolute commitment of the centre to this way of working. No alternative would be acceptable. People were clear that these were developmental principles that the centre would ensure were implemented across all locations. It was a powerful mixture of:

- **supporting** people with a full time coach to help them realise their potential, but with the quid pro quo that

- the change **had to happen**

Initiative taking, the anticipation and resolution of problems, the commitment to agreed solutions, and the cooperation between functional groups all became features of the new operation. The business benefited and job security was enhanced. The real reward was the improved quality of people's working lives as they grew and revelled in their capacity to directly influence their own operations.

As mentioned at the start of this section, the remaining two selected structural changes are detailed in Attachment One. They were no less pivotal to the organisation's sustained success than the above four, but are placed in the Attachment so as not to overburden this section.

B.   What happened procedurally and what were the effects?

With such fundamental changes happening to the organisation's structure, new procedures naturally had to be created to enable it to carry out its everyday business. This was an ideal opportunity to avoid the mistakes of the past, and the pitfalls of the conventional process of producing procedures. Instead, developing the new procedures covering every aspect of the running of the organisation featured a different process.

Those who carried out the procedures created them.
Management steered the process by which that happened.

- **Those who 'do it', create it.**

    The people directly responsible for a procedure created it. In cases where others' operation or service were affected, they were consulted on the effects of the procedure.

- **Fundamental aspirations of procedures decided.**

    Those writing the procedures were supported to first agree the fundamental aspirations that they would pursue. Such a process nurtured a sustained focus on and ownership of those aspirations by those who carried out procedures. The natural result was a much more secure repeatability and quality of subsequent action.
    They have simultaneously been able to take sensible decisions as to how to flex the procedure, should the needs of the business demand it. In these instances they have modified the detail of a procedure, but ensured that its aspirations have nonetheless always been met.

- **The best resources were made available to those who created procedures.**

    Those actioning procedures decided how best to take account of the expertise and resources made available to them. Managers involved ensured that however this was done produced a result that met the required technical and operational standards. If it didn't, they took care not to correct the decision themselves, but ensured it was rethought and rechecked until standards were met. Whilst this seemed a slower process at the time, it has always turned out to be a quicker one in the longer term. The people creating the procedure intimately learned the fundamental technical and operational bases for that procedure. The longer term impact on the quality of their work saved much time. Errors did not occur that have traditionally plagued those who weren't completely aware of the technical reasons behind what they habitually had to do.

- **Style and format to suit those who have to 'do it'**

    The style and format of each procedure was chosen by those operating it. Consequently they intimately understood it, and had firm ownership of its entirety.

- **Procedures flexed to reflect business changes**

    The same group regularly reviewed the procedure in the light of the changes they frequently saw happening in the business.

The effects

- **Repeatability and commitment significantly improved**

  The results from this process proved to be quite different from those produced from conventionally generated procedures. People had generally experienced those to be handed down from whatever group/person was deemed the most technically or operationally expert. They appeared as instructions.

  In contrast, the effects of following the above process were :

  o **a greatly improved understanding of the detail and rationale** for a procedure amongst those directly responsible for it

  o **a determined commitment** to its repeatability

  o **a capacity to flex** it appropriately

  o **an appetite to train newcomers** on the rationale and detail of the procedure

  At a practical level, these effects proved to be valuable advantages to the business. In essence this process recognised that a procedure was not a bit of paper to be handed to those who have to carry it out. Instead, it was an agreed way of behaving. To achieve this reality, the above process is needed to engage the hearts and minds of those who continuously deliver the action. Not to make that effort carries the message that managers judge that their subordinates have no valuable thinking to offer. That is the real root of the commonly experienced poor repeatability and standards on procedures within organisations.

- **This difference in 'process' proved operationally critical in the new Multinational**

  Reliable procedures became a particular priority in the Multinational where different cultures needed to operate consistently.

  The above process became vital in achieving repeatable standards across national locations. It allowed local variations to occur that did not compromise the fundamental aspirations that the procedures were intended to deliver. This ensured the repeatability of standards that is so necessary in sustaining a secure overseas operation.

  These issues are described in more detail within the Procedures section of the collated principles in Chapter Three (p.121).

C. What happened in the Man Management area, and what were the effects?

- **Changes were led by each management line.**
  The senior manager initiated all changes

  I remember an early pivotal discussion with the senior manager – whom I shall rename Jack – who was to become the Operations Director.

  He asked, 'Frank, how on earth are you going to coach and support the entire set of managers in the outfit on your own? There's only one of you. There just aren't enough hours in the day – or night.'

  ' Well, there you have the heart of it,' I said. 'I'm not. And you're right – it can't be done in the way you're imagining. It can only be done by each the management line learning to operate differently in its every day business. Your managers and their subordinates will only do that work together if you personally lead them to do it. So actually you're going to do it – and I'm going to show you how, and support your efforts. I shall be guided by you to lend additional support wherever you judge it's needed within the different management lines. But it must be clear that this is your initiative, and that the work is transparently led and done by you. The additional support from me is to happen only when there is no other way of achieving the end result needed.'

  He wryly commented, 'How did I guess that I would end up doing the work?'

  I replied, 'It will have no permanent value unless you do. If we want this to be nine day wonder, then stand aside and I'll lead the work. That will guarantee any change will be superficial, short lived, and be based on conformity.'

  He was of course unclear exactly how he was going to make this fundamental development happen. He did grasp that only he could lead it. Over a number of intense discussions he started to absorb that the matter was conceptually simple:

  - **He would set up the standard one-to-one reporting**
    between himself and the heads of the various management lines. The same discipline was to occur all the way through the organisation. Installing this habit alone has proved no mean achievement in any enterprise

  - **He would review progress frequently within those one-to-one reviews,**
    and focus on hearing an analysis of how every day business problems were being solved. Previous discussions with each manager would have agreed which particular managing habits he was to focus on improving. Jack would then be looking for improvements in those habits within the reviewed solutions.

  - **He would ensure that his direct reports followed the same discipline** with their subordinates.

Of course he realised that simple in concept though these guidelines were, turning them into habitual disciplines would be hard work. Additionally, he understood that experience offered two proven pieces of advice:

- o He was to take no prisoners if he heard comments like 'I only work at those managing habits within projects, or at meetings' (the two most quoted excuses/rationalisations by non-performers and posers). The need was to check that efforts to embed these different habits happened within every one of the activities that the business routinely demanded. Failure was guaranteed if the practice of these habits was isolated to any one activity.

- o He was persistently to probe for the tangible business results that came about from people's work at their new habits. Again he was to take no prisoners if he heard that effort was going into the managing habits for 'cultural' or 'ideological' reasons alone. These 'reasons' have been most commonly advanced by those who seek to evade the obligation to produce tangible business results from such habits. He needed to firmly establish that his men's first duty was to be demonstrably competent.

I assured him that the good news was that nothing in this work was going to be more complicated than this issue. All the work on all the other issues was going to be just as easy to understand.

I assured him that the bad news was that working at all the other issues to produce improved managing habits would require similar hard work. However, the way to do that work would remain precisely the same. It would require sustained practice at the new habits within the tackling of everyday business problems.

- **Each of the seven Man Management disciplines was grown within the Line Management relationship.**

Jack fully realised the scale of the commercial prizes that success at this work would bring. He was also aware that the success of his recent promotion to Operations Director hung in the balance. He rigorously pursued the above strategy and installed it as the normal way business was transacted. Its successful implementation revolved around the line management relationship between manager and subordinate. He ensured that his managers lived that relationship as a guided partnership for which they were solely responsible. It is key to understanding his success to see clearly the exact nature of that guided partnership, and where the accountabilities within it lay:

- o **Each line manager developed their skill at seeing and tackling the broader issues** that a particular problem posed. Their subordinates' duty was to tackle the more narrowly focused issues raised by that problem. The total needs of the business were consequently met by tackling these differing but complementary types of issues.

- o **Each line manager saw it as their responsibility to continuously develop the skill with which their subordinates tackled their issues**. They supported and guided their subordinates' efforts to implement the appropriate combination of man management skills within their work. Those are described in detail within the principles collated in Chapter Three (p.135). However, they are listed here as :

- **Responding to Success and Failure**
  Reviewing matters in such a way that success energises the un-defensive tackling of weaknesses.

- **Understanding, Creating and Using Strategy**
  Pursuing fundamental aspirations for the key issues concerned and simultaneously supporting those being pursued by one's manager.

- **Decision Making Methods**
  Appropriately using the seven naturally occurring decision making steps to both complete work and cooperate with others' efforts

- **Taking Initiatives**
  Foreseeing difficulties and creating and implementing proposals that help resolve the issues.

- **Managing Ideas**
  The capacity to support others, or synthesise different ideas, or appropriately offer alternatives.

- **Managing Time**
  The skill of using all three elements of time management: planning, monitoring, and time effective practices.

- **Leadership**
  The capacity to steer all the processes needed to complete work effectively with the commitment of those involved.

- **(Teamwork)**
  The above seven skills are the complete elements of teamwork. It does not exist as a separate additional skill set. This is explained in detail in Chapter Three's collation of principles.

- **Each manager ensured that their subordinates' efforts were appropriately coordinated with other work being carried out in the organisation**

These elements created the guided partnership between manager and subordinate, in which the manager was responsible for both the guiding and the partnership.

The effects

Some key results:

- **it produced business-effective work** within the management lines. Tangible targets were consistently met or exceeded

- **it grew individual habits that enabled any set of people to form an effective team** to tackle any challenge. Consequently, it became possible to work in cross-functional or multi-locational teams of any required composition with competent standards of achievement

- **it rapidly grew management talent** capable of taking up increasingly senior positions and duties in the organisation. If one feature stood out about this organisation it was the rate at which it was capable of securely developing such talent

Such effects were a key basis for the enterprise's rapid, sustained success and growth.

KEY LESSONS LEARNED

There were too many to completely list here, but their entire meanings are captured in the collation of principles noted in Chapter Three.

A selection of highlights is:

- **Seeing and deploying the connection between principles generates significant wealth. However, the vogue is 'quick, easy to understand, and impressive to say'**

  There is a trend to frequent the 'Management Accessorise' shop. There seems to be an infatuation with the quickly accessible, the easy to understand, the instant bit of wisdom, the sound-bite management insight that can be paraded to burnish the image, the one-liner from the latest academic management theory, etc., all packaged in verbal glitter and demanding little careful repeated reflection. The unyielding reality has been that successfully tackling complex challenges in organisations has not resulted from pursuing such superficialities.

  My experience is also that a penetrative analysis that strikes at the very root of an issue has always been characterised by an elegant simplicity. I have noticed that when I do not understand the core of a problem deeply enough, my summary of it has an opaque complexity. Truths from this work have not turned out to be complex when the heart of the matter is finally laid bare. However, the analyses on which they are based have always involved sustained effort. Their many layers have rewarded repeated reflection. Their outward appearance has not tended to instantly glitter. The gold has turned up later – but only after much panning. However, the results show that it is high quality gold.

The interdependence between the principles of this work is a case in point. Not an immediately attractive sounding idea, I grant you – can't be used in that snappy Power point presentation beloved of people desperate to quickly impress. But when effort has been spent to fathom its meaning and use, the effects in the business have been potent.

Patient, careful reflection can yield the deeper truth.
Looks less impressive, but gets better results

As recalled above, a key basis for the organisation's extraordinary sustained success was its method of new product development. It put intense pressure on its competition within the market place. Careful analysis shows that it was the direct result of the interdependence between certain principles operated in the structure, procedures and man management areas of the organisation. Referring to the detail described in p.56, examples of those principles were:

- o **Structurally :**
  Simultaneous access to the experts servicing a business where they worked in a group responding to the same manager was fundamental to success. It could only happen within the structure of the Business Unit.

- o **Procedurally :**
  Having the functional experts in direct control of the procedures their functions would operate during each phase of the product's development gave the best basis for success.

- o **Man management :**
  Business Unit team members were obviously used to working towards the fundamental aspirations generated with their Business Unit Head. This was automatically the ideal perspective for them to similarly generate the aspirations that they intended to pursue with the Product Development Manager. This close interlinking of two sets of mutually supportive, self generated aspirations proved to be a powerful basis for their commitment to the product development programme.

These were by no means the only principles that interacted to sustain product development in the pre-eminent position it enjoyed for so long, but it serves to illustrate the reality that appropriately deploying such interactions can put serious money onto the bottom line. That reality is not immediately obvious, but rewards those who deliberately pause to think and reflect about its implications. If I could have one wish, it would be that our management population give up the pursuit of the 'quick, easy, outwardly impressive', and start to explore the value instead of pursuing action based on thoughtful, careful reflection. This work is evidence that there is significant wealth to be generated by it.

● **Just because it's the largest organisation doesn't mean what it's doing is either right, or the best.**

Large, well established, profitable organisations such as multinationals can easily be assumed to be running a fundamentally thought-through, coherent, tried and tested way of managing things.

That is the appearance of matters.

However, there is an unrelenting truth that stalks the corridors of all large enterprises: the difficulty of running groups of people trying to do anything at all rises geometrically with the number of people involved. The added complications of different cultures, nations, locations, that beset multinationals simply compounds this truth. The result is that the larger the organisation, the more numerous and the denser are the thickets of personal interests, and the stronger are the many political undercurrents that need to be navigated. I'm not saying that the smaller organisation is not riven on occasions by precisely the same symptoms. I have experienced that too. However, in the larger organisation, these effects tend to be much more predominant.

The consequence has been that it is particularly difficult to consistently achieve fundamentally thought-through, coherent, tried and tested ways of managing things in these larger groups. The inherent resistance and inertia to such changes can be significant.

The appearance of matters can easily belie the truth of the situation.

The setting up and success of the above dairy foods multinational illustrates some ways of systematically 'thinning out those thickets' and calming those 'political undercurrents', i.e.:

- ○ **A genuine partnership between the Centre and National operations**

  It proved strikingly effective to operate a mutually supportive partnership between the centre and the national teams. The combination of the national operations being accountable for their business and national strategy, with the centre having accountability for overall strategy and developmental processes helped minimise both personal vested interests and political undercurrents. Instead, this concentration on different but complementary focuses meant that both central and national teams pursued mutually supportive business priorities.

  The continuous process of each partner looking to appropriately resource the other e.g. the centre providing coaching support, and the national teams providing information that anticipated their business issues – has been the practical basis for success. At a deeper level, the core difficulty in the conventional multinational is the continuous attempt to do business via establishing a balance of power between the centre and national groups – hence the centre's conventional stance as recalled on p.58 'A different type of Multinational structure...'.

This alternative view of the multinational pictures quite different sets of accountabilities. These remove any need to seek such a balance. It becomes clear that for both to succeed, each needs the other's help to succeed at their different focus. The basis for a mutually beneficial relationship is laid. Personal interests and political undercurrents are deprived of the manure of competition to thrive and grow strong.

- **Capturing both local diversity and business consistency**

The habit of translating organisation wide principles into specific local practices that take account of local information yields two key advantages:

- o Delivering the same aspirations and targets for each local practice ensures business consistency

- o Taking account of local information within the detailed plans produces appropriate diversity

Those experienced in the operation of multinationals will well know this to be an elusive and valuable combination.

BUSINESS CHALLENGE FIVE

DAIRY FOODS COOPERATIVE :

A NEW COOPERATIVE SETS OUT TO BREAK THE MOULD – AND SUCCEEDS

CONTEXT OF THE CHALLENGE AND THE PERCEIVED PROBLEM

A former Board member of the previous multinational dairy food company already ran a highly successful multinational company in a different but related industry. He had personally started his company from small and humble beginnings and grew it as a hands-on entrepreneur. He decided to enter the dairy food industry, and succeeded in buying a failing dairy cooperative.

Having watched the success of the operation described in Challenge Four, he asked to meet, and made me an offer I couldn't refuse.

He drew out a blank piece of paper and said, 'Create the ideal organisation that is an order of magnitude better than anything around, and I'll back its installation one hundred percent.'

I asked for clarification, 'Do you mean you want a copy of what you saw work in the multinational on whose Board you sat?' (described in Challenge Four).

'No,' he said. 'I want something better.'

I knew I'd never again get the chance to build an operation from the ground upwards that pursued every successful principle I had so far unearthed. The opportunity to create a living business operation unfettered by the past, and more importantly unhampered by the usual political constraints, was just too good a chance to pass up.

'What if I'm proposing something you've never seen before?' I enquired.

'I'm not paying you to install something I already know,' was his instant and unequivocal answer. 'You realise this operation is at the centre of this nation's media concern – and will remain there. My personal reputation is on the line. Everything we do will be done in the full glare of publicity. Failure is not an option.'

We agreed to meet after I'd surveyed the existing operation and talked with all its managers. I would then be in a position to describe to him how that ideal organisation would look.

We met a week later. He reviewed the proposal with meticulous care, and agreed its total scope. Throughout all the difficulties and pressures of installing the new organisation and getting it to run effectively, his commitment and support never faltered for a single moment. It was to prove an intense period of personal history for myself and the people involved.

WHAT HAPPENED

- **The Unions called an immediate strike**

A strike was called over redundancy arrangements for those who were to leave the company. This was resolved, leaving the enterprise free to install the new organisation.

Again, I will try and recall the key features of the structure, procedures, and man management areas.

What happened structurally and its effects.

- **A radical step change in entrepreneurial drive was created right at the bottom of the organisation.**

The key to raising the game dramatically at the operator level in the organisation was to set up a collection of small businesses run by chosen operators in long-term partnerships with the company. Each business would be owned and run by a nominated person running a group containing up to six or seven positions.

This was about as different as the men, or the managers, had ever experienced or heard of. It took careful, detailed and repeated discussions to come to a mutual understanding of what the proposed structure was really trying to achieve. Key elements of that understanding were:

- o **the partnership was a serious, long term, mutual commitment – not the traditional 'out sourcing/contracting out'**

- o **the cooperative was totally committed to the success of the small businesses**

The company remained vitally interested in every detail of each small business, its progress and its prospects. This was not to be the 'treat the activity at arm's length, and disown it if it gets into trouble – we've more important things to worry about' way of viewing things, which so characterises out sourcing/contracting. On the contrary, the company would do everything in its power to ensure the sustained success of the businesses. Support in setting up accountancy, pensions, insurance, health and safety were all seriously undertaken. It closely and regularly liaised with every business to ensure each knew the forthcoming operational plans and the effects on them. It provided a monthly lump sum payment to each business to reflect the service needed. It rapidly adjusted payment should the actuality of what occurred not match the plans. It had an approved list of people whom the business owners could man their operations from. They were encouraged to suggest additions/modifications to that list.

- o **the quid pro quo – the small businesses delivered entrepreneurial drive
into the base of the operation.**

Each business leader manned up his operation in the manner he judged appropriate from the approved list of people. He took great care that in doing so he could meet all the criteria for the operation. Payment was dependent on it. He was continuously aware – as were his men – that issues of flexible work practices, cooperation within the team and with other teams, and the extent to which team members could back up other operations in other groups all automatically increased their take-home share of the lump sum provided for the small business. He consequently saw it as a vital commercial need to develop his team in those three areas of work practices: support within and outside the team, and the ability to technically stand in for other teams' needs. This was strongly encouraged by the company providing a training and reward scheme for expanding an operator's capacity to work in different teams. It goes without saying that the small business leaders mainly looked for initiatives from their crews that delivered a better operation at the lowest cost. This was the main key to an increased take-home share of the lump sum. The common example was for them to continuously alter their manning levels to accurately reflect the level and types of operation that they undertook. 'Fixed costs' came to mean something quite different in this way of working.

- o **each small business was intimately linked into the running and optimisation of the
whole manufacturing activity**

  - ▪ **all small business leaders answered to 'Key Operators'**
  who ran specific sectors of the whole operation

The Small Business leaders were appropriately grouped according to what parts of the operation they worked in, to answer into a permanent staff member – a Key Operator. He would be responsible for the planning, optimisation, efficiencies, and financial performance of a discrete part of the operation. This automatically meant that each small business was continuously updated by the information the Key Operator regularly shared with its leader. Their consequent initiatives were therefore based on the direction of the overall operation.

  - ▪ **all Key Operators worked in the same business unit,**
  ensuring consistency across all small businesses

All the Key Operators answered to a Business Unit Head who had responsibility for the whole business in the same way as previously described in Business Challenge Four. This ensured that consistent information and priorities were continuously fed into all the small businesses.

- ● **Designed to enable middle and senior levels to work in the market place, and on strategy.**

  - o **the small businesses released middle and senior levels
  from crisis management**

The ability of the small businesses to run the core basis of the manufacturing operation enabled another fundamental change to take place. It was a yet more radical, unusual and far reaching change.

In the conventional structure, middle and senior managers commonly spend significant time and energy dealing with the effects of operational problems. It's the well known 'my life is continuously overfilled by the inescapable treadmill of crisis management' symptom. In contrast, once the new structure enabled the bottom levels to take charge of operational problem-solving, a key opportunity opened up for more senior levels. They then had the opportunity to do what they were actually paid to do: not to solve problems, but to create wealth by taking business initiatives.

○ **the upper management levels focused on the market place and the company's strategy**

A central strategic challenge confronted managers in the market place. Secure success would be built on resolving it. Failing at it, or ignoring it, would bring mediocrity at best and failure as a more likely outcome. The manufacturing units would inexorably produce perishable dairy products. The clear commercial goal was to market these products within their unforgiving deadlines, to a point as close to the eventual customer as possible.

Typically, the above structure succeeded at the challenge by releasing the Business Unit Head to spend over 90% of his time in the market place. He was able to influence the customer base in a way that could not be matched by the competition. His direct line authority over an integrated team containing all the business expertises (e.g. technical support, manufacturing, etc.), gave him the sort of direct influence that customers greatly valued, and could not access elsewhere. His instant capacity to make and reliably deliver the appropriate deal told customers that they were working directly with the key decision maker.

The bottom line demonstrated secure success.

Direct and continuous contact with the market place enabled the Business Unit Head to also appropriately modify the organisation's strategy at speed. This gave the enterprise great agility and 'sureness of foot' in its ability to respond to changes it saw in the market place. Not unsurprisingly, the commercial performance of the company put significant pressure on its competitors.

SOME KEY EFFECTS

The most obvious overall effect was to change the company's bottom line from its previous losses to one of sustained and growing profit. Several factors underpinned this turnaround:

- Enabling the bottom level to take responsibility for the operation grew a robust sense of their own self respect. The scale of their initiatives markedly increased as a result.

- Continuously updating the Small Business leaders with the planning and optimisation work of the Key Operators gave those leaders the bigger picture of the operation. One fundamental ingredient for generating appropriate initiatives was therefore always in place.

- Directly linking responsibility and reward led the small business leaders to make incisive and rapid changes. Typically, one leader correctly saw that his particular business would greatly benefit if his total crew were of graduate standard. He rapidly and smoothly made that happen with the minimum disruption to his working crew and was proud to enjoy the rewards that came from quickly managing that change. The total operation also significantly benefited from the upgrading of his team. Such a change would have been either unthinkable in the previous way of working, or would have been the unsuccessful subject of interminable negotiation.

- Combining the entrepreneurial drive of the small businesses at the bottom level with the integrated service that the business units could deliver into the market place produced a commercial performance that could not be bettered by the competition.

This turnaround was sustained in a highly competitive and continuously falling market. The results were so consistent and threatening to the company's closest competitor that they put in intense effort into copying the structure. Such replication proved simple and totally ineffective. The client company already knew from the start that their real commercial advantages could not be copied. What was visible was the new and highly unusual structure. What was not visible were the procedures and man management practices that drove and integrated with the structure. These required experience, skill, and diligence to develop. They could easily copy what they saw of the shape of the new racing car, but they could not develop the formula for the specialised fuel on which it ran. Their efforts failed.

What happened procedurally and the effects

The same opportunities existed as in Business Challenge Four.

Such radical changes in structure automatically called for new procedures right across the company. The same principles were applied as detailed in the previous case history. The particular procedures developed were very specific to the operation and the people concerned. Nonetheless, the same effects and benefits were inevitably produced in the business and the organisation. The detailed explanations of Challenge Four are therefore not repeated here, save to give a flavour of the particular effect of the small businesses.

The company closely supported each group's efforts to develop its own set of procedures in whatever form they felt comfortable with – always provided operational standards were met. The necessary consistency between different small business groups was resolved between their leaders and the relevant Key Operators. This resulted in particular teams delivering their own procedures with high reproducibility, but which were also consistent with other teams on essential operational matters.

What happened in the Man Management area and the effects

As for the issue of procedures, the man management factor presented the same opportunity as for Challenge Four, but on a much wider scale. The effect of the small businesses taking up the responsibility for the daily problem-solving was far reaching. It usefully altered the focus of the man management practices at each level in the organisation, i.e.:

- **Disciplines of initiative taking, cohesive use of the decision making steps, and managing ideas became critical at the small business level.**

The day-to-day cutting edge of the operation depended on the ability of the small businesses to incisively take initiatives on the problems confronting them. The fact that they realised the rewards for doing so would directly and reliably show up in their pay packets was a strong incentive for achieving sustainable solutions. Having created this situation, the company naturally invested considerable effort in training and supporting the operating crews to become skilful at the range of man management practices detailed in Chapter Three. It was very much in its interests to encourage the highest standards it could in this concern. This represents an entirely different attitude to that of the traditional contracting out/out-sourcing arrangement.

The response to the training and support was outstanding. The small business groups revelled in their new-found freedom to influence their work situation, and be equitably rewarded for it. They took carefully measured risks that conventionally managed structures would not have dreamed of, and reaped deservedly effective results. The level of support between business groups reached levels that no 'flexibility agreement' I have ever heard of or witnessed has reached. It was driven by their own commitment to performance levels and their consequent pay –not the reluctant foot-dragging acquiescence so commonly seen from negotiated industrial relations arrangements.

- **Upper management levels focused on strategy, and influencing how teams responded to the needs of the market place.**

As described above, the performance of the small businesses at the base of the organisation enabled a fundamental change in the role of the upper management levels. Their focus usefully shifted away from reacting to operational problems to being proactive in the business. Their lives had previously been too heavily justified by their capacity to respond to operational crises.

In contrast, their new management challenge was to rapidly set and modify strategy in the light of their direct contact with the market place. They spent significant time understanding and discerning the strategy and long-term aspirations that both customers and their market place were pursuing. Considerable effort was also spent to create that same understanding within the teams working back in the operation. That regular briefing enabled the support teams to anticipate changes to match the needs of the market place. Practising these skills was aided by the business unit structure placing all the functions within the one team accountable to the Business Unit Head.

SOME EFFECTS AND LESSONS LEARNED

- **The most visible effect was the speed and quality of cooperative decision making at the operational level.**

  The impact of the small businesses surpassed all expectations. It was as if the impenetrable dam that had long held back the pent-up energy, commitment and latent talent of the work force had burst open at a stroke. The transformation in the quality of the operation on every single index of performance was both extremely rapid – in some cases instant – and sustained. The transformation in the quality of their lives was startling: work became something they relished, enjoyed, and could express themselves in. They seemed to become whole people instead of the diminished people they were in the old conventional system. It was a truly rewarding effect to witness and one that remains a vivid memory.

- **The impact of the man management practices within this structure was to bind it into one unit linked closely to the market place.**

  Anyone who has grappled with trying to improve how organisations work will know how elusive, critical, and difficult it is to achieve this effect. Customers quickly realised that this was a company that was seriously interested in their short to long term needs. They also saw that all its responses were coordinated across all functions. It delivered them at a speed that spoke of a complete absence of bureaucracy. This was, of course, because there wasn't any. The work on both the structural and man management factors had eliminated that from the enterprise.

- **Sustained support, and the absence of politics at the senior level, enabled spectacular success.**

  I found the opportunity of creating this experience exhilarating at many levels.

  Sadly, it also illustrated by contrast how constrained we usually are by the tides and currents of vested interests and politics that normally feature at the senior levels. They diminish the scale and invention of what can be achieved in organisations. They diminish us as people. Removing them, and replacing them with sustained support, allowed us to explore our true potential – as organisations and as people.

BUSINESS CHALLENGE SIX

A CHEMICALS MULTINATIONAL :

A HIGH-PROFILE NEW OPERATION MOVES FROM IMPENDING FAILURE TO OUTSTANDING SUCCESS

CONTEXT OF THE CHALLENGE AND THE PERCEIVED PROBLEM

A multinational chemicals company had a well established business that manufactured and sold packaging material. It put very significant investment into designing and building the world's largest and fastest production plant for making that material. They planned to make a substantial profit from selling the output from the new plant to their well established worldwide customer base. It was such a large project that failure would affect the bottom line of the whole multinational – not to mention doing significant damage to its reputation. The new plant also broke into new technological ground, and would operate in hitherto unknown territory. This was by any standards a 'milestone' technical and commercial challenge that the company needed to succeed at.

The project was in its last phase of construction and rapidly approaching its commissioning deadline. The first sign of trouble emerged as a significant concern about delivering that deadline. Punitive penalty clauses were signed with customers who had already bought the plant's expected output. More bad news emerged as significant operational and technical problems remained unresolved. Previously less technically advanced plants had traditionally suffered fraught and protracted commissioning start ups. They had never delivered their design performance on time and on budget. There was a palpable air of unease and a lack of confidence within the commissioning team. The commercial and reputational outlook appeared forbidding. No consistent understanding existed either about the difficulties with the project or what should be done to improve matters. Great pressure was felt from the fast approaching deadline and commercial commitments with key customers.

WHAT HAPPENED

● **The manufacturing manager had the courage to step back and think anew.**

Sean, the manager (not his actual name) could clearly see the potential danger to the company and himself. He decided to seek help, as neither he nor anyone else could see a clear way forward, and time was of the essence. His HR manager had seen the work described in Business Challenge Three and suggested we meet and explore the problem. We agreed after that meeting that I would look at his operation and talk with a range of the managers involved. We would then meet again to consider the analysis and recommendations from that survey.

The survey disclosed very uncomfortable realities, and posed a career-threatening solution.

Asking the staff to give concrete and specific examples of both the successes and difficulties within the operation gave an entirely consistent picture. When all the information was collated and fed back to them they had no amendments to make, and agreed with the picture of the operation that emerged.

- ○ **The facts said that continuing as before would bring failure.**

    Talking through the implications of the survey with Sean, the conclusion was that continuing without any change would lead to operational and commercial failure on a significant scale. Despite its considerable size, the company would be badly affected by the likely losses. Sean's career would be irretrievable.

    However, there was an operationally sound solution. It was equally clear that the organisation would regard it as heretically unconventional. Nonetheless, the key benefit of completing the survey and validating it with the management team was that it clearly confirmed the factual basis for that solution. It stands to Sean's considerable credit that he did not buckle under the pressure, and proceeded to propose a solution to his boss that unleashed a storm of protest about his head. Senior managers poured unreserved scorn on the need to even consider such an idea. They cited long company practice that said it just did not do such things, had never done them, and should never do them. It was made clear that should the smallest thing go wrong with what was clearly a 'lunatic idea', then Sean had no future in the company, and probably no future in the industry. Sean remained steadfast, and was left a lonely figure in implementing an entirely unsupported solution. Only his HR manager thought he had a point.

- ○ **The facts said that a politically incorrect solution would succeed.**

    The way forward was to replace the senior management of the project with particular non graduate replacements who were operationally and technically experienced. Critically, these managers had a track record in the man management skills (as defined in this work – Chapter Three) that the project urgently needed. The organisation had technical back-up in considerable depth to support the new non graduate operational team should they need it.

    The existing management of the project was academically and intellectually gifted, but had neither the managing skills to bring it to a successful conclusion nor the inclination to acquire them. Their ingrained habit was to micro-manage every issue and take every decision themselves, no matter how small they might be. Their response to the pressure of the project rapidly grinding to a frustrated and confused halt was to increase the energy they put into yet smaller scale management – nano-management – not even the tiniest decisions escaped their full attention.

    However, the organisation firmly regarded these managers as typical of the sort of people they recognised as leaders – academically bright, intellectually gifted, excellent presenters, and articulate to a fault. Their policy for many years exclusively promoted such graduate qualified managers to pivotal positions in their operations. It was an absolute article of faith. In their view, to depart from this fixed mantra of management choice was heresy.

○ **Other proposals dealt with how the project should be managed and how the basic operation could support it.**

The strength of the storm that raged over changing the management control of the key project in the company obscured the other equally radical proposals that Sean was suggesting. These described how the standard structure could best support the project and the normal operation. The paradoxical effect was to allow him to quietly get on and implement them.

They hinged around setting up business unit style groups at operating plant level involving all the functions needed to run the operation. The multinational ran a deeply functionalised structure, and this change was a radical departure. All the changes in procedures and man management described in the previous Business Challenges were worked through by staff in their own particular way.

Sean implemented all the necessary changes with commendable speed, and gave the new management team his firm support.

○ **a famous victory was won.**

For the first time in the company's long operational history for this type of plant, the commissioning was completed on time and on budget. Again for the first time in the company's history, the tested sustained production levels achieved by the plant met or exceeded design targets. The commercial results from worldwide sales were a shot in the arm for the whole organisation. The company's reputation in that market place was secured.

People now fell over themselves to claim some reflected glory from being associated with the now 'innovative' idea' of managing the project 'differently'. Sean's career became secure. I noted with wry amusement, however, that this was the last and only time the organisation followed the 'innovative' practice of matching management skills to the job in hand, regardless of people's academic track record or intellectual verbal ability.

Old prejudices die hard – if ever. They certainly didn't seem to be in the least affected by the success of implementing management habits that were entirely inconsistent with them.

SOME EFFECTS AND LESSONS LEARNED

We needn't spend too much time on this section, as the reader can by now well guess from the recount of previous Challenges what the effects were.

Some highlights were:

● **Reality – even a spectacular success – is impenetrable to the closed mind.**

The reader will notice the echo of what happened in Business Challenge One, within the American Oil Multinational. At least, this multinational noted the commercial success of the work, and a seemingly Houdini-like escape from an apparently inevitable debacle. However like its American cousin, it chose not to learn from how that success came about. It made not the smallest move to investigate the basis for the key proposal that it originally derided as heretical nonsense. Once it succeeded, they simply gave Sean back his career and closed the matter. Like the American multinational, success was accepted and its causes raised no interest. Fundamental lessons from that experience resolutely went unlearned. The organisation was short and medium term richer, but not a whit wiser. To some, the comfort of closed minded convention seems much more attractive than the real causes of proven commercial success.

● **The balance between managerial skill and technical ability is critical**

> **Leadership by managerial skill backed by technical ability can be highly successful.**
> **Leadership by technical ability alone has a very low potential for success.**

The above example is one of many that I have seen where leaders need first and foremost to be competent managers. This does not mean that they haven't also worked hard at ensuring they have a sharp grasp of the technology of their business. However, their prime strength has been in a detailed, factual, skilful grasp of effective management habits.

This work illustrates what happens when we reverse this balance. When I first ventured into this work, I was invited to look at why a well known company manufacturing and selling fridges was struggling to be profitable. It had a long and enviable reputation in the market, and the public felt that their product was synonymous with quality – and it was. How could it possibly go wrong?

It had a policy of promoting its most successful engineers/technical people to senior managerial positions. Most critically, these very able people had no interest in management issues, and regarded all such concerns as 'soft' matters filled with opinionated psycho-babble. They prided themselves as only being interested in 'hard' numbers. The effects were stark: the organisation lost all ability to commonly agree where it was heading, how to operate in teams, how to nurture the anticipation of problems, and how to instil initiative taking, etc. It became non functional. It did continue to provide a technically competent back up service to its customers. The sad reality was that its senior levels were now staffed with people unable to appreciate the real nature of the serious problem facing them. They had implacably closed minds to the possibility that their fundamental problem lay outside their technology. Of course, that was their prerogative – as was their responsibility to face the ensuing commercial effects. Speaking as an engineer, I found the experience chastening, and a lesson that has never left me.

CHAPTER THREE

A COLLATION OF THE PRINCIPLES USED TO RESOLVE THE ONSITE BUSINESS CHALLENGES

INTENT AND FORMAT

<u>Intent</u>

The first purpose is to draw together the principles used to tackle the onsite business challenges described in Chapter Two.

A description of each principle, the context of its use, and its key effects are detailed in the following sections. The hope is that managers can internalise this information and re-apply it in ways that suit their individual needs.

The nature and scale of the business challenges described in the previous chapter required the principles to reach into every part of how the organisations ran. The second purpose is therefore to capture how they were used to develop the organisation as a whole. My hope is that managers can similarly absorb this information so that they can re-apply it to meet their organisation's needs.

<u>Format</u>

Section One of this chapter recalls the three starting conditions that have given organisations the best basis to commence applying the principles within this work. They could then successfully develop their managing habits in a systematic fashion.

Solving the business challenges encountered on site has inevitably called for work to be done within the key factors: structures, procedures, and man management. Section Two details the principles that emerge from the work in each of those operational areas.

SECTION ONE: **THREE STARTING REQUIREMENTS THAT ENABLE AN ORGANISATION TO FURTHER DEVELOP ITS MANAGING HABITS**

1. Tackling core issues

The senior level has demonstrated a determination to identify and fundamentally resolve the core issues underlying the challenges facing the organisation.

The senior managers led by the CEO have seen the task of identifying those issues as a pivotal, separate project. They have relentlessly pursued the findings of that work, so that the fundamental needs of the business are met. The significant political risks that have usually accompanied these efforts have been skilfully managed, and not allowed to daunt or divert the team.

2. Using first-hand operational information

They have carefully established the first-hand operational facts that describe those issues, and continuously taken accurate account of them.

The analysis of the relevant issues has been based on operational information from the level(s) who directly deal with them as part of their job. Senior managers have consequently taken care to check assumptions about those issues that have inadvertently become part of their 'accepted wisdom'. A number of these assumptions have usually had to be significantly changed.

3. Continuously developing daily managing habits

Individual managers heading each of the management lines have shown an appetite to continuously develop their own daily managing habits.

The CEO and senior team have realised that secure commercial results only came from the continuous development of the daily managing habits used in each management line. They have further grasped that that can only be achieved if the line manager concerned pursues his own development in the same issues. It is unglamorous, painstaking, and highly demanding work, yet has proved a key basis for sustainable, quality business results.

These three requirements may seem the most trite of common sense statements – indeed, at a conceptual level, they are. Nonetheless, two things have been relentlessly proved over the years of successfully doing this work:

- firstly, the extensive effort built into meeting these requirements make them a difficult path for managers to tread. Each of them has required consistent, long term, tenacious effort. The challenge of confronting deep seated difficulties, usually created over a long history, has naturally posed significant practical and political obstacles to overcome.

- secondly, simple though they are in concept, there are many layers of work, and many implications that inexorably flow from each requirement.

The individual development by each line manager is on its own a significant challenge. It has brought many personal 'cross roads' into focus. People have for instance had to explore difficult changes in their approach to encourage key members of their teams to grapple with bottlenecks in their performance.

This has proved to be no 'soft option'. Indeed, managers who have set out to pursue this development work would claim they found it demanded continuous effort. Nonetheless, their experience has been that it has brought sustainable success.

The revealing result of these demands is that only a minority of CEO's and senior teams are prepared to undertake the rigours of this work. The majority have always agreed the logical need to have the above bases in position. They have, however, always felt that easier paths were more attractive. I would certainly feel that is entirely their prerogative to make such a choice and have never sought to dissuade them from that judgement. Those people who have attempted and succeeded at this work and posted its exceptional results have needed every ounce of their own commitment to accomplish the task. If such conviction is not there at the beginning, it has not been worth starting this work. It would fail, and the 100% success rate of the work be jeopardised.

As the operational principles are explained in Section Two, it will become obvious that the absence of any of the above starting conditions will significantly hinder their implementation. With all three requirements in position, a secure basis is created for the work to progress.

SECTION TWO   **PRINCIPLES FOR THE OPERATIONAL AREAS**

Exploring the structural, procedural and man management components in turn:

PRINCIPLES FOR THE STRUCTURAL AREA

Broader context

● **A highly emotional area with deep efficiency implications**

The structure describes how accountability will be shared out and linked up in the organisation. The issue of accountability has proved to be a powder keg of emotions, intense ambition, and the focus of persistent manoeuvring and personal effort. Managers have often decided to see their entire identity justified by and reflected in this struggle. They have happily deemed their whole lives well spent if they achieve their desired positions. Consequently, they have worked their hardest to avoid what they would consider as a failure to reach those positions, or their equivalent.

With people feeling that key personal interests were at stake, the decisions on structure have had business effects that are hard to overstate. The impact on the quality of decisions, and on people's capacity to grapple with challenges and difficulties, has been fundamental and widespread.

● **Success has been marked by a factual, integrated view of how the organisation works**

Effective judgements made in this area have had two key characteristics:

   o   firstly, they have explained an integrated picture of how the total organisation structure would work. People have then seen how the different parts of it would interact to deal with business issues

   o   secondly, they presented a consistent view of how work on all the major challenges within the operation would be aided by the structure

Where managers found the organisation's analyses and judgements in this area to be helpful, two results have followed. Firstly, the speed and quality of decisions, which had firm and broad support, became a feature of its work. Secondly, the level of commitment to grapple with difficulties that naturally arise when implementing any ambitious set of plans was palpably strong, and full of confidence.

Format

The following section recalls the principles for the structural area. To aid an over view, the key issues around which the work centred are relisted below.

Issue 3 – 2.1   Structures that face the customer:
Business Unit and Functional structures

Issue 3 – 2.2   Accountability:
How accountabilities vary across the different levels in an organisation, and the key role of the Management Line

Issue 3 – 2.3   Interfaces:
Dealing with business issues that lie at the interfaces between different parts of the organisation

Issue 3 – 2.4   Business Units, and Functional Groups

Issue 3 – 2.5   Regaining management control of Production:
Enabling business priorities to guide Production

Each of these issues is examined below following a format of :

Summary ....Key conclusions from the work on that issue

Background context..Main information relevant to the issue

Principle(s) ....Effective principle(s) applied to the issue

Explanation...Operational detail of principle(s)

Some beneficial effects and implications........Some experienced positive effects

Commonly encountered difficulties.................Some challenges

Issues

Issue 3 – 2.1:   **STRUCTURES THAT FACE THE CUSTOMER :**

Business Unit versus Functional structures

SUMMARY

The conventional structure is split into functions (e.g. manufacturing, technical support, marketing, etc.) that are primarily concerned with how they operate. Essentially, this structure faces inwards. The consequence has been a strong trend towards bureaucracy, with market place performance being the significant loser.

In contrast, the business unit structure consists of multidisciplinary groups of experts clustered around customer bases to service their needs. The result is an organisation that continuously faces outwards to the customer. All actions become prioritised by the central need of the business to excel in the market place.
Each group of experts is led by a Business Unit Head who has total operational and financial responsibility for that section of the operation. Alongside these teams is a set of Functional Heads (Finance, Systems etc.), who represent the organisation's best technical talent within those expertises. They are responsible for defining the standards and technical strategies that the organisation pursues in each of those functions.

This structure has produced a far higher quality, speed and cohesiveness of initiative taking than any other alternative. Its accountability and speed of response to problems has also proved to be significantly sharper than the traditional functionally based structures.

However, to harness the potential of the Business Unit structure, significant effort has had to be spent in developing its managing habits. Experience shows that without that development work, the above business advantages are not achievable. Such work represents a hidden commercial advantage, which competitors in copying the structure have failed to realise, and hence never replicated its significantly better business results.

BACKGROUND CONTEXT

Functional structures

One strongly held conventional view is that an organisation needs to be split into functions. Each would contain its particular experts, with a senior team positioned above the functional departments. All the accountants would therefore work in a finance function with a Finance Director at its head. Similarly, all the sales and marketing staff would be located in the marketing function headed by a Marketing Director, etc. The senior team would typically comprise the CEO and the Functional Heads. The key characteristic of the functionally based structure has inevitably been an overwhelming focus on the operation of its functions. Everything – including the market place – is seen in the perspective of that focus.

Business Unit structures

At the other end of the continuum is an organisation consisting of multidisciplinary teams focused on servicing delegated sections of the total customer base. Each team answers directly to a Business Unit Head with total operational and financial responsibility for his part of the total business. He would be aided at his level by Functional Heads (such as a Finance Director, etc.), who carry particular technical responsibilities that only experts in those functions can discharge. The senior team is positioned directly above the Business Unit and Functional Heads, and typically comprises a selection of those same managers, headed by the CEO.

The key characteristic of this very flat structure is its continuous outward facing concern for its customer base. All activities and functional needs become prioritised by that overriding market focus.

The organisation's choice of where to operate on the continuum between functional and business unit structures has had far reaching commercial effects. Yet it has been particularly vulnerable to very strong vested interests, intense loyalties at the senior level, and the strong political tides of power and influence that have surged through the organisation. It has been extremely rare to see this decision led by the needs of the business.

Intertwined with this choice has been the CEO's decision as to how he has elected to lead the senior team. The CEO's personal view and management of that responsibility has had a pivotal effect on the choice of structure the organisation has made and how it has operated it.

At one end of the continuum, I have witnessed CEOs with a particular personal skill (e.g. in product development) use that talent to rule over what he sees as his feudal fiefdom. His decisions on all matters are the writ that runs through the organisation. His personal leaning towards, for instance product development has dominated all decisions. In such situations, there has naturally been no appetite for a structure that faces outwards to the customer – only a structure that faces the CEO.

At the other end of the continuum, skilful CEOs have relentlessly managed all key issues through the senior teams' individual abilities, and their capacity to operate as a team. In such situations, structures that prioritise the needs of customers have become a possibility.

PRINCIPLE	**A structure that faces outwards to the customer significantly improves performance.**

EXPLANATION

There were five basic components to this principle:

- dividing the total enterprise into component businesses that inevitably had appropriate links

- maximising the accountability for each business, i.e. delegating it to one manager

- organising how each business was run to deliberately maximise the quality and speed of response to challenges

- organising information systems to monitor progress in each business that helped speed the response to indicated difficulties, and were also transparent to everyone in the organisation

- having a senior team that operated as a Business Unit for the whole enterprise

Explaining each of these in turn:

1. **Dividing the total enterprise into component businesses**

   Organisations have either focused their operations on appropriate customer bases or product groupings, depending on the exact nature of their business. Their choice was always made on the basis of which option, or mix of options, best aided the quality of service to customers.

   Business Unit teams have then been set up to service the range of businesses sectors that that analysis has identified.

2. **Maximising the accountability for each business**

   Each business thrived when accountability for it rested with one manager and his team. Accordingly, that manager – the Business Unit Head – had full financial and operational responsibility for that business. It has then always been unequivocally clear:

   - **what the scope for initiative taking** was in any situation

   - **what the causes** were for any action taken

   - **and what could be learned** from any subsequent results

   Equally, the business has thrived when functional experts were simultaneously accountable for both the setting of technical standards and the delivery of technical strategies.

   Both these sets of responsibilities, and their interdependence are detailed later (in Issue 3 – 2.4 'The partnership between the accountabilities of Business Units and Function focussed groups' p.110). Suffice it to say at this point that a critical ingredient in the business unit structure has proved to be the combination of Business Unit Heads and Functional Heads, working as one operational team.

3. **Maximising the quality and speed of response to challenges**

   The Business Unit Head and his team created their own aspirations for their business. The quality and speed of their response to subsequent challenges reflected that they:

   - had the appropriate mix of technical skills to respond

- owned the aspirations that drove that response

- had direct and sole control over all the resources to meet the challenge

- realised that it was their sole obligation, and that of their manager, to succeed at 'their' business

These four conditions have powerfully encouraged quality responses at speed within each business.

4. Transparent information systems that speed the response to difficulties

The above three features have sharpened accountability within the separate businesses. However, this has only been possible when appropriate information systems have been installed to monitor each operation.

Great effort and attention has been spent by each business on designing and commissioning its own systems to monitor its performance. Continuous effort has gone into ensuring that information could be easily checked at all times throughout the organisation. Experience shows that the appetite for anticipating difficulties and the speed of responding to them were significantly higher than when the businesses relied on a centrally based accounts system. Ownership of the local systems was high, and they were continuously reviewed to sharpen their relevance and consequent use.

Systems were also installed that collated the separate business information sets to produce regular monitoring data for the entire enterprise.

5. The senior team was the Business Unit for the whole business

The senior team has of course been the level that focused on prioritising the needs of the total organisation.

Senior managers have therefore set aside line management responsibilities they may also have had for particular parts of the business or functions. As a result, that level has concentrated on relentlessly supporting the CEO in clarifying and pursuing organisation-wide aims and priorities. This has never been an easy task to achieve. Unity at the most senior level has rarely occurred as a natural starting condition. Sustained efforts have had to be made to grow that unity by implementing the principles detailed in the Man Management Section (p.135 - 199). Though difficult, the efforts to succeed at it have been handsomely repaid in the beneficial effects detailed below.

SOME BENEFICIAL EFFECTS AND IMPLICATIONS

- **The organisation has better served its market place.** Specific effects have been:

  o **Significant energy and drive has been unleashed on the business,** where before it had been dissipated and blocked by the unending internecine manoeuvring within and between functions.

  o **The rate of initiative taking and preparedness to carefully undertake the creative and unusual significantly increased**. People's habit became 'let's see what could be possible to achieve' rather than the previous view of being continuously constrained by the 'roadblocks' that were a feature of the deep hierarchical structures of the functional departments.

  o **Minimising the management levels and number of people involved** in decision taking had a significant effect on initiative taking. Both the speed and level of ambition of decisions rose. These were commonly taken directly by the relevant functional expert within the business unit, or by his immediate manager. It became continuously clear how they were taken and what their effects were. By the same token, prevarication and fudging issues were immediately and transparently obvious. This latter feature rapidly decayed and disappeared altogether after an initial induction period.

- **Customers greatly valued forming close and direct operational relationships with a wide range of experts** within the business units.

  Highly influential links between customers and technical, production, distribution, and product development managers etc., were easy to nurture. These significantly enhanced the traditional connections with sales and marketing staff. Customers grew a strong commitment to what they experienced as a real and direct influence on all aspects of the service they were receiving. The commercial impact of closely coordinating this network of relationships was considerable. It proved to be a significant competitive advantage that could not be copied by the functionally based structures operated by the competition.

- **A more integrated and effective service to the customer was achieved by having specific managers deal with issues at the interfaces between business units.**

  Commercially significant issues had previously either 'got lost' at the interfaces between functional departments or perversely ignored in favour of functional priorities. Specific managers and their teams were now delegated responsibility for such issues. They pursued business-wide priorities, and delivered significant profit that was previously 'missing'. They additionally provided a more integrated service to the customer. This matter is explored in more detail in Issue 3–2.3 Interfaces, p. 107.

- **The efforts of business and functional teams became integrated** as each became clear what their separate yet mutually supportive responsibilities were.

  The operational team of Business Unit Head and Functional Heads was particularly effective. It naturally had control of all the business priorities and interfaces.

- **Most importantly, the senior team's cohesiveness gave clarity of direction and improved initiative taking throughout the organisation.**
  The senior team's unity gave the organisation a consistent view of its direction. This led to all levels being crystal clear about the nature of appropriate initiatives to seek out, and a confidence that they would be supported without falling prey to the previously encountered political cross-currents at the senior level.

COMMONLY ENCOUNTERED DIFFICULTIES AND CHALLENGES

- **Hard and persistent work was needed to develop the skills required to operate the business unit structure.**
  There were significant challenges in both changing to a business unit structure and operating it to its potential. To capture the scale of the commercial prizes described above would inevitably require much developmental effort. This has made the commercial advantages of the structure almost impossible to copy. Simply replicating the structure – which competitors have been driven to attempt a number of times to try and halt the significant erosion of their market position – did not produce the commercial results it was capable of. The required skills to operate it needed determined diligence to acquire and grow, and were invisible and unknown to any competitor.

  A particular case in point has been developing a different view and practice of teamwork. Typically, people needed to work in a range of different teams across the structure to deliver its full potential. As a result, they needed to develop past the conventional behaviour of identifying with a fixed 'home team', with the inevitable belief that 'it was the best team'. This produced a limited toleration of others in the organisation who ironically became regarded as 'outsiders'. Attitudes to these unfortunate people then ranged from neutrality through to hostility. Business Unit team members had to work hard at skills to make any team become rapidly effective, regardless of where other team members came from in the organisation. This is explored in more detail in Issue 3 – 2.3 Commonly encountered Difficulties... Team xenophobia – p. 109.

- **All functions need to be seen in the perspective of the needs of the total business.**

  The main difficulties lay in the area of deeply entrenched vested interests, and a fear of developing different managing habits. Those vested interests were centred on two focuses.

  - **Firstly, the desire of managers to create and sustain the power base** of their own expertise within large functional departments.

    Sadly the majority of senior managers who had devoted their working lives to this pursuit found it extremely difficult to learn to put the needs of the business first. This priority is of course entirely inconsistent with the pursuit of personal power. The hard experience is that CEOs have had to accept that certain managers had decided not to support the business ahead of their personal needs. Painful adjustments had to follow. Unpleasant though this was at times, prudent CEOs have realised that they had to grasp the nettle of that inconsistency. The alternative was the decline of their business.

- o **Secondly, the ingrained habit of such functions has been to see the business from the perspective of their own needs**.

This was entirely inconsistent with the habit of always viewing a function's obligations from the needs of the total business. One is the use of a technical expertise as the foundation of a hierarchical bureaucracy within a functional department. The other is the sole pursuit of an integrated service to the market place and its customers. Again, people struggled to make the 'shift in view' to prioritise the needs of the total business. Tellingly the more senior the manager, the more difficult he found the adjustment.

ISSUE 3 – 2.2: **ACCOUNTABILITY :**

How accountability varies across the different levels in an organisation
and the key role of the Management Line.

SUMMARY

Competence is minimised when the accountability at each level is distinguished by the amount of power and influence it wields.

It is maximised when increasing seniority has been characterised by:

- a growing ability to rigorously resolve increasingly intangible challenges and

- an increasing ability to help develop how the organisation works as a unit

Importantly, both these abilities have been focused on improving the handling of daily business problems.

The pursuit of these skills has encouraged managers to grow effective partnerships with their subordinates. These have been key to developing managers, their subordinates, the business and the organisation. This type of leadership strongly seeks out the strategic issues within the business. The partnership element encourages subordinates to maximise their application of operational information to the challenges facing them.

Senior levels, and particularly the CEO, have had to be continuously vigilant to sustain this direction. They have needed to remain alert to the occasional but destructive drift by particular managers towards the pursuit of power.

The key benefit to the way the organisation works has been to establish results focused, mutually respectful partnerships between managers and subordinates throughout the enterprise.

BACKGROUND CONTEXT

The way accountability varies across the different levels in an organisation has fundamentally affected every aspect of its commercial performance. It has simultaneously had powerful emotional effects on people working within the outfit. Indeed, the experience is that for better or worse it has deeply affected the very quality of their working lives, and the core nature of the entire organisation.

The pursuit of power

The convention is that the key difference between managers at different levels is the power they wield over resources, people, and decisions. Where this has been the conviction, people have spent every last effort, and their very best talents, manoeuvring to amass more of that power, and even more effort protecting it. It has unleashed a determined pursuit of intense politics.

Subordinates working for such managers quickly understand the feudal nature of their position. They instantly realise that job security will be paid for with personal loyalty. Initiatives have been carefully sanitised to specifically support their manager's ambitions. The danger of suggesting ones that might be appropriate for the business but do not fit those ambitions has been quickly grasped.

Colleagues of such managers have looked to the defence of their territories. A serious political fight for survival has been clearly signalled. They have been sure to be fleet of foot in all the well recognised manoeuvres of such a competition. The partial disclosing of information and motives, advancing the cause of 'supporters' and disparaging the worth of 'competitors', massaging information to favour personal views and undermine opposing views , and all the rest of the tried and tested political 'trickery', have been urgently pressed into service. The commercial impact has been significantly negative. Initiative taking, for instance, markedly deteriorated, as the key focus became internal politics. The business became a second priority. The capacity to anticipate difficulties and respond cohesively across the organisation all but disappeared. The emotional impact on people's levels of motivation, commitment and enjoyment of work life became memorably unpleasant. No development of individual managing talent occurred during such a period.

An alternative view of how responsibilities have been nurtured across different levels in the organisation is described in the following principles.

PRINCIPLES

1. Increasing seniority has meant increasing accountability for:

   a) handling the more intangible business issues

   b) developing how the organisation operates

2. The management line is the arena where the organisation's habits of accountability are grown

EXPLANATION

Detailing the operational background of each principle in turn:

1a) Accountability for more intangible business issues

The more intangible business issues have wider and deeper implications.

A typical example has been: 'Significantly improve the business relationship with a highly respected multinational customer'.

The relatively more tangible business issues have had a narrower and shallower range of implications. A typical example has been: 'Significantly improve the quality of a key range of products'.

The business patently requires equally effective solutions to both types of issues.

Recognising this reality requires the more senior levels to demonstrate increasing ability to rigorously manage the more intangible issues. Rigour has meant a demonstrated capacity to habitually achieve two things:

A. to consistently develop a fact based analysis of those issues

B. to be able to implement comprehensive plans based on that analysis. These have needed to gain the watertight commitment of all the affected parties

Exploring each of these abilities in more detail:

A. **A high quality fact based analysis of intangible issues** that so far have eluded resolution is challenging to produce.

However, once done it has actually been relatively easy to recognise. It is comprehensive in its scope and contains no opinion that is not backed by relevant operational detail. A lot of careful work has invariably had to be done to achieve that standard. It usually involves sifting first hand through that operational data, and checking it face-to-face with appropriate people.

Sadly, the common experience is that organisations are tempted to base their actions on a series of eloquently presented opinions formed from assumptions that have been accumulated over time. Some of those assumptions have turned out to be factually correct when they have been checked out against operational reality. However, a significant number of them have usually not satisfied that test. The habit of diligently doing carefully researched analyses is not a conventional one, and we are much the poorer for its absence. Our businesses are also poorer.

B. **Implementing comprehensive plans. These have needed to gain the watertight commitment of all affected parties.**

Skilful senior managers realise that they need to be meticulous in gaining the commitment of others to their plans, especially when they involve unresolved, intangible issues. They realise that is a separate job in its own right, which deserves careful thought. Particular effort needs to be spent in involving people affected by those issues at the earliest stages of the work. A common example has been the need to include their input into the fundamental aspirations that will underpin those plans. Other work at other stages of the decision making steps (see Issue 3–2.10, p.154) has been needed to reliably win people's hearts and minds.

Regrettably this practice is not the conventional norm. Usually it is assumed that the hearts and minds issue is a 'done job' that automatically results from presenting the plans to change matters. We have no such automatic right to anyone's commitment, no matter how senior we may be. It is something that is commercially precious – literally –and we always need to plan to earn it. The norm is to put in the little effort that's described, and we consequently generate conformity instead of commitment. We all lose as a result.

1b) <u>Accountability for how the organisation operates</u>

Developing how the organisation operates has always been the most intangible task of all. The opportunity for piecemeal non factual analyses of the issues involved is at its largest, and the risk of assuming commitment from the management rank and file to any corrective plans is at its very highest. The scope for subsequent inappropriate action that can do significant damage to the business and create cynical disillusion amongst managers is also at its largest. Responsible senior managers have therefore striven to tackle this challenge with 'their best' care and accuracy. There have been two key ingredients for their success:

- line managers lead organisation-wide development via their own personal development

- Organisation-wide development has been led within the tackling of everyday business problems

Both these factors are recalled in detail in the section on Leadership – Principle 3, p.216. There is an inevitable overlap between the issues of accountability and leadership, and the fuller explanation is given in the later section. However, for the sake of continuity, a summary follows below.

- **Line managers lead organisation-wide development via their own personal development.**

  The convention is to create energy sapping, specifically created activities that are extra to normal business demands to achieve organisational changes. These have exactly the same effects as the 'management band wagons' described in Chapter One. They distract from key business needs, do not produce the desired results, and foster frustrated cynicism amongst line managers.

  The effective alternative is for managers to translate such desired changes into developments that they will seek within their own managing habits. The result has been to focus that work within the daily routines of individual managers.

- **Organisation-wide development has been led within the tackling of everyday business problems.**

  Convention focuses organisation development as a separate 'philosophical' concern (e.g. 'culture changing activities') resulting in all the 'band wagon' effects mentioned above. Few things have earned as much disrespect from effective line managers as this view of matters.

  The successful alternative is for such managers to translate the required changes into differences in how their subordinates will tackle their daily work. This embeds organisation development within the practical detail of routine activity. Such development has therefore become an inescapable part of 'normal business'.

Increasing accountability has therefore been characterised by an increasing ability to steer both these factors to happen in the above fashion. The key essence of this different view of accountability is to base it on the manager's drive to continuously develop his personal managing habits.

2) <u>The management line is the arena where the organisation's habits for accountability are grown</u>

A person's view and convictions about any management issue are built on what he does about that issue within his daily work. So it is with the organisation as a whole. Its view and convictions about accountability are built on how its management lines regularly handle that issue. The habits that the line manager and his subordinate use to agree and understand their responsibilities are the seedbed for the organisation's view of accountability. This is true for every managing habit. This simple unyielding reality has driven the CEO and his senior team to pay the highest priority to leading how their management lines operate.

The following example of how such a 'line' works is therefore central to understanding how the whole enterprise views accountability. I make no apologies for the detail in this section, and its length. It explains the very heart of the matter. The specifics of how a particular 'line' has worked are described below. We can then use that experience to highlight the different focuses that the 'line' concentrated on.

EXAMPLE :   **INTRODUCING A CRITICAL RANGE OF FOOD PRODUCTS**

A client organisation was in the business of manufacturing and marketing dairy food products. It was at the early stages of working with a highly successful, national supermarket chain whose reputation was built on quality. As a new provider to the supermarket, it was critical that the organisation's first major range of products should be successfully developed and delivered. It was equally important that the supermarket customer become convinced of the value of forming a long-term relationship with the organisation.

● **The more senior manager concerned focused on the broader strategic issues**.

These included:

o **Product development aspirations:**

Making sure the product development aspirations of both companies were consistent and mutually supportive.

- o **Influencing quality**:

    Enabling the customer to have real, rapid, and sustained influence
    on all the processes that affected the quality of all the products.

The more senior manager's position gave him first-hand information about these issues at the highest levels in both companies. Some aspects of the plans he devised that took account of that information were:

- o Informal joint working groups were set up involving key customer managers, which reviewed and set directions for future product development. Key changes in that direction regularly involved both management teams. The development programme was backed by appropriate investment, and the best talent allocated to it. Regular reviews of the work happened at the highest level in both organisations.

- o He fostered direct and on-going contact between the operational experts in both organisations, for every function that affected product quality – technical services, procurement, production, distribution, etc. Work in all these areas was systematically communicated and coordinated.

- **The more junior managers concentrated on the narrower focused, more operational issues. These were nonetheless seen as equally important as the above more strategic matters, and therefore as deserving of the necessary resources and time.**

These included:

- o **Speeding up product development**:

    Improving the commitment of each function to the development activities they needed to tackle.

- o **Prioritising quality in all functional activities**:

    Ensuring procedures on quality became an integral part of each developmental activity.

The more junior levels had far more detailed information about both these issues than more senior levels. Some aspects of the plans they devised that took account of that information were:

- o Wherever possible, the product development work happened within the normal daily operations of each function. This led to firm ownership of the product and its operational requirements.

- o Quality became the concern of each functional activity that took part in the development work. The procedures ensuring that quality was sustained were coordinated and overseen by the manager responsible for the overall project.

Both senior and more junior managers used the maximum first-hand information at their levels to identify concerns that needed to be tackled. This ensured that issues ranging from the most strategic to the most detailed were grappled with. No concern throughout that continuum was allowed to escape attention. The work on both the broader strategic and the narrower operational issues were mutually supportive. Both senior and more junior managers therefore added considerable value to each other's work.

● **Additionally, the more senior manager was aware of the key processes that his subordinates were using, and regularly monitored their progress.**

The senior manager's judgement was that the commitment of the manufacturing function to the testing work on new products was the most difficult and critical to gain. He therefore ensured that his subordinates had a comprehensive plan to achieve that. His priority was also to double check that the Manufacturing Head was committed to the arrangements that had been put in place.

● **He satisfied himself that key results on quality were anticipated well ahead of time.**

The results of quality criteria that the customer would especially focus on became a particular concern. He therefore reassured himself that the new procedures that his subordinates were setting up with the various functions would deliver early warnings of any imminent problems with any of those criteria. More importantly, he put high priority on his men pursuing proactive plans to anticipate any difficulties in this area.

Key Focusses

of the Management Line that are illustrated by this example:

● the 'line' operates **a guided partnership**

● **the manager is responsible** for both the 'guiding' and the 'partnership'

Summarising each element:

○ **'Guiding'** :   of processes, personal strengths, interfaces, and end results

The 'guiding' ensures that:

▪ **all the appropriate processes** are tackled within his subordinate's work

▪ **the detail of personal strengths and weaknesses** are built into in the way he supports those processes

▪ **all the necessary interfaces** are taken account of in the subordinate's work

▪ **appropriate end results** are delivered

○ **'Partnership'** : of different information sets, and mutually supportive plans

The 'partnership' ensures that:

- **between them, the manager and subordinate tackle the widest range of issues** that they can access for the particular challenge

- **both colleagues use the maximum information** they can accumulate about those issues

- **both colleagues create plans for their respective issues that are mutually supportive**

SOME BENEFICIAL EFFECTS AND IMPLICATIONS

The above recall of accountability is a particular view of the nature of power. Its key effects and implications have been:

- **It generates power from an increasing skill at applying the principles** capable of resolving complex issues.

  The effect of basing power on skill has been to prioritise the manager's efforts to continuously improve his own skill levels at deploying those principles. People led by managers who demonstrate this commitment typically say, 'Boss never asks me to do what he doesn't do himself to a higher standard'.

  The organisation-wide impact is that only business issues are focused.
  Power is not dissipated on personal issues or attachments. Energy is not wasted.

- **It exercises that power within the guided partnerships of the management line.**

  It is only the manager's increasing skill at the above principles that can allow him to deliver the above two focuses within the guided partnership. He can only nurture that particular relationship from the position of practised skill. Subordinates are best developed by practitioners.

  Equally, such experience led coaching has the sharpest of teeth. The personal scar tissue that the manager collects from his own continued development is the best tutor for rapidly spotting others' errors of principle or shortcomings of application. There is little room for complacent treading of water in management lines led by those who still pursue their own development. The opposite has proved equally true.

The core essence of these effects and implications is that power is habitually generated from an inner pursuit of personal development. This is then harnessed to nurture mutually beneficial work relationships with colleagues: the guided partnership of the management line.

It is the very antithesis of power in pursuit of external influence and 'territory'. That is the essence of feudalism: the pursuit of dependent work relationships where the business takes second priority.

Instead, inwardly generated power with its core focus on skill development prioritises the business. As importantly, it has had profoundly healthy effects on the quality of people's lives. It has had a consequent fundamental effect on the core nature of our organisations.

COMMONLY ENCOUNTERED DIFFICULTIES AND CHALLENGES

1.   **Courage, vigilance, and tenacity are needed at the most senior level.**

● **Courage**

The pursuit of feudal power for influence and territorial reasons has been entirely inconsistent with meeting the business's overall needs.

The first is the indulgence of personal attachments of one kind or another.

The second is evidence of a more mature outlook, which is capable of personal development within the pursuit of the business's needs.

The mistake often made at the most senior level is to fudge the issue of the absolute inconsistency between these two different directions. People can mistakenly indulge in the wishful thinking that there is a soft option of a compromise. There has never been any viable middle ground between these two directions. Any compromise attempted at the senior level has been instantly recognised as such throughout the organisation. People have then correctly concluded that politics reigns, and adjusted their behaviour to survive. The business has then been the significant loser.

Of course, it is the particular obligation of the CEO to have the courage to make a definitive and irrevocable choice. That has, on occasions, brought difficult changes at the senior level. Managers whose fundamental prime motivation was not the well being of the business have had to depart. The experience has been that to fudge that decision in any way eventually causes much more damage to the business and organisation than the short term adjustments of a clean departure. Equally, there have been powerful and long lasting benefits from demonstrating that seniority does not excuse non business focused behaviour. It has, for instance, convinced managers throughout the organisation of the safety of raising their game on such key issues as the ambition level of their initiatives.

- **Vigilance**

Even in successful client organisations, people have drifted towards the pursuit of power for influence and territory. This has even happened in the case of managers who have tasted spectacular success by previously prioritising the business's needs. The senior team, and in particular the CEO, have had to be continuously vigilant in observing and reviewing these tendencies. The experience has been that assumptions have built up about managers, especially when they have been successful. It can be automatically assumed that such people will always stay constant in their outlook and priorities. It has blinded the CEO to the unpalatable truth that negative changes were occurring in once business focused managers. This work has never been a bed of roses, and a Walt Disney ending is not promised for every story. CEOs have missed the drift of key managers towards the siren voices of feudal power. The price paid for failing to observe that drift has always been considerable, and laced with copious pain. The payment for sustained success at this work has been continuous vigilance.

- **Tenacity**

This work has always called for deliberate, sustained effort. There has never been an 'auto pilot' that one can switch on, then rest on the nearest laurel and assume that things will continue to be successful because they have been so in the past. Doing this development work has meant that effective managers have needed the tenacity to make success happen on each day. They have needed to find that the work is continuously its own reward. They have needed to revel in the results it brings and have an insatiable curiosity as to what is around the next bend on their developmental journey. My own experience of that journey so far is that it is intense, exciting, deeply rewarding, and always surprising.

2. **The sound of trumpets is the sound of danger.**
   The sound of silent thinking is the sound of successful accountability.

As described earlier, there seems to be an irresistible urge to focus changes around 'something visibly new' – the new change programme, the redesigned/new company seminar, the new policy statement, the new series of workshops, the new consultant, the new imported modular training on this or that issue, the new 'in jargon for the new insight', etc. The list is endless, as people strive to be seen to take some identifiably different initiative. All these activities are invariably heralded by much blowing of trumpets and earnest calls to demonstrate loyalty by climbing on board the latest band wagon.

Over the many years of observing every type of band wagon ever invented, I have yet to witness the sound of trumpets as heralding anything other than inevitable danger, disillusion, long term failure, and ensuing cynicism. Nonetheless, it does not seem to dent our enthusiasm for continuously inventing yet more band wagons, and louder ways of blowing trumpets.

The unglamorous reality is that quiet, persistent, low key attention to how the everyday challenges are met holds the proven key to sustainable success. More importantly, the core of how to handle those challenges differently has inevitably come from the intense silent thinking that first has to happen in the management line. That thinking needs to be the instinctive habit the manager uses to decide how 'his patch' needs to modify its operation. He has to penetrate to the real core of the difference needed, and how it can be brought about by the people in his management line when they carry out their normal business. That change cannot happen, and has never happened, without that careful thinking. The heart of success is in the use of the mind. The sound of successful accountability is the sound of intense silent thinking.

Issue 3 – 2.3   **INTERFACES :**

Dealing with the business issues that lie at the interfaces
between different parts of the organisation.

SUMMARY

Business issues have generally been left insufficiently attended at the interfaces between the different parts of
the organisation.

Successfully dealing with such issues, has always had significant financial and reputational incentives. However,
lack of accountability and teamwork have routinely prevented that happening. Managed teams containing the
relevant expertise have been set up to specifically deal with them. Such teams working at the various interfaces
have answered into one of the standard management lines. When significant improvements have occurred in
the issues concerned, leadership and team composition have often altered to reflect those changes.
Alternatively, if the commercial and reputational benefits have been permanently gained, then the teams have
been disbanded.

BACKGROUND CONTEXT

- **Resolving issues left unattended at the interfaces within any structure
  has had significant incentives.**

  No matter what the structure of the organisation, the interfaces between the different groups within it have
  not been as meticulously run as the groups themselves. Issues that arise at those interfaces do not receive
  the attention they deserve. Successfully resolving them has always had significant commercial incentives. As
  importantly, customers perceive that they are paying for a quality of service that includes the competent
  handling of those issues.

  Their incompetent handling has certainly caused significant irritation to that customer base.

- **Functional structures apply functional priorities at these interfaces.**
  Business unit structures vary in their competence at handling such work.

  Organisations whose structures are divided into functions have found it extraordinarily difficult to deal
  competently with issues at their interfaces. Priorities within the functions have not encouraged a business-
  wide view of the tasks to be tackled. Perversely, in a lot of cases the tendency has been to regard them as a
  'nuisance' distraction that gets in the way of delivering functional priorities. Whilst this is a business
  nonsense, it has been driven by the way that success is measured and reviewed within the functions
  concerned.

Business units are not immune to this difficulty. Some have dealt competently with issues at their interfaces, and some have not. It is true, however, that their record is significantly better than the function based structure, because they are far closer to the concerns directly expressed by their customer base. Nonetheless, their responses have not been unfailingly reliably and competent.

PRINCIPLE

- **The structure needs to deliberately build in teamwork and accountability at the interfaces between groups**

EXPLANATION

Managers and teams have been selected to specifically tackle the issues at these interfaces. Their members have been drawn from various business areas to provide the technical and business expertise needed. They have reported via their manager into one of the standard management lines within the organisation. Team membership and indeed its leadership have often been modified to reflect significant changes in the interface issues. When they have been permanently resolved, the teams have been disbanded.

SOME BENEFICIAL EFFECTS AND IMPLICATIONS

Some of the experienced effects have been:

- **accountability has been sharpened** by the specific allocation of a team and its manager to those interfaces. It enabled the business issues to be resolved, the financial incentives to be captured, and customer service to be securely managed.

- **it has provided an ideal opportunity to develop up and coming talent** from different parts of the organisation. It has offered particularly valuable development to new managers experiencing their first assignment within the management line.

- **productive working relationships** have been forged between people from different parts of the organisation. Very often, memories of people's observed skills have subsequently surfaced in the planning of future work.

'Working as one team' has therefore been given some substance, instead of being the empty rhetoric/slogan that it often is.

COMMONLY ENCOUNTERED DIFFICULTIES AND CHALLENGES

- **Team xenophobia has been a phase to deal with.**

A common early result of forming effective teams within a business unit based structure has been that team members form a very strong identity with that group. Understandably, they start to regard the team as very much a secure, reliable and competent 'home base'. Unfortunately, that usually gets translated during the earlier stages of that team's development into a mild to strong hostility to 'outsiders' to that team. These unfortunate colleagues have then been regarded as second-class citizens who don't 'belong to the best team'. Cooperation with 'outsiders' on wider issues of importance to the total business has then significantly suffered.

Distinct and sustained effort has always had to be put in to develop the business unit team past this xenophobic phase. Hard work has been needed to see its true mission as serving the total business in whatever way came to hand. In that wider perspective, they can begin to see developing effective teamwork as a vital tool to be used in any business setting. They cease seeing it as an end in itself, and only associated with their own business unit. Without moving through this particular stage of development, the irony can be that the setting up of business units results in creating 'management islands'. Their 'borders' are then fiercely defended against all comers, to the detriment of the total business.

Issue 3 – 2.4   **BUSINESS UNITS AND FUNCTION FOCUSSED GROUPS**

SUMMARY

The enterprise has been best served when the business units and functional groups work in close partnership.

The business unit's accountability includes the implementation of every technical standard within the operation. It relies heavily on the functional groups' expertise in setting those standards, as well as their ability to create and deliver the organisation's strategy for that expertise.

The composition of the groups and the close partnership between them have created great flexibility for the developmental career paths of the people involved. The direct commercial benefits and the effects on teamwork have been significant.

BACKGROUND CONTEXT

This interaction between business units and functional groups has at times suffered from the pursuit of influence and standing. Each set of groups has been tempted to either see itself as more important than the other, or been favoured by senior managers with vested interests.

In contrast, when the optimum arrangement of responsibilities has been carefully thought through, it has always emerged as a close cooperation between the two groups.

Strong and determined leadership has been needed to both instil that thinking, and eliminate the 'pursuit of power and influence' whilst encouraging the 'pursuit of business needs'.

PRINCIPLE

> **A close partnership between Business Unit responsibilities
> and those of the Functional Groups for setting standards and technical strategy
> has met all the needs of the operation.**

EXPLANATION

The Business Unit Head has been directly responsible for implementing all functional standards within his business (e.g. such areas as product quality). He has also had full responsibility for creating all the strategies pursued in his business and for delivering their consequences on to the bottom line.

Equally, the business has flourished by giving responsibility to the relevant Functional Head for two areas. Firstly, each Head has been directly responsible for creating, communicating, and gaining commitment to the technical standards for that expertise. These have then been operated by all business units.

Secondly, each Functional Head has been responsible for creating and delivering all the future strategies that the organisation will pursue for his function. That naturally implies an obligation to communicate and gain commitment to those technically focused strategies.

SOME BENEFICIAL EFFECTS AND IMPLICATIONS

Highlights have been:

- **Cooperation between business units and functional teams has produced faster and more effective decisions.**

Both the business and functional areas have become crystal clear about their responsibilities. As importantly, each has come to realise how the other's duties complement their own within the total business. This has led to much faster and more effective decision making, as each became more confident of the other's valued support.

The frequent decisions made by any of the functional experts within the business units have been typical examples of this speed and quality. The speed has resulted from the one functional expert formulating the decision, and checking with the appropriate Functional Head, if he judges that is needed for quality reasons. His direct line manager – the Business Unit Head – is then in a position to immediately support the decision. This process has proved many times faster and more secure on its quality basis than any alternative structure.

Regular reviews between the Business Unit Head and Functional Heads have underpinned this process. These check through issues of quality and look ahead at forthcoming strategically important work.

- **The business unit structure removes all barriers between functional experts and accelerates career development.**

One striking effect of the business unit structure has been its capacity to develop talent many times faster than the norm. The multidisciplinary teams continuously provided members with a means of assessing how they could best serve the business differently, and simultaneously advance their own career development. It provided a means of quickly spotting and testing people's potential for areas they may not have considered or ventured into.

Technical experts have become effective sales managers, production people have become much respected financial managers, etc. Whilst such developmental moves are unconventional they have occurred with confidence, ease and speed. The decisions were taken with the benefit of witnessing the balance of strengths and weaknesses demonstrated by each person as they worked with their colleagues to pursue the business's full range of activities. This accuracy, speed, and flexibility of promotional development has had the most significant effects on commercial results.

The effect on teamwork has been very marked. People with a varied development path progressing through areas as diverse as, for example, technical back up, production and marketing, inevitably accumulated a wide background knowledge. They also formed a firm and wide spread network of dependable relationships across the disciplines within the particular business. These significantly aided the speed and depth of teamwork when the organisation had most need of it.

COMMONLY ENCOUNTERED DIFFICULTIES AND CHALLENGES

Managers reach the most senior team via routes that have favoured either the function focused groups or the business units. Some may then fail to cross over into the stage of development that prioritises the needs of the total business above any part of its operation. This has then sometimes tempted them to exert strong political pressure to favour the influence of the groups and relationships that they have an historical affinity with. People became instantly aware of that preference. They have then spent considerable effort and time trying to take account of that bias on the decisions that they were contemplating making. This has on occasions consumed more energy, time and talent than was spent on the actual business in hand.

Issue 3 – 2.5   **REGAINING MANAGEMENT CONTROL OF PRODUCTION :**

Enabling business priorities to guide Production.

SUMMARY

Our own management mistakes have ceded control of our production areas to interests that do not prioritise the needs of the business.

Line-managed groups, using the standard practices of all such groups, have regained that control. They have dramatically improved the commercial performance of the production area, the rewards package of the people involved, and their job security. These groups have operated the business in long term partnerships with the core organisation, and have wrought equally dramatic changes in every aspect of production performance. The scale of the changes and the speed of implementing them have been well beyond that achieved by any other structure.

More importantly, this sharp rise in competence at the operational level has released middle and senior levels of management from incessant crisis management. Those who gave up their previous dependence on the seductive drug of dealing with constant crises went on to effectively tackle more valuable marketing and strategic issues in the business. This has achieved the elusive and potent change from crisis to business management.

The overall effect has been to put inexorable pressure on competitors to the point where they saw no other option but to attempt copying this structure. They were not to understand that the structure alone could not yield such remarkable results. They were unable to observe the procedural and man management practices – described in later sections – that enabled the structure to deliver such a powerful commercial advantage. Neither could they see the considerable effort that went into the installation of those practices. Inevitably, their replications of the structure failed to produce the business results they so urgently sought.

BACKGROUND CONTEXT

Symptoms

● **A patchy to poor performance, with poor work practices.**

The common experience is that most organisations significantly under perform in the production area. Indeed all the ones who engaged successfully with this development work were similarly disadvantaged at the start of their work. The candid view would be that those performances ranged from being patchily acceptable to being intermittently troublesome. They commonly experienced difficulties with productivity, flexibility, manning levels, levels of initiative-taking, speed of response to problems, people understanding the wider implications to the business of actions taken and not taken, an inability to remove commonly agreed non-performers, an excessive cost basis for the operation, etc.

- **An area where the need for fundamental changes was not faced up to and the business's writ did not run.**

The equally common experience has been that the management teams regarded their work as more important than what was happening on the shop floor. They also felt that the further away one got from the production area, the more important the work was. This view was reinforced by the production area being heavily unionised, and consequently not consistently prioritising the business's needs. The result was that the ownership and sheer drive to improve and manage the production area's fundamental bottlenecks have largely been absent. It only tended to come into sharp focus when some aspect of the service and or delivery to a customer was threatened. This is of course a typical sign of responding to a situation rather than proactively managing it.

In addition managers commonly felt that this problem was 'too big'. They would correctly point to occasional very troublesome performances in this area as being an industry norm. 'It's a cross we all have to bear' has been a common and resigned refrain, accompanied by a frustrated, pained acceptance of what they viewed as 'inevitable'.

Causes

This is a typical example of an extremely visible difficulty that affects a whole range of the performance indices regularly reviewed in management teams. The core processes that cause the problem are inevitably intangible. That doesn't mean to say that the solutions are intangible – very far from it – but their accurate creation cannot come about without first deeply understanding the nature of those processes and how we came to operate them. They are:

- **We accept practices in production that we wouldn't tolerate anywhere else in the organisation.**

We don't prioritise managing the production area to the same level as other structural issues we readily grapple with in the business. We will, for example, quite naturally and appropriately consider fundamentally overhauling the distribution, or sales areas, or any other area if that seems needed. In contrast, we resignedly accept features in the production area, such as restrictive practices, inconsistent reward schemes, inconsistent productivities, people and teams who all agree don't belong in the organisation, etc., as inevitable and immovable limitations.

- **We abrogate our responsibility to manage people as individuals. We treat them as one total group.**

We don't prioritise the effort to manage people at this level on a one-to-one basis. This is a pivotal mistake, which sets off an automatic negative spiral of fundamental damage.

The inevitable result is that there is no continuous dialogue that can build the key relationship with individuals working for us. Neither can we develop a close understanding of their unique potential and strengths. We consequently treat all our production people as one amorphous group. We then exacerbate this error by making it clear that we regard that group as inferior to the 'management group'. Understandably, they deeply resent that attitude, and resort to unionisation to restore what they see as an imbalance of power. We then complain of the inevitable result that the unions' interests don't align with those of the business. This negative spiral, which we initiated, has then inexorably led to the industrial relations difficulties that we continuously suffer.

We truly created these difficulties as a direct result of how we have chosen to manage. Only our management teams are responsible for the outcomes we suffer. Our work forces are essentially blameless, and have only responded to the way we have chosen to manage their situation.

- **We don't harness individual talent when it emerges, nor think to realise what it really means**.

We are prepared to accept that our people have gleaned significant experience and knowledge over their years of working in the production area. However, in no way do we demonstrate the same determination to harness it as we do, for instance, with our managers. This has been read with great clarity as a message of how we evaluate the worth of our production operators as people – and it is perilously close to sustained disrespect.

We consistently fail to see the significance of the sense of pride and ownership that our people have, when they individually come up with their initiatives and views. They are of course intensely proud of them. Most importantly, when these occasions occur, we fail to give them the respect of careful thought, and therefore we miss the deeper inference they have for our businesses. We totally miscalculate and are unaware of the much wider potential that exists for people to take initiatives. Instead, we grow a view that is wary of them doing so, because our current framework for managing them does not have the infrastructure to harness, guide and grow their contributions.

We therefore commit the cardinal error of not realising that powerful alternatives do exist that tap into that potential for initiatives and so release its value to the business.

- **We have allowed a non-business writ to run production.**
  We have exacerbated matters by persistent expediency,
  and created a Gordian knot of inconsistent work practices and reward schemes.

In many ways we have mainly given up the very ground on which our businesses are based: the creation of their end products. We have grown accustomed to accept that another writ will run across that ground, which habitually does not prioritise the business's needs. We have strongly tended in the past to take the expedient route out of industrial relations difficulties that have arisen out of that acceptance. We habitually passed by the challenge of grappling with the core issues at stake. Over time, we have failed to fundamentally solve those difficulties. Instead, we have institutionalised the energy and morale-sapping activity of negotiating compromises. We have justified this failure of management by the short-term benefits that we claim the business has gained as a result of any compromise. As a direct result, we have gradually created an intricate web of inconsistencies (e.g. pay structures, work practices, manning levels, flexibility arrangements, etc., – the list is depressingly long), which we then continuously stumble over in future years. Worse still has been that the business inevitably paid handsomely over the long-term for this failure of management.

There is a proven effective alternative.

PRINCIPLES

- **Implement the proven principles of line-managed groups:**
  - **responsible for creating and delivering their business aspirations**
  - **accountable to the management line within the organisation**
- **Reward the operational groups in a way that is equitable to the business and the groups**

EXPLANATION

- **Accountable, line-managed groups creating and delivering their business aspirations.**

  The successful experience is that we can build on all the effective principles detailed previously to put in place structures for the production of our end products and services that:

  - **Repeat the success of the Business Unit:**
    small managed working teams, entirely accountable for their performance.

    - **Teams of up to six people, or at most seven, totally manage discrete parts** of the operation, answering to their own working manager. He has been accountable for their performance against all the aspirations and criteria for that section of the operation.

    - **The teams apply all the disciplines** that other working teams within the organisation operate, and have received the support and training to do so. As with other teams, their managers have been responsible for their problem solving, their initiatives to improve matters, their efforts to improve how their interfaces work with other groups, etc.

    - **Establish normal line management practices of reviews and regular dialogues between the manager and individuals**
      The standard individual reviews have taken place with the full range of positive to negative observations being worked through between managers and subordinates.

    - **The managers have been accountable for the manning levels** in their areas, who is on their teams, and who is not.

● **Reward the operational groups in a way that is equitable to the business and the groups.**

   ○ **This principle has delivered better results than the industry-best standards.**

The resulting levels of initiative taking and cooperative work practices within the working teams have far exceeded the best standards of the industry.

There are many ways of implementing these mutual benefits, depending on the precise company situation that exists. Business Challenge Five described in Chapter Two detailed the most direct way of doing it. It represents a way to achieve it without making any compromises that dilute the principle.

   ○ **The key is to create a structure that maximises the scope to take initiatives, and then rewards people on the results they achieve.**

The essence of any effective arrangement is that the manager and working group should be rewarded for the actual results that they have produced. They then should have the freedom to share those rewards amongst however many men they have used to generate those results. Pay-out is dependent on meeting the usual operational prerequisites specifying quality, safe working conditions, etc.

SOME BENEFICIAL EFFECTS AND IMPLICATIONS

● **The principles give unrivalled commercial results that competitors have tried to copy, and failed.**

The bottom line is that experience has shown that this type of structure enables a sustained rise in productivity and quality of operation (i.e. all service and quality criteria), unmatched by any other structure. The proven absolute minimum is 40%. The highest number has three figures in it. Competitors have tried to copy the structure that has produced such startling increases in productivity, but have always failed to replicate its results. The point has been explained elsewhere that the structure alone cannot produce such effects. The key to success is the combination of the structure with its appropriate procedural and man management habits. These are detailed in later sections.

● **The resultant structure continuously self regulates quality and costs bases.**
It rapidly develops individual talent.

Specifically:

   ○ **Levels of initiative taking and the speed of problem solving far outstripped** any level associated with the previous structures. These had provided individuals with no ownership of how things were done, or capacity to influence it. By contrast, the managed group structure was able to immediately implement fundamental changes within their teams at speed, and with no controversy within them. Such changes as improvements in working practices, alterations to team membership, and flexibility with other working areas all happened with total commitment, and without delay. None of these self generated initiatives had ever been contemplated within the previous conventional structure.

- o **The competency and intensity of following procedures**, combined with appropriately adjusting them, were several step changes better than that achieved in the previous operation. This is the very heartland of production efficiency and is the core basis of performing well on every success criterion. Teams correctly saw for themselves that better pay rewards automatically came from such procedural competence. They required no encouragement to pay sustained attention to this area.

- o **The level of manning was continuously minimised to match whatever operation was in hand, whilst achieving all quality and safety criteria.** The level of flexibility was continuously stretched to its practical limits, and the costs of the operation were automatically minimised as the nature of the operations changed. Periodic headcount cuts were never needed, nor was any outside influence ever required to encourage the operator teams and their managers to minimise their running costs to suit the changing operation. They saw it as in their own interests to manage that as 'tightly' as possible in order to maximise their earnings.

- o **People who took on more initiatives** in wider parts of the operation were automatically rewarded. Those that proved unwilling or unable to pull their weight within the teams were instantly spotted by their colleagues. They were automatically seen as adversely affecting their fellow team members' take home pay. Trial support was immediately put in, and they were appropriately exited if that proved to be unsuccessful. The pressure from within the teams and their managers to protect their performance, and thence their rewards, meant that no difficulty was allowed to grow into a problem. There was never any suggestion of a poor performance issue – or indeed any other issue – being permitted to escalate and damage their earning capacity.

- o **The groups grow self respect, have better job security, and are better rewarded than before**. The lives of working groups have been transformed as their self respect has grown with their ability to directly influence how their work place operates, and the confidence that they will be transparently and fairly rewarded for their initiatives. This has produced both better job security and benefits packages than the conventional structure could have ever provided. Neither could unionisation remotely match these rewards.

In essence this structural change reclaimed the operational ground where the action takes place in our organisations. It re-establishes the managing structures and accountabilities that operate throughout the rest of the enterprise. It re-establishes that it is the business's writ that runs across this territory, and not that of any outside organisation. Most importantly, it establishes individual respect for **our** people, which has been absent for far too long.

- **Middle and senior managers were able to upgrade the work they did.**
  Competitors were unable to match their effects in the market place.

Significantly improving the operational competence at the very base of the organisation had yet more significant benefits for more senior levels. They were:

- **It reduced management levels and numbers**
  and allowed them to focus on growing the business in the market place.

Operational problem solving used to occupy the attention of the supervisory level and the next two levels of management within the previous conventional structure. Removing this burden had a dramatic impact: it enabled the above reductions and change in focus to take place. More importantly it released, for example, a typical factory manager equivalent to virtual full time face-to-face involvement with customers. He was then able to form the sort of connections that they were keen to take advantage of and had never had access to. The resulting effects on areas such as marketing and sales were highly significant. The competition had no way of matching that performance. They could not position the depth of technical and operational expertise next to the customer as his regular sales contact. Neither could they provide the customer with the direct and immediate authoritative access back into the operational areas. This was the extreme pressure in their market place that forced them to attempt to copy the above structure.

- **The additional advantage was to form business strategy**
  as low down in the organisation as possible.

Managers were strongly influenced by their continuous exposure to the market place and key customers. This automatically gave them the first-hand information needed to continuously shape the business strategy. They could then take best advantage of the changing market place. This gave the business a fleetness and accuracy of foot in meeting and anticipating customers' needs, which the competition found no way of matching.

In essence, only the enabling of the operational front line to take competent charge of their own areas could release talent at the middle and senior levels. That talent could then be unshackled from inappropriate crisis management, and grapple with its true obligation of creating wealth for the business in the market place.

COMMONLY ENCOUNTERED DIFFICULTIES AND CHALLENGES

- **Managers had to 'detox' from the habits of crisis management and focus on wider business issues.**

Inevitably, the first difficulty in gaining commitment to the above structural change lay in winning the hearts and minds of the management teams. They needed to grasp that the real eventual prize was their release from the burden of short term problem solving, and their consequent chance to grow the business. Whilst this was seen as common sense, it posed an inescapable and testing challenge.

Managers had developed personal habits over a long period to cope with the treadmill of short term problem solving, i.e. crisis management, that the conventional structure had conditioned them to. They had become used to seeing their capacity to cope with this situation as evidence of their 'worth'. However, responding to crises did not hone the managing habits needed to grow the business. Necessarily, such managers faced a significant challenge in developing those habits. None would claim that they found it easy. Some wryly observed that they experienced withdrawal symptoms for the easier to understand, more tangible, old style 'treadmill of crisis management'.

● **Vested interest groups outside the organisation see the writing on the wall.**

Powerful vested interests strongly opposed these managed groups working in the production area in close partnership with the organisation. The principle that they could significantly influence their own pay and reward in cooperation with the organisation was total anathema to such interests.

One national union official went on record in the national media as saying that, 'This is the greatest threat to trade unionism since the start of the industrial revolution'.

It is true to say that none of the operational people concerned was interested in joining a union. Their pay, rewards, and degree of control over their jobs were at levels that no union could possibly match. The unions plainly saw this reality. The organisation also spent considerable effort and time ensuring that all the needs of both managers and team members – from pay, to support for operational matters, to welfare issues, etc., – were meticulously anticipated and met. The company regarded this venture as very much a long term partnership. They recognised that if people were prepared to break with the tradition of relying on the union to 'protect them', then they were particularly deserving of the very best of careful and sustained support.

This work sets out to fundamentally pursue business competence to benefit the enterprise and the people within it. It sets out to threaten no one. However, the inescapable effect of that pursuit is that any vested or personal interests that do not contribute to the benefit of the business and its people will be excluded. That is a natural prerogative of any business. It is not a sign of aggressive intent to outside interests such as the unions. It is only a standard necessity of commercial survival and excellence.

PRINCIPLES FOR THE PROCEDURAL AREA

Broader context

This is a much neglected, undervalued, and misunderstood area, yet it is the most common focus of the majority of activities within an organisation. It is also the way that customers and the outside world mainly experience the enterprise.

- **Most things that happen are old procedures in action, or new ones in the making**

   The vast majority of activities within an organisation are repetitions of regular attempts to progress some ongoing/intermittent activity. Only rarely does an organisation undertake an activity that is totally unique, one-off, and contain no element of something it has attempted in the past. People therefore spend the majority of their working lives carrying out procedures of one sort or another. It is noticeable that the well run organisation has distilled the majority of what it does down to clearly understood and implemented procedures. That of course is a key reason that work within them seems calm, unhurried, yet rapid and focused. In addition, the very best of them follow procedures that have disciplined repeatability yet can also flex to suit the needs of any particular situation.

- **A company 'is' its procedures to its customers**

   Customers, and others who interact with the company, are generally seeking a repeated operation or one for which there is commonly a standard procedure. Alternatively, they are making a request that is often a repeat of something dealt with in the past. People consequently experience the organisation mainly through how it handles its procedures. They are necessarily the working interface that the organisation has with the outside world. Given this reality, they receive remarkably little determined and ongoing attention. The priority they attract at senior management level is minimal to zero. This is an inconsistency that prevents achieving effectiveness in this neglected yet pivotal activity.

This section seeks to make some amends for the inappropriately low priority that procedures have in the scheme of things. It recalls an effective way of creating and operating them that is very different from the norm. As a result it reveals an equally different picture as to what is at the heart of procedural success and failure.

Two key challenges in creating procedures are recounted:

- ensuring reproducible quality and commitment

- achieving consistency as well as flexibility

Detailing each aspect in turn:

Issue 3 – 2.6   **REPRODUCIBLE QUALITY AND COMMITMENT :**

How and where can procedures be generated so that reproducibility and quality
are achieved across different locations and cultures?

SUMMARY

The key has been to grasp two facts. Procedures are:

- an organisation's managing habits

- not a bit of paper – they are an agreed way of behaving

The managing habits of the organisation as a total unit are its procedures. Once senior managers have accepted this reality, they have then seen effective procedures to be a key basis for improving the business's commercial performance. Only then have the appropriate resources and focused thinking been applied to this issue.

The fact that procedures are an agreed way of behaving inevitably means that the management levels carrying them out, have to create them. Only then does the resultant action have reliable quality and commitment. The job of the more senior levels is to think through and support the process by which that best happens. There are a number of distinct steps in that process. Long experience has shown that there are no short cuts to any of them. Senior managers have needed to find ways of guiding the process and resourcing it with the necessary expertise.

Consistently managing the creation and maintenance of procedures in this fashion has had other deep-seated benefits. It has for instance helped to grow an unconventional yet business effective view of authority. The common wisdom is to take decisions at the point of maximum hierarchical power / authority. The practice of taking them at the level where the maximum operational information exists about those decisions has greatly improved their quality and speed. It has helped to foster mutual respect across the organisation for the different sets of information, which different levels can offer to decisions. Whilst unconventional this view of authority has proved commercially effective.

BACKGROUND CONTEXT

The 'top-down' way of creating procedures is the normal habit.

The convention is that the most senior and technically experienced manager will be delegated the responsibility of producing, for example, 'the Procedures Manual' for a given area or operation. If the scope of the work is large enough, he will head up a small team of similarly senior managers to produce the desired tome. A disappointed, baffled, and frustrated director in a successful multinational, operating in the hotel and leisure industry, takes up the story of what is a very typical sequence of events :

' We spent many man-months in our team distilling our considerable experience of how procedures
should work world wide in our best hotels. We spent considerable monies producing high quality leather

bound manuals, personalised to each relevant manager, and covering every aspect of the operations involved. We convened an extremely expensive, worldwide, top level seminar for all the managers involved. All senior executives attended to voice their support. The content and rationale for the procedures we had created were carefully explained. We ended by formally presenting the manuals to each manager in a well publicised ceremony. We visited key hotels some months later to find that not one of them had used any of the manuals once. They were all put away in places that most people could not even remember. What is going on?'

Of course, there have been endless variations of this pattern of steps that people have used to develop procedures. However, whatever the variations, the key features of this way of creating procedures are:

1) **Top priority will have been given to the production of the procedures on to paper.** No effort, expense and management expertise will have been spared. Even the paper will be the very best!

2) **The very best management or technical talent will have direct responsibility** for devising the procedures.

3) **Those responsible will personally create the entire content** of the procedures.

4) **Those implementing the procedures will be in no doubt about the commitment of those managers who created them** when they tell them what to do. Those doing the telling will be convinced that people's commitment is automatically gained by talking at them.

In essence, this most common way of generating procedures pays a lot of attention to what it sees as the end product: the written procedures. The belief is that provided we put significant effort, time, expense, and expertise into producing that product, then by and large it will be 'job done'. Of course we will put effort into all the administrative activities involved with their presentation, and give them a 'gloss' to demonstrate the work's importance and the need for attendees to 'give their commitment'. The latest bells and whistles will be pressed into service at some upmarket venue.

No matter how many times pursuing this belief has failed to produce high quality, consistently implemented procedures, there remains a great reluctance to fundamentally examine and rethink this approach. Ironically, the most clients have claimed for this conventional process is that their procedures have been patchily acceptable, with disconcerting and unpredictable lurches into embarrassing failure. Even so, they have continued focusing on producing yet more impressive looking descriptions of their new procedures. The technology will be the latest and the best and all the glitz of moving Power point demos, complete with the latest sophistications will be embraced. It remains the same strategy. The results remain the same. The new packaging has not improved procedural performance.

PRINCIPLE

Procedures are the managing habits of the organisation.

- **a procedure is not a bit of paper**

- **it's an agreed, consistent way of behaving**

- **necessarily, all the appropriate work has to be done to generate understanding and commitment amongst those actioning the procedures**

EXPLANATION

What all organisations seek, is consistent, quality focused behaviour by those operating any procedure, anywhere in its enterprise.

The levels operating the procedures have to be involved in carefully thought through activities in order to achieve this type of uniform, committed behaviour. These activities have proved yet more critical for a multinational trying to achieve this consistency across many different locations, in many different cultures. To mount and sustain the systematic effort for this work first requires the management teams to deeply understand the real context of this issue.

Seen from the view of the organisation, its procedures are in fact its managing habits. They are played out within and across various groups. Just as a manager's personal managing habits are a key to him developing his own performance, so too are procedures, a key to the whole organisation developing its performance as a unit. Management teams – and in particular the senior one – have not approached this area with the appropriate priority and determination until they are committed to this view of matters. Its challenges and its potential rewards then become clear.

Procedures are therefore the organisation's managing habits, and are built on an agreed way of behaving amongst its managers. To ensure that happens, certain activities have to be put in place. These entail the managers directly responsible for operating those procedures:

- **thinking through and agreeing the fundamental aspirations that the procedures are to pursue.** The managers and men directly responsible for carrying out the procedures need to identify the aspirations that they will satisfy. These need to be described in their own language and style. A more senior and more experienced level of managers cannot, and must not, do this work. It has been common to have them review the work and offer information when appropriate.

- **agreeing the operational information** that they deal with on a regular basis, which those procedures need to take into account.

- **involving the people actually carrying out the procedures**
  in formulating all the detail of how they will carry out any non technical operation.

- **coordinating technical support into that work**
  to ensure that it meets the required operational standards

- **specifying the tangible end results and targets**,
  which will act as some of the indicators as to whether the procedures are delivering the aspirations originally selected. Again, these need to be written up by the operational managers in the manner and style that best suits their needs.

This pattern of activities enables those implementing the procedures to think through and internalise certain decision making steps associated with those procedures:

- **the fundamental aspirations** they are to pursue

- **the operational information** they need to take into account

- **the detail of exactly how** they will be carried out

- **the targets** they will meet

Experience says that none of these steps can be bypassed without jeopardising the understanding and commitment of the managers and operating teams involved. For example, none of them can be created by a 'better informed/more expert' outsider. Diligently working through these steps nurtures the maximum contribution from operating staff whilst ensuring that technical standards are sustained. Such a process has enabled three critical things to be achieved:

A) **The senior managers overseeing the work have given prime priority to the process** by which the procedures will be produced by operational colleagues. They have further ensured that other groups such as operating staff and technical support are appropriately integrated into the work. It has been the effort and time spent on guiding that process that has ultimately produced consistent behaviour in applying the procedures.

Note the direct contrast with points, 1), 2),and 3) of the previous conventional process.

B) **The very best collective technical and operational expertise at the more senior levels has been made available** to those creating the procedures. That expertise has not 'taken over' the production of those procedures.

Note the direct contrast with points 2) and 3) of the conventional process.

C) **The operational level actioning those procedures had the opportunity to think through the necessary decision making steps** i.e. the procedure's fundamental aspirations, operational information, detailed working plan, and targets.

Note the direct contrast with point 4) of the conventional process

The direction and content of this process is diametrically opposite to the conventional 'top-down' option.

SOME BENEFICIAL EFFECTS AND IMPLICATIONS

- **Living through the process delivers consistent repeatable procedures.**
  Talking at people doesn't.

At the practical level, the above steps have consistently produced quality results that cannot be matched by any variation of the conventional 'top-down' process. Previous to starting this development work, clients have endlessly tried conferences, seminars, boot camps, changes in policy statements, new mission statements, external consultants, monitoring committees, etc., to achieve the elusive goal of consistent, quality procedures. All efforts have followed the same belief that the key was louder, more weighty, or more attractive explanations and exhortations from the senior levels/experts. The different habits needed by the new procedures stubbornly did not consistently appear. The simple reality being endlessly rediscovered was that it is not possible to talk new habits into existence.

They have only been nurtured into being by appropriately involving those who are to implement the habits. They need the opportunity to work at the appropriate decision making steps (see issue 3–2.10, p.154 for full set of steps) associated with the procedure. It is worth noting in passing that this is another example of the interactive interdependence between principles within the three basic factors: Structure, Procedures, and Man Management. In this case, the principles of setting up effective procedures have to involve appropriate principles within the Man Management factor, from the decision making area.

- **The process produces the 'holy grail' of procedures – the capacity to flex procedures but still deliver their essence.**

One benefit of such a process has been that procedures can differ in detail at different locations. This variation has allowed managers to reflect particular local and cultural factors. Multinationals facing the need to manage such factors have a particular need to take account of such variations. This has not been at the expense of the quality or reproducibility of the procedures. Judgements as to how to vary the detail of them have been guided by the need to meet the fundamental aspirations selected for those procedures, and the targets identified for them. No other way of generating and sustaining procedures achieves this operational necessity. Most certainly the conventional 'top- down' method has a poor track record of doing so.

The process has two additional deeper implications:

- **the optimum point of decision making is the point of maximum information**

- **respect and initiative taking are affected**

Detailing each element in turn:

- **The optimum point of decision making is the point of maximum information.**

  The organisation has been seen to place authority with managers whose core jobs involve the first-hand operational information that the procedures are concerned with. In contrast to the 'top-down' way of developing procedures, it has not placed authority with the most senior level available for the task in hand. Instead, it places first-hand factual information at the heart of decision making, not status, position, or power. This results in faster and more accurate decision making, which takes place much lower down in the organisation. The added effect is that more senior levels have a greater opportunity to deal with strategic issues.

- **Respect and initiative taking are affected.**

  Decision making led by those at the point of maximum information – and not by those at the point of maximum hierarchical position – has a further effect. When consistently applied, people became confident of the organisation's habit of respecting all levels equally, based on their ability to offer relevant information into important decisions. This has had pronounced effects on the level of initiative taking throughout the organisation.

COMMONLY ENCOUNTERED DIFFICULTIES AND CHALLENGES

Despite its well publicised troubles, rebooking the Titanic remains a popular trip.

Managers have proved deeply attached to the 'top-down', dictating and exhortation way of trying to create procedures. Despite the resulting inconsistent procedural performance the response has generally been to invent yet more ways of repeating the same process. The attraction to this convention seems rooted in some strong convictions. They are:

- **A belief that talking at people changes their behaviour.**

  Many of us firmly believe that when we explain our view of what is 'obviously correct' to someone, it should be sufficient to change the way they then do things, particularly if we are their manager. We imbue the issue of authority combined with being 'obviously correct' with the Walt Disney-like fairy dust of 'instant change'. I wave the wand of my manager's clearer understanding of what you should be doing, the fairy dust sparkles its magic, and – 'POW!' – you're instantly transformed. The old you has disappeared! Only the new you remains!

  Intellectually of course, we all know this is horse manure. But the fantasy that you can instantly change others through a combination of 'authority' and asserting something as 'obviously correct' is truly powerful. It's true power is revealed when it fails – as it always must – and the manager proceeds to repeat it again and again.

Only when the manager grasps the true nature of the hard road people need to be travel to change, and their need for his support, will he give up this fantasy. Even then, only some managers have stopped believing in the wand and the magic fairy dust. Some can still be seen regularly giving the wand 'what-for'.

- ○ **Mixed in with that belief is a fixation about 'leading from the front'.**

  Managers fiercely committed to this view are convinced that 'telling them how it is' demonstrates their capacity for 'leading from the front'. They are deeply attached to what they see as the need to display 'charisma', 'presence', and 'leadership potential'. Any expense and effort is therefore justified to keep on trying variations and repeats of the 'top-down' exhortation process.

- ○ **The additional belief is that the most hierarchically senior manager must take the decisions.**

  The conviction has been to maximise the standing, power, and influence of the figure taking decisions. The mantra is: "We must use the 'biggest hitters' we've got". The firm belief is that commitment to the new procedures rises with the seniority of the decision maker involved. There is absolutely no evidence to support this assumption. On the contrary, the experience amongst clients is that the more senior – and hence more remote – the manager taking the decisions is from those who have the most relevant operational information, the more cynical and conformist is the response. 'What does he know about what really goes on?' is the common remark. This is of course the very poorest basis for commitment.

The extent to which managers have persisted with a convention that doesn't produce results of the required standards is simply an indication of their deep commitment to the above three unfounded convictions. Of course, the hope has been that people having repeatedly experienced the poor performance of the conventional process, will reconsider their views when exposed to an alternative that consistently works. Indeed, some managers have seen the obvious common sense of that alternative. Much more to the point, they have realised the results it achieves. They have decided to pursue the principles that underpin it. It very much stands to their credit, integrity, and strength of purpose that they have gone down the path of developing their own managing habits so that they become able to reapply the principles for themselves.

Others have exercised their prerogative to continue booking further trips on the Titanic

Issue 3 – 2.7   **CONSISTENCY WITH FLEXIBILITY :**

How can procedures retain disciplined repeatability,
yet be kept continuously alive and flexible to reflect changes in the needs of the business?

SUMMARY

The key has been to remain focused on the fundamental aspirations that the procedure is designed to deliver.

The procedure's operational plan and its targets are useful preparatory thinking that need to inform what may happen. They should not restrict or dictate what actually happens. The optimum commercial results stem from consistently delivering the full range of the procedure's aspirations, especially when conditions confronting the operation have changed. At times, this has meant flexing the prepared plans and or targets to reflect those conditions. The optimum commercial results have not come from the robotic delivery of the same plans and targets regardless of changed circumstances. That has only increased the chances of deteriorating competence, damaging the organisation's reputation, and/or irritating its customers.

BACKGROUND CONTEXT

Customers have sometimes been exasperated by an organisation's rigidity in following set procedures. They have felt that on certain occasions it was just common sense to make some modification to reflect the needs of a particular situation. Effective procedures need both disciplined repeatability and ways of being flexed. Without that ability to appropriately modify what it does, the organisation has been seen as prioritising bureaucracy ahead of their customers' needs.

At other times, procedures have outlived the circumstances that gave rise to them. Managers in this instance have sometimes inadvertently continued to operate them because they've become 'part of the fabric of what happens'. Again, the challenge is to retain the repeatability of an agreed procedure, yet have a means of responding to changes in the business. Those changes can then inform how that procedure is flexed, or in the extreme case, totally altered or removed altogether.

<u>PRINCIPLE</u>

- Procedures need to be **led by the fundamental aspirations** they were designed to pursue, and the operational information they were intended to respond to.

- **Their preset plan of operation is useful preparatory thinking.**
  However, it should not be allowed to restrict or dictate what is actually done.

- **Their preset targets are useful preparatory thinking** as to what would be effective to deliver. However, they should not prescribe the judgement/assessment as to what to deliver, or how things have gone.

<u>EXPLANATION</u>

The aspirations chosen for a procedure describe the widest perspective within which to see its use. They paint the bigger picture the procedure is trying to bring about. Managers who continually focus on those aspirations have always seen the broader context of the work in hand.

They realise that the key obligation is to satisfy the fundamental aspirations a procedure is pursuing – not the robotic delivery of its previously prepared detailed plan. That plan is based on the known/assumed operational information at the time the procedure was created. If that information later changes, then the plan needs to take account of those changes.

Similarly, by focusing on the aspirations, targets are seen as a limited and arbitrary way of deciding if those aspirations are being achieved. Instead, the real challenge is to have an ongoing, rapid, and balanced grasp of the progress towards the full set of aspirations selected for the job. Progress against updated targets has proven to be just a useful part of that balanced grasp – not a substitute for it.

SOME BENEFICIAL EFFECTS AND IMPLICATIONS

- **Reliable, repeatable quality service that flexes to respond to changing circumstances**

  The practical result has been that customers have seen the organisation as delivering a quality service. They equally see it as one capable of flexing appropriately to meet changing circumstances. They therefore feel the organisation is genuinely interested in people's concerns. It's a way of combining the benefits of a large enterprise with those of smaller entrepreneurial businesses.

  The two factors producing this key result are:

- o **Managers who are mindful of the bigger picture the procedure is serving are more focused on customer needs and market place requirements.** That has meant that they have been alive to changes in that area, and well predisposed to respond quickly to them.

- o **People can use the procedure's aspirations to make reasoned judgements about appropriate changes to its operation.** They have a common sense basis for responding to changed circumstances.

The deeper effect of both these benefits has been to keep those directly responsible for delivering procedures closely linked to changing business needs.

- ● **It has provided a useful template for managers to use in other challenges**

Managers experiencing these effects within their work on procedures have had the chance to see the business relevance of applying the principle to every activity they undertake. The commercial prize is very considerable. As opposed to today's norm of obsessing about targets and preset operational plans (dealt with below under **Difficulties**), the habit of tackling all activity whilst keeping in mind its fundamental aspirations produces entirely different effects. It has:

- o alerted them to a wider and more relevant set of business issues for the challenge in hand.

- o exposed managers to a wider scope for appropriate initiatives

These have proved to be bedrock habits that have underpinned the commercial success of this work.

COMMONLY ENCOUNTERED DIFFICULTIES AND CHALLENGES

- ● **We misunderstand the nature and use of targets and operational plans.**
  We have become their slaves and not their masters.

We currently seem to be hopelessly besotted with targets and operationally detailed plans as a sole means of achieving anything. We appear to believe that either one of these on its own, or together, is sufficient to bring about quality, sustainable solutions to our challenges. This belief appears to be bomb-proof against endlessly repeated and clearly demonstrated failure when it is operated. We endlessly complain about it, but mysteriously seem to find no alternative to repeating it.

Two sets of difficulties have caused these inevitable failures:

- o one is centred around not deeply understanding the true nature of targets and operational plans o   the other is centred around the pattern of personal strengths and difficulties managers sometimes use on this issue

Exploring each of these in turn:

<u>Understanding targets</u>

▪ **Targets are a useful 'back up' way to partially assess what happened.**
They are never a fixed or complete truth.

Targets are sensibly necessary. However, they are creatures born of the set of operational and business information that applied at the time they were conceived.

As the business inexorably changes, so does the set of information describing its key issues. If those changes become large enough, then inevitably the appropriate targets will also change. Targets are necessarily just an informed guess at what we expect the business to look like at a particular time. They are not a fixed truth. Should, therefore, the key issues change sufficiently within the business, then the targets have usually had to appropriately alter. This has especially been the case when the work has a long time frame. Significant changes in the business information then become almost inevitable.

Targets are also merely a selection from many possible indicators that can be used to help judge if the aspirations for the procedure are being met. They are a small chosen key-hole picture of what might happen. Targets are therefore never ever a complete truth. Reliable and sustainable success is not meeting the hypothetical and partial picture painted by the targets. Reliable and sustainable success is completely meeting all the fundamental aspirations about which we have concerns. This needs to be backed up by satisfying the limited and partial indications of the targets. The convention is to make the fundamental error of using the limited 'back up' of the targets to substitute for answering the wider and deeper question of 'did we meet all the aspirations set for the job?'. Our much more pernicious error is to become so besotted with targets that we lose sight altogether of the aspirations we were supposed to be pursuing. I have witnessed times without number where this obsession has produced small scale results that satisfy the narrow vision of the targets. It completely missed delivering the far larger scope required by the full aspirations of the work.

That is the position of a slave to a particular tool and not the master of the total process of which that tool is part. In contrast, such mastery has delivered quality results meeting every aspect of the challenge in hand.

Understanding operational plans

- **Plans also reflect the operational information of the time.**
  They are useful preparation.
  They should aid the judgement as to what to do – not substitute it.

  Plans are a list of detailed operational instructions that are a way of delivering all the aspirations being pursued. They achieve that by taking accurate account of all the relevant information.

  Like targets, plans are not a fixed truth. They simply reflect the operational information about the procedure, at the time they were created. Should that information change, then the certainty is that the plans will need to take account of that change. Only in this way can they accurately deliver the original aspirations of the work. Simply ignoring the change, and rigidly implementing the plans, has delivered inappropriate results.

  To the skilful and competent manager, plans are a useful basis for action. He may in the event judge not to carry them out. His first obligation is to successfully deliver the aspirations he sets out to pursue. The real test of his skill is to always achieve that. He will therefore regard his plans as useful preparatory thinking, which will inform what he chooses to do – but not rigidly dictate it or restrict it.

The interaction with personal strengths and difficulties

- **It can be inviting to avoid dealing with the bigger, more relevant questions**
  and become busy with the detail of targets and plans.

  The very nature of targets and operational plans means that they offer a lot of detail to think about. People have sometimes found it easier to busy themselves in that detail. It can provide an excuse to avoid grappling with the broader and more difficult business questions:

  - what are the **key issues** within any problem that we need to prioritise and work at?

  - what is the **range of aspirations** that will take us to the appropriate position with those issues?

  These are more difficult questions to answer. They have always required much effort, and careful, persistent thought – not least because – managers have known that in answering them they are nailing their colours to the mast about a future that they are promising to deliver.

  Faced with this harder, riskier and more necessary thinking, people have sometimes sought shelter in the comfort of dealing with familiar and tangible detail. Targets and plans have appeared to be a safe harbour, necessarily full of that type of detail. It has proved inviting to seek continual shelter in that harbour, and avoid setting out to sea to undertake the much more uncertain voyage of grappling with the broader issues.

- **We commonly promote people because they demonstrate an appetite for lots of detail.**

  The consequence has been that managers can become habit-formed to respond to challenges by instinctively diving into considerable operational detail – and staying there. Their experience has not readied them to be familiar with thinking about the non detailed, broader, intangible core issues of the business. They can naturally assume that the managing habits that got them to their position are surely the ones to repeat. Some have had the open mindedness and courage to recognise their need to learn and develop different thinking habits from the ones that got them promotion. It is a testament to their humility and strength of character. It is perhaps understandable, but regrettable, that others have exercised their prerogative not to make that choice.

This combination of difficulties has encouraged managers to lose sight of the fundamental aspirations of the work in hand. Instead they become wedded to the much smaller scale, preset detail of their targets and operational plans. Sadly, this has produced the stiff necked bureaucracy that brooks no flexibility and that so enrages those who suffer it. Organisations can ill afford to gain that reputation amongst customers about any service they offer.

PRINCIPLES FOR THE MAN MANAGEMENT AREA

Broader context

- **Work on the least tangible factor has had to be strongly rooted in common sense, and be directly capable of producing tangible business results**

  This factor explains the processes used in taking and implementing all decisions about every resource the enterprise has access to.

  This is the least tangible of the three organisation factors – Structure, Procedures, and Man Management. It has consequently been the one most vulnerable to emotionalism, vogues, 'sacred cows', ideology, dogma, endless contrived jargon, blizzards of acronyms, and a seemingly endless avalanche of modular training.

  By contrast, ordinary managers facing urgent operational difficulties require practical, well reasoned, proven solutions. These need to:

  - o take into account all the issues that face them

  - o recognise that those issues interact to produce the many faceted problems that confront them

  - o be described in everyday language, without being obscured by any created jargon

  - o offer a means of doing something practical to fundamentally solve those problems

  This section describes the principles within the successful work done by managers that met all these criteria. Those principles meet the most stringent criterion– that of common sense. That doesn't mean to say that people haven't found themselves doing highly unconventional things. Indeed they often have. However, they have made sure that whatever they have done firstly makes sense to them and accords with the business information they have about the situation. Secondly, they have made certain that their work is capable of delivering the necessary commercial results.

- **Developing managing habits in this factor has been best achieved as part of tackling the everyday business challenges**

  This issue has already been described in the work on 'Accountability' (Issue 3 – 2.2: 'Accountability for how the organisation operates', p. 96.). However the man management area is the main marketing target for 'special activities' that claim to help managers to develop skill in it. In contrast, this work has encouraged managers to focus on developments within their every-day work. Offsite training has on occasions become appropriate. However it has been a minority focus compared to the major effort focussed within the businesses.

To aid an over view of this section, relisted below are the key issues first detailed in Chapter One, which comprise the Man Management factor:

● **The Management Line is the seedbed for developing habits in the above issues**

The guided partnership of the management line is the very cornerstone of developing skill in the above areas.
To the extent that that partnership is variable and confused across an organisation, then so too is its performance in the above issues.
To the extent that that partnership is consistent and thought through across an organisation, then so too is its performance in those issues.

Taking each of the above issues in turn and detailing how the effective management line has grown the above managing habits within its handling of every-day business:

Issue 3 – 2.8   **RESPONDING TO SUCCESS AND FAILURE.**

SUMMARY

The discipline of regularly reviewing how daily challenges are being tackled is the root basis for developing effective managing habits.

By the same token, compulsive continuous activity has produced at best a temporary plateau in performance, followed by an inevitable erratic deterioration.

Effective reviews have been based on the unconventional practice of analysing the detail of how any success occurred – no matter how minor. Analysing success has had the practical business effect of significantly improving people's ability and appetite to take initiatives – especially with ambitious challenges. The emotional impact has been to create the confident un-defensiveness needed to examine any error.

People's appetite for improvement can only be energised by seeing their difficulties in the full perspective of their strengths. Our convention of only analysing failure condemns people to see their weaknesses in the perspective of their weaknesses. Not unsurprisingly, this has consistently minimised or eliminated the appetite for sustained improvement.

Every aspect of how we currently run organisations gives priority attention to error. We always have a different opportunity open to us. Error is critical to examine. If we want improvement – and not blame – then it must be done in the perspective of analysing what successes have occurred. If we want to institutionalise blame, then we need to continue our current practice of analysing errors in the perspective of only ever examining error.

BACKGROUND CONTEXT

- **Disciplined skilful reviewing has proved to be the very spring board of long term success. Its habits are learned within the management line.**

  The way in which individuals and teams respond to the results of their work has controlled their capacity to improve their performance. It is the key to their ability to develop their full range of managing habits.

  All of the organisations that have undertaken this work have regarded themselves as being very much 'long term players'. They see their efforts to be set for a triathlon, and not a sprint. In this perspective, those who will outperform the competition have been those with the most robust capacity to continuously improve and develop. That ability fundamentally depends on the two habits of reviewing work, and the analysis of success and failure within those reviews.

  How both these habits are dealt with has had the most fundamental effects on such key issues as: the level of initiative taking within challenging situations, the appetite to implement difficult changes, and the level of confidence when faced with testing situations, etc. This has therefore proved to be a vital business issue, whose effects and interactions have been deep and very widespread.

Nurturing these two habits within the guided partnership of the management line has always had a fundamental impact on the commercial performance of the whole organisation.

- **The convention is to ignore it in favour of endless activity, or bureaucratise it.**

Very few organisations have either of these habits in position. Certainly none of the ones who successfully did this work commenced with any realisation of their relevance to their businesses.

In their defence, it has to be said that the convention is not to waste time on something as apparently unproductive as 'reviewing'. Managers very often see this activity as a third priority to 'getting on with the business in hand'. They only attempt an in-depth review when something has gone badly wrong. Compulsive activity combined with the pressures of a perpetual busy schedule have powerfully groomed this habit.

The more 'enlightened' organisations have so bureaucratised reviews (e.g. by ossifying them within periodic, infrequent, and ritualistic 'assessments') as to drain them of all operational relevance. They have become parodies of living regular reviews, and are universally resented and disrespected. The absence of regular reviews has sucked in the dangerous substitute of the grapevine gossip rumour machine. This has greatly encouraged management by politics, and the rule of feudal power.

These habits, or their absence and common substitutes, centrally influence how the organisation operates.

PRINCIPLE

- **The review is very much the 'engine' that can drive sustained progress**

- **A full, and factual analysis of successes within a piece of work needs to be the basis for analysing any failures or difficulties that might have occurred within it**

- **That analysis needs to be the basis for a person creating his own improvement plans.**

  His manager will need to see this as his opportunity to support his efforts

EXPLANATION

Clarifying each of these elements in turn:

- **The review is very much the engine that can drive sustained progress**

  It has proved to have three effects:

    o Continuous deliberate improvement becomes possible by applying sustained attention to the way matters are being handled.

    o People become increasingly aware of the exact nature of the processes underpinning what they are doing that can increase their chances of success.

    o Crucially, it is a practical way of gradually improving the skill of awareness itself. This starts to open the door to more rapid development of a wider range of managing habits.

  I once regularly interviewed applicants for jobs within the oil multinational alongside an acerbic but sharply observant middle European manager, Kosovitch (not his real name). He was getting irritated by one candidate who insisted on repeatedly referring to his ten years of experience in his existing job as a key point in his favour. Kosovitch carefully probed what the interviewee had learned from the various successes and failures he had in the ten years. The answer was very little if anything at all. When the unfortunate man next referred to the fact that he'd got ten years experience at his job, Kosovitch could contain himself no longer and enquired, 'Tell me, is that ten different years' experience or the one year repeated ten times?'

- **A full and factual analysis of successes within a piece of work**
  needs to be the basis for analysing any failures or difficulties that might have occurred within it

  Analysis means recalling the specific detail of precisely who said and did what, how, and when, that led to the successes that occurred. It is the opposite to statements of congratulation or praise – both of which are generalised opinions.

  In contrast, this analysis nurtures the habit of detailed factual observation of what actually occurred, suspends any judgement, and accepts no generalisation that can hide an opinion or a prejudice. It is a means of training an acute awareness of the exact way work is being accomplished. I hasten to add that this is the most deceptive of skills to develop. All the managers (including myself) who have ever worked at improving their ability to analyse in this fashion have had to spend considerable effort and time to make any headway with this skill.

  It provides two critical ingredients needed for successfully looking at failures or difficulties.

    o Firstly, the specific detail that such an analysis yields automatically provides the procedure for repeating that success. Disciplined success analysis inexorably equips the reviewer with an increasing bank of proven effective practices. He can then turn to these managing tools when faced with future challenges.

- o   Secondly, such an analysis remains a factual undeniable record of success that provides the securest platform of confidence from which to view any failure.

- **That analysis needs to be the basis for a person creating his own improvement plans. His manager will need to see this as his opportunity to support his efforts**

This illustrates the vital opportunity for each person to practise his responsibility for his own improvement. It explains why not having regular reviews has such a debilitating effect on personal development, and hence organisational competence. By contrast, reviews of this nature are the very heart of continuous improvement.

The supervising manager's support for his subordinate's improvement plan(s) has been key to nurturing the guided partnership between them.

SOME BENEFICIAL EFFECTS AND IMPLICATIONS

The vast majority of activities yield a mixture of partial successes and failures to learn from. If the management line has grown the habit of responding to this mixture by analysing it in the pattern described above, then certain effects have been achieved:

- **The basis is laid for increased initiative taking.**

Responding to successes and failures in the above fashion significantly changed how people responded to business challenges. They were more prepared to take initiatives and undertake the unusual and ambitious. They have only been willing to face that risk if they are sure that their efforts will be reviewed with the above discipline. If assessments of people's efforts do not satisfy these principles, then exhortations by senior managers for 'the troops' to take more initiatives have inevitably fallen on deaf ears. The troops have rightly concluded that the more dangerous enemy is not in front of them: it lurks behind them in the shape of how their leaders will evaluate their work. Best not to risk partial failure and fall victim to a court martial containing little or no account of any successes.

- **A platform of secure confidence has been built.**

The unearthing of the detail of how any success came about established facts that could not be subsequently eroded or dismissed in any way. They remained the facts of what actually happened. This grew a secure level of legitimate confidence in people that could not be shaken or taken away by subsequent examination of any failure that took place. They were consequently best placed to examine failure with an appetite for improvement.

- **An accurate perspective of difficulties emerges**.

Additionally, when difficulties and failures are seen in the light of all the successes within an activity, their true significance has become clear. If they have been small difficulties or failures, then they have been seen as such. If they have been large difficulties or failures, then they have been accepted as such. People become confident that the unexaggerated reality of what they have done will consistently be seen. A basis has been laid to prevent defensiveness and create an open mindedness to difficulties and failures.

- **The conditions for continuous improvement are in place.**

Having completed the above analysis, the person is then best placed to create his own improvement plans for the future.

It has proved vital that his supervising manager takes every opportunity to support his subordinate in those plans. The prize for encouraging a subordinate's independent habit of reviewing his work in this fashion is considerable. It is arguably the biggest prize a manager can secure. It enables subordinates to grow the self driven, fact based development of their own managing habits. Managers who have achieved this know that it is a watershed, beyond which lies the subordinate's independent, self sustained success.

- **The working line management relationship is greatly strengthened.**

The relationship between manager and subordinate becomes founded in facing detailed truths whilst tackling actual business challenges. Importantly, its roots are in the open, regular, fact based, joint analysis of both successes and failures. If the subordinate then becomes confident that his manager will always support his plans for improvement, then a vital basis of the guided partnership of the management line is in position.

COMMONLY ENCOUNTERED DIFFICULTIES AND CHALLENGES

- **The convention is a total focus on failure analysis.**

In contrast to the above discipline, the conventional response is the exact opposite. It is to examine failure first, and most usually, it is only to examine failure. High powered 'business review meetings' regularly do that. People then publically account for only their failures. Social convention has then often encouraged the habit of lacing these reviews with preliminary praise as the means of dispensing with any successes that might have occurred. The effects of practising this process have always been pernicious and very far reaching.

- **Failures are heightened, and defensive responses set in.**

Examining failure in the sole context of other failures has inevitably heightened and distorted the importance of each incident. It has made it impossible to grasp their true significance. Small failures have been enlarged by solely looking at them amongst other failures. Large failures have taken on the appearance of catastrophies. This habit has rapidly raised deep defensiveness in those being reviewed. They quickly sense the injustice of artificially distorting the scale of their shortcomings. A rapid spiral of defensive habits inexorably sets in, and levels of competence quickly start to erode. People start to devise numerous ways of:

- **hiding the reality of what has happened**, for fear of any part of it being reviewed.

- **minimising the information about work issues** that reaches the review agenda, so as to limit the damage it can do them.

- **avoiding the really ambitious and potentially high yielding projects**. 'Whatever you do round here is wrong', 'However hard you try, you can never satisfy them', ' You wouldn't want to fall into their bad books', 'You don't get any support round here if anything goes wrong'– these are all quotes that people use to explain that it's far too risky to venture into work that has the smallest chance of failure. These of course are precisely the potentially high yielding pieces of work that the business needs to have competently tackled.

- **prioritising the political games** of creating allies and friends so that they can best survive what they correctly see as a threatening situation. This has absorbed effort, energy, and time that are denied the business.

● **Sole analysis of failure focuses people on what they can't do, and defocuses them from their skills.**

Over the many years of this work, everyone I know (including myself) can readily offer rapid, detailed and factual observations of what has gone wrong – particularly what has gone wrong in someone else's work. Our capacity for rapid failure analysis is extremely well developed. I confess mine to be at Olympic standard. The practical effects of first analysing, or worse, only analysing failure, has been to fill people's minds solely with a detailed picture of what they either can't do at all, or are currently not very good at doing. We actually enshrine this practice in our computerised systems. Important business review meetings invite people to go through the 'exception reporting' analysis of the business. That's the one where you get to look at the computerised print out of the highlighted negative variances in your performance and everyone else's. You then get to explain publically what you've done wrong, and what you're going to do about it. The positive variances that capture any successes are neither highlighted nor commented on. Such behaviour would be regarded as bizarre in the setting of a business review meeting. Subsequently facing such people with a demanding business challenge inevitably has them defocused from whatever skills they have to meet that challenge. We succeed only in shooting ourselves in the foot.

● **Sole analysis of failure maximises the chances of future failure.**

The response to consistently and only presenting people with a picture of what they aren't good at or can't do has either been trenchant defensiveness, or palpable anxiety, or both. This combination of being focused on what one isn't good at, and an emotional response of defensive anxiety, has proved an insurmountable barrier to developing the appetite for improvement. When people reviewed in this fashion have been faced with a demanding business challenge, they have naturally shied away from taking initiatives or the pursuit of the ambitious or unusual. The mind is too full of what it can't do, and the heart too full of defensive anxiety.

Having shot ourselves in one foot, we effectively do the same to the other one. The total focus on failure begets further failure.

- **Praise is of no practical use. It deteriorates the situation by potentially encouraging a dependent, feudal relationship.**

Giving praise as part of a review has proven to be a truly poisoned chalice.

The first reality is that praise has no practical benefit. It is by its nature a generalisation, and cannot reveal any of the detail of how to repeat the matter being praised. It is merely an opinion. It is a nice opinion that may give a warm glow. Nonetheless, it can offer no practical benefit.

Secondly, it has proved insidiously dangerous at a relationship level. It's an opinion, usually built on the sands of a person's emotional need to soften the impact of subsequent failure analysis. It has not been possible for people who have been praised to work out how much of that sand has been washed away by the following discussion on failure. Praise is solely in the gift of the person praising. The person praised has not known, and indeed cannot know, the basis on which that gift of 'brownie points' will be withdrawn or eroded. He can only hope to notice it when it has already happened, and adjust to it the best way he can. It takes the direction of a feudal relationship where praise is at the level of largesse, and the subordinate is encouraged towards a dependent relationship. This has never proved to be the basis for him to develop the sturdy independent relationship needed to nurture his own pattern of effective managing habits.

- **The conventional business review meeting has become a powerful negative force for both the business and its people.**

In the light of these difficulties, the way in which we run the conventional business review meeting is revealing. Its standard pattern is uncomfortably close to the above description.

Its sustained effects have been powerfully negative. The level of initiative taking and the capacity to anticipate problems and challenges, have both deteriorated. When these consequences have occurred, it has been a powerful reminder that the negative commercial effects of conventional but ill thought out managing processes are inevitable.

The good news is that the opposite is equally true. The choice as to which we operate is fortunately entirely in our hands.

SUMMARY

Creating strategy has been the ideal opportunity to draw together the thinking and concerns right across the organisation. It is a pivotal activity for producing focussed cohesion within all the business activities of the enterprise.

The opportunity exists to focus the key issues of concern at every level in the whole organisation. Managers throughout the structure get the chance to create their statements of aspiration for the issues they have prioritised. Additionally, they have to be supportive of aspirations specified by the level above. A continuum of mutually supportive business aspirations is therefore created. The whole organisation can then subsequently tackle the entire range of its daily business in a cohesive fashion. At a deeper level, it is one key platform on which real functional mutual respect can grow between the different levels in the organisation.

Creating strategy in this way depends on the habit of opening the mind to the full range of issues that can be tackled for any given challenge. The further skill has been to devise statements of aspiration that are broad enough to take account of those issues, yet specific enough to offer guidance on the operational decisions that will need to be faced later in implementing the strategy.

In contrast, the conventional conditioning of being solely focussed on targets and detailed planning has trained managers to habitually close their minds and continuously narrow their focus of attention. This habit is exactly counter to the above need to open the mind to accurately form strategy. Whilst targets and detailed planning have proved deeply unhelpful to the creation of appropriate strategies, they have of course remained vital in the implementation phase.

BACKGROUND CONTEXT

- **Companies have positioned their strategies anywhere on the continuum from being very specific to very generalised.**

  Wherever they have chosen to be on this continuum has had deep and widespread effects on the business. Examining those effects for each end of the range:

  - **'Strategy' has been narrowed down to a series of targets.**
    This immediately restricted people's focus and minimised the quality of the end results.
    At one extreme, organisations have narrowed down their 'strategy statements' to merely being targets, e.g. 'Our mission is to become number one in such and such market', etc. Such a desire is easy to understand because a target is by its nature specific enough to picture. It gives people something comfortingly tangible to relate to. However, this inevitably has the effect of instantly narrowing

people's focus at all levels in the organisation. It prematurely restricts people's thinking to a pre-selected band of actions. Its other effect has been that it provided no guidance within that band, as to exactly what type of decisions were acceptable to the organisation. As a result, people felt they had carte blanche to do anything in pursuit of any target. This has opened the door to actions ranging from being short sighted to outright unscrupulousness/illegality. At the very best, some temporary benefits resulted. Inevitable long term, long lasting, and deeply regrettable disadvantages followed. The key is to understand that a target is merely a possible picture of a very particular end result. When used as such it has proved to be helpful. However it is not a statement of fundamental aspiration. It is incapable of stimulating and guiding the wide range of cohesive, high quality initiatives that commercial challenges have invariably required. The way to achieve this valuable characteristic is detailed in the section below – **Some benefits and implications.**

- ○ **'Strategy' can be broadened to become statements of philosophical belief.**
  Intellectually interesting, but operationally useless and vulnerable to manipulation.
  Some organisations have gone to the other extreme and broadened their strategy statements to the point of generalisations. These then rapidly become 'motherhood and apple pie' in nature, e.g. 'We want to be a responsible member of such and such community', etc. Naturally in this day and age, any well meaning sentiment is welcome. It's certainly better than the malign ones that can lurk at any level in the organisation. However, the nature of such a broad strategy statement is that it is too vague to give any useful guidance on which band of actions people lower down in the organisation should seek out. It offers little help in difficult decisions of choice that happen throughout the business. The organisation becomes rudderless in its handling of every day issues. That has opened the door to rule by personality, and the absence of any sort of logical common sense basis for decision taking. People have responded to such strategy statements by posturing. In the worst cases, they have seen the opportunity to manipulate matters within the excessively broad band of interpretations that such generalised statements allow. The key is to understand that as statements of direction become more generalised, they inevitably become ones of philosophical belief. Though they have proved to be interesting subjects for intellectual debate, they have not proved helpful to managers grappling with difficult operational choices.

- ● **Strategy is most commonly seen as the sole preserve of the senior level.**

The convention is that strategy is created by much thought and effort in a piece of work exclusively set within the senior team. Of course, the most extreme version of this has been to set in within a team of consultants. It has then been rolled out to the rest of the organisation.

Some of the inevitable effects have been:

- ○ **Genuine commitment has not been possible**

  Managers have been dutiful in their response when the strategy has been accurately thought through, and prudent enough to conform if not. That is not commitment. People don't truly own the views as if they were their own. They therefore don't engage that spark of individual initiatives that signals people's creativity is aroused.

- ○ **The result is narrowly focused**
  compared to the range of issues confronting the organisation

  The automatic effect of the senior team working on its own is that the strategy is based only on the information and issues they focus on. Whatever the process they carry out cannot intimately engage with the extensive range of information and issues that exist throughout the organisation. It has the effect of distancing the business's strategy from the full range of its operational issues – a steep and slippery slope that deteriorates commercial results.

- ○ **It unnecessarily fosters an 'us' and 'them' mentality**

  Visibly dividing into two camps when preparing to work together as a united team has never proved a strategically wise move. Having one camp create a solution in isolation, then tell the other what direction they're both going to work towards, is at best insensitive.

  It enshrines status and position as the key elements of authority. It relegates operational information at every level except the most senior one to an irrelevance in the most critical piece of decision making in the organisation.

- ● **An alternative exists that meets the real needs of the business.**

  The reality is that any business presents a continuum of challenges ranging from the broadest and least tangible to the most specific and highly tangible. For the organisation to perform well, it is obliged to meet all of these challenges all of the time and produce consistent mutually supportive solutions. The most appropriate arrangement is to have the more intangible issues tackled by the more senior levels, whilst the more tangible ones are focussed by the more junior levels. This view of responsibilities leads to a quite different picture of what a useful strategy needs to contain, how it needs to be generated and then used.

  This is summarised in the following principle, and detailed in the benefits and implications section.

PRINCIPLE

- **The key issues selected by every level in the organisation form the basis for this type of strategy.** Aspirations for those issues are created by each level, and comprise the full strategy. A key requirement is that each statement supports those created by the level above.

- **These strategy statements closely inform operational and commercial decisions, and flex with changing information about those issues.**

EXPLANATION

Recounting the detail of each element in turn:

- **The key issues selected by every level in the organisation form the basis for this type of strategy.** Aspirations for those issues are created by each level ....

The organisation's strategy starts with the CEO selecting key issues of concern to him, for which he will state aspirations that he wants to pursue. Each of the subsequent levels will similarly choose key issues of concern to it, for which it will state aspirations that it wants to pursue. The key proviso is that each statement must support the set of aspirations created by the level above.

This therefore creates a continuum of mutually supportive aspirations, built around the key issues facing each level. Crucially, it is led by the CEO's concerns, and is thence underpinned by those of everyone else. It gives the maximum support to the strategy statements chosen at the most senior level. They receive the backing of all the other levels' increasingly more detailed strategic thinking. The chances of them actually happening within the business then become much higher than the norm.

- **These strategy statements closely inform operational and commercial decisions, and flex with changing information about those issues.**

Basing the strategy on the key issues facing each level ensures that the business concerns throughout the whole organisation are taken into account. It then becomes a common sense need at every level in the operation to refer major and difficult every day decisions to that thinking. Intended plans can then be checked out to ensure that their results will help to deliver the strategy. This is a view of the future that lives within all the commercial decisions taken in the daily business.

Subsequent business changes have of course continuously altered the information about the key issues at various levels in the organisation. The first people who will become aware of these changes will be the operational managers who generated that part of the strategy. They are then ideally placed to recast their strategy appropriately. If necessary, they have flagged to other levels the need to make changes in their sections of the overall strategy. This automatically ensures that the strategy flexes with the inevitable developments in the business.

SOME BENEFICIAL EFFECTS AND IMPLICATIONS

● **A key skill is creating a strategy consisting of statements of aspiration.**

The challenge is to look into the future for a chosen issue and create an aspiration that describes 'where we're trying to head to' with that issue. Critically, it needs to be of use to managers faced with the difficult choices that tackling that concern will undoubtedly raise. As mentioned in the above Background Context, if the stated aspiration is too generalised, then it will give no guidance. If it is too specific, it starts to take on the characteristics of a target, and prematurely closes down people's thinking to an inappropriately narrow band of activities. The key skill is to create a statement broad enough to stimulate an appropriate range of activities, yet specific enough to offer guidance about subsequent decisions within those activities. An example may help with illustrating how to achieve this important balance and some of the critical benefits that it brings.

EXAMPLE   **SETTING UP THE NEW FOOD MULTINATIONAL** (Business Challenge Two)

The sequence in which the strategic statement was developed was unconventional, and is a major key to its success.

Basis for strategy

○ **A key issue of concern (i.e. a selected vital piece of information about the situation)**

Examining all the information about the situation, the key factor was selected for which the strategy statement would articulate an aspiration. In the case of setting up the multinational, that factor was:

The links between the accountabilities of the national organisations, and those of the centre.

This issue would fundamentally influence the commercial success of the whole venture. Its effect on the operation of conventional multinationals had proved to be pivotal. It had significantly influenced the quality and speed of decision making throughout all teams, at all levels. It had heavily affected the level of cohesiveness across the entire organisation and its capacity to respond to any significant business challenge.

Strategy statement

The key aspiration was to establish a mutually beneficial partnership between the centre and each national team.

The latter would have total business accountability for their enterprise. They would accordingly create their own local strategy, but ensure that it actively supported the company wide strategy developed by the centre.

The centre would also be accountable for the developmental processes used throughout the multinational, i.e. responsibility for all principles related to structure, procedures, and man management.

Features of the strategy statement

● <u>It originates from key pieces of information, i.e. key issues</u>

The first thing of note is that choosing to base the strategy on selected pieces of information about the situation helps the end result to be focused on existing realities. It stops unfettered flights of imagination, philosophising, and producing cosmically broad statements of the motherhood and apple pie variety. Instead, it challenges managers to prioritise the issues facing them that will most affect the business. You can never be proved wrong when you philosophise. You only run that risk when you have the courage to publically declare your choice of priorities amongst today's scene.

● <u>The statement chooses an unequivocal direction and demonstrates it with a few clear decisions</u>

The chosen strategy opts for a very definitive option: it clarifies that choice with a very small number of decisions. However, they illustrate the operational heart of the option. This helps to stop the strategy becoming mere rhetoric and fine words. The decisions become an aid to help managers subsequently choose between difficult alternatives that will face them when they implement the strategy. This is a key success criterion that effective strategies have met.

● <u>The statement carefully refrains from encroaching on the detail of how things will happen, and contains no vestige of any target</u>

Having made the few big decisions necessary to outline the operational heart of the strategy, no further detail is offered as to how they will be achieved (i.e. plans), or what effects are expected (i.e. targets). That is appropriately worked out later by managers using the detailed operational information within their work arenas. This helps prevent the temptation to micro-manage.

Most importantly, the total absence of any targets prevents the early narrowing of people's thinking. It helps to prevent that thinking from being closed down to a prematurely restricted set of actions, and thence minimising the scope of their endeavours.

Instead, it helps people to focus on the real core of the strategic choice being made, and not be distracted by an early mesmerisation with numbers.

The combination of these three features helps to appropriately position the strategy statement. It prevents it being a woolly minded statement of philosophy at one extreme, or a myopically detailed target at the other extreme.

- **Support is an undervalued and misunderstood skill**

  The requirement that the strategy statements of each level actively support those of the level above has had important effects. Conventionally, support is regarded as a second rate skill – it's for the 'also rans', with just the hint of the lickspittle, and bordering on the unctuous. The reality is quite the opposite.

  Those who have ensured that their strategy directions support those of the level above have found it requires real effort and focused creativity. It calls for the mind to be open to what may be the quite different views that others see as important. In short, it asks those who practise it to be agile of mind, and to always put the interests of the business first.

  The effects have been marked.

  - On the business front it has produced a tightly cohesive strategy that has given the organisation a discernible identity. It is the identity of consistent action. It is not the duplicitous froth that expensive PR fantasies attempt to conjure up as corporate identities in the make believe world of advertising. It is the durable, real identity that comes from consistent delivery at each level in the organisation. Its bedrock is the mutual support built into its strategy.

  - On the relationship front, it has welded the different levels together in a closeness that has proved invaluable, particularly when significant difficulties have beset the organisation.

  The experience has been that it is the truest sign of leadership to both give support and earn it from others.

COMMONLY ENCOUNTERED DIFFICULTIES AND CHALLENGES

- **We have conditioned our managers not to think strategically.**

  It has consistently proved remarkably difficult for managers to create statements of strategy.

Understandably, it is always challenging to look searchingly into the future, and then choose an unequivocal direction to pursue for the issues in hand. To then 'pitch' a statement about that direction that is at just the appropriate point on the continuum from 'too generalised' to 'too specific' is yet more testing.

Having said that, the experience has been that managers find this exceptionally troublesome to do. Their instinctive habit has been to produce either statements defining targets (i.e. quoting options for numbers or tangible end effects that might be striven for), or statements of very wide generality. Even when they realise the error they are making, they have still found it intensely difficult to produce the above strategic thinking. Their problems have stemmed from two causes:

- o **The very common conviction that numerical targets and other tangible end results are the only key** to successful commercial endeavours

- o **The grooved habit of focusing on targets has minimised developing skill at penetrating to the core issues of a situation**

To help clarify the point, here is an example from the development work done by a particular client.

EXAMPLE   **A NEW MULTINATIONAL NARROWLY AVOIDS KNEE JERKING ITS RESPONSE TO FINANCIAL TARGETS**

- o **Strong gut response to their targets invites them to expand into the neighbouring country.**

    An aspiring food industry multinational had just reached the initial stages of trying to break into foreign markets. The senior management felt strong pressure from the need to be successful at that challenge. They were totally focused on the critical need to deliver certain growth and return targets within a set time deadline. They were acutely aware that success or failure with those targets would have a powerful effect on the enterprise's financial standing. It was familiar with how the market place operated in the country geographically closest to them, and had information that it was possible to succeed with the plans they were capable of. Their estimate was that those plans would deliver the targets needed. They were excited, very optimistic, confident, and on the very point of getting into action.

- o **Last minute strategic thinking prevented the business error.**

    Very fortunately, cooler heads prevailed. One voice asked, 'What exactly is our strategy in expanding into this country? What are the fundamental and long term advantages of us becoming a significant player there? What exactly does the future hold for us if we stay there?' Up to that point, the sole concern had been to meet the targets on time, avoid the considerable penalties involved, and simultaneously gain the financial benefits. Fortunately, they then realised they hadn't yet crystallised their strategy, and had knee jerked their response to the pressure they felt in meeting their targets.

Their previous long-grooved obsession with only being concerned with 'producing good numbers' had swept away their strategic grip of running the business. No systematic thought had been given to the core issues facing them in operating abroad, and the key directions they would pursue were not clear. They therefore had no answers to the sort of questions being asked. It is very much to their credit that they had the humility, wisdom, and appetite to recognise the mistake, and immediately started to do the needed strategic thinking. Necessary information was rapidly researched, key issues identified, and directions for the business abroad identified. Their priorities became clear to them, and they identified markets that fitted this thinking. They then checked that their financial targets would simultaneously be met.

○ **Subsequent successful expansions into new markets led by strategy – not by targets.**

They expanded into markets that were further away than the original selected country. Continued expansion into yet other countries proved successful. They did later choose to operate within the nearest country, but only in businesses that exactly fitted their overall strategy. It proved highly successful for the total business. It was certainly orders of magnitude more effective than the original knee jerk response of operating within the neighbouring country on the sole basis of meeting the targeted financial returns.

● **We have rewarded and groomed our managers to prove they can consistently narrow their focus of attention to only targets.**

Ingraining the habit of being focused on numerical targets has inexorably conditioned our managers to only think of a selected portion of a performance issue. They become used to only being comfortable with those portions that can be easily measured. This has then generally grown into believing that they can ignore all other aspects of the issue, and more damagingly, that they are commercially unimportant. In addition, the public approval and promotion of those who primarily deliver their targets has relentlessly driven other managers to redouble their efforts to ingrain the same behaviour. The inevitable effect has been to embed the mental habit of automatically narrowing the focus of one's thinking and attention to just one aspect of any issue: its potential targets.

They have consequently found it extraordinarily difficult to attempt strategic thinking, which demands the opposite mental approach. This asks the person to identify and think deeply about the full width of core issues that underpin an area of the operation. It asks the mind to open to the full perspective indicated by those issues, and have the courage to choose a clear direction to pursue that takes account of all of them. When managers have achieved this, they experience that a far wider and deeper set of issues has to be tackled than that implied by any set of selected targets. The irony is that diligently pursuing those issues has always produced better numerical results than the knee jerk conditioning of instinctively and only chasing targets.

The real need is to grow an increasingly sharper grasp of all the fundamental issues within a particular challenge. This habit is not nurtured by conditioning managers to automatically close their minds down to only delivering targets. It is in essence about growing the habit of appropriately opening the mind, and not habitually closing it down.

- **Targets do have an important part to play in delivering a strategy.**

The above recall of how strategy can be understood, created and used is not saying that numerical targets are not relevant or useful. Successful commercial work requires the discipline of having tangible, objective indications of our success. Quantifiable targets have offered a secure way of providing some of those indications.

Having said that, the experience shows that targets, and their pursuit, have to be resolutely set aside when creating strategy. It then frees the mind to achieve the depth and width of thinking needed for such work. The setting and pursuit of targets have been a natural and useful part of subsequently implementing a strategy. They have proved a powerful and misleading hindrance during its creation.

ISSUE 3 – 2.10   **DECISION MAKING METHODS :**

Some of the implications

SUMMARY

There are seven naturally occurring decision making steps.

They can be used in a multitude of different selections and patterns in making and implementing every decision. Their application to all the work problems I've encountered and those I've observed others tackling has successfully solved those challenges. In the majority of cases the end numerical results exceeded all expectations.

The power of these steps lies in the fact that there are no formulaic ways of using them. Whilst clear guidelines have emerged that help their use, judgement and skill have to be developed by continuously practising them on live problems.

The coaching of subordinates to develop that ability has been the bedrock focus within the guided partnership of the management line. This work has been the cornerstone of systematically developing the quality of everyday business work. It has simultaneously laid the key basis for effective teamwork across the organisation.

The deeper reality has been that every other management skill has been rooted in a person's ability to use these steps. It is therefore the very core discipline that has to be mastered.

Simultaneously, such work has steered the organisation as a whole towards the habit of tackling issues on the basis of commonly shared fact and logic.

- It is the shared logic that stems from pursuing a common set of aspirations

- It is the shared set of facts that emerge from the information jointly collated about those aspirations and the job in hand

This has had the fundamental effect of moving the organisation towards a rational way of deciding matters, and usefully guiding it away from becoming overrun by 'politics'.

BACKGROUND CONTEXT

● **A wide variety of methods is used**

Three categories of decision making methods are available:

- o 'methods' that are led by people's intuition

- o hypothesised models for decision making that someone has invented

- o decision making steps that are naturally occurring. Extraordinarily, however, they were first presented by Ralf Coverdale and Bernard Babington Smith as a concept of 'A Systematic Approach to Getting Things Done'

People also combine bits and pieces from any of these methods in whatever manner seems appropriate to them at the time. As a result an extremely wide variety of decision making methods are used.

Briefly looking at each of the three basic alternatives:

- o **Intuitive**

  The 'methods' – if that's the right word for them – led by personal intuition are as numerous as the number of people using them. Each person's intuition works in ways that are unique to them. Each decision making 'method' in this category has been similarly unique. By definition, this way of handling matters has varied in ways that are not predictable to anyone else, apart, possibly, from the decision taker. Subordinates who work for managers who decide things in this fashion have lived a life of confusion and uncertainty. They have sometimes chosen to form a closer relationship with their manager to get a better feel for the way his intuition works. The alternative has been to minimise interactions with their manager, or in the extreme case 'escape' from him, or the organisation.

- o **Hypotheses**

  The hypothesised models of decision making steps offer a predictability as to how things will be tackled. People have had a common language to both describe what stage in the decision they are at, and also understand the stage colleagues have reached in their work. The sequence(s) between the different steps used to take decisions and solve problems tend to be fixed to certain patterns. Some of the steps defined by the various models are similar or identical. Organisations have commonly institutionalised one or more of these models across their operations, to aid the interactions between different working groups and areas.

- o **Naturally occurring steps**

  Close examination of every single statement during any piece of work discloses that it belongs to one of seven fundamental steps. They are consistent with every step in all of the hypothesised models of decision making, as well as those created by any person's intuition. Uniquely, however, the seven steps include the full range of different steps that occur partially in each of the other methods. The selection and sequence in which the naturally occurring steps can be used is entirely a matter of judgement, and is infinitely variable. More information about them, and their use, is detailed below.

- **Powerful commercial and emotional effects**

The decision making method being used has the most fundamental effect on the commercial results achieved. People have correctly felt that a lot is at stake when deciding which particular method is chosen and used. Appropriately, intense dialogues have taken place to reach a conclusion on this issue.

People often see their standing, capacity to influence, and personal power, as tied up with exactly what decisions get taken on various matters. Their interest and motivation to see the 'right' method being used to bring about decisions consistent with their views have added to the intensity of those dialogues.

As with all the issues in this section, this one is coached within the guided partnership of the management line.

- **This work has used the naturally occurring steps**

This development work has used the above steps throughout the last forty years to tackle all of the business challenges encountered. Every one of those problems and their many complexities have been successfully solved. Most of the challenges were regarded at the start as being intractable, with a history of previously failed attempts to solve them. Others had not been attempted before. These steps are therefore thoroughly proven in the most testing of situations, and have yet to fail in illuminating a successful way forward. It is worth repeating at this point that there is no fixed universally applicable pattern or sequence in which these steps can be used. The selection of steps from the fundamental seven that are chosen for use on the problem in hand is also entirely a matter of judgement. This way of handling matters is not restricted by any formulaic way of working. Indeed, a key source of its considerable power lies in inviting managers to become increasingly skilful at two judgements: firstly in choosing the decision making steps that best suit the challenge facing them, and secondly in selecting which pattern(s) they are then used in.

Whilst they were brought to prominence by Ralph Coverdale's and Bernard Babington Smith's 'A Systematic Approach to Getting Things Done', the steps within the approach have been in existence for as long as men and women have attempted to solve any problem. They are inherent to the nature of any task, and have the apparent and deceiving simplicity of common sense. The multitude of labels that can be used to identify the different steps are not important, and are simply the arbitrary choice of whoever uses them. They are just to aid short hand communication about them within working groups. Instead, what has proved vital is to understand the fundamental meaning of each step. Those meanings are listed below, so that we can refer to them during the recall of work on this issue.

Decision making steps:

- o choosing the aspirations to pursue for the challenge in hand

- o exploring the knowledge, facts, experience, and resources that are relevant to those aspirations and the above challenge

- o identifying the key activities that need to be tackled

- o specifying the practicalities of how each activity will be carried out. The precise detail of who, what, when, where, and how things will happen needs to be set out

- o specifying the targets, and end results that need to be seen during and after the work, to indicate that the challenge and its aspirations have been met

- o carrying out the action

- o reviewing what has occurred, so as to improve the current work and the tackling of future challenges

● **It is possible to describe the outline flavour of this issue but it needs to be experienced to grasp its real meaning and relevance**

Long experience of personally working at these steps, both on my own and with many other managers, shows that any explanation of them has a superficial and very incomplete value. Indeed at times my explanations of them seem to have hindered rather than helped people's understanding of these critical steps. Their actual meaning, relevance, and use have only been revealed to people when they continually experiment with applying them to real problems. It is that application that has developed people's understanding of and skill at using these steps. This simply means that whilst I will try my very best to share some information about this issue, the reader faces the task of gaining real understanding by trying out the steps for himself. Of course, following his initial trials, the long journey that opens before him is the more demanding and productive stage of gaining real operational skill at their use.

The analogy with developing high levels of physical skill at a complex sport is a very close one. Explanations about various techniques, positions and movements can only give a mere intellectual and rudimentary view of the sport. Consistent practice and exploration under the pressure of actual performance offers the only route to operational skill and real understanding. The same is true of developing ability at the mental habits of decision taking.

The rewards for such effort have been far reaching and cannot be overstated. They are detailed in the section below, **Some beneficial effects and implications.**

PRINCIPLE

The challenge is for individuals to:

- **become personally skilful**
  at using the naturally occurring decision making steps within their own thinking and work

- **make contributions when working in teams**
  that both aid the resolution of the challenge in hand
  and the steps that others are considering

- **become skilled at selecting the steps, and their sequence of use**
  to resolve the challenge being worked at

EXPLANATION

This has proved to be the most fundamental and influential issue coached within the management line. The commercial effects of successfully accomplishing it have been sustained and significant. Ignoring or failing at this challenge has always significantly deteriorated the business.

The manager has worked persistently to coach his subordinate within his handling of everyday problems to:

- **firstly, develop the skill of knowing which decision making step(s) his thinking is focused on**, before he decides to pursue or share that thinking.

- **secondly, to develop the skill of knowing when to time that thinking into any discussion**, so that his contribution aids the step others are considering

- **thirdly, to develop the skill of choosing the optimum pattern of decision making steps** for particular challenges. There is no fixed pattern or sequence of decision making steps, which is universally applicable to all decisions or even the majority of decisions. Life is never that simplistic. The real challenge is to become increasingly skilful at perceiving which sequence of which steps best fits the work in hand.

SOME BENEFICIAL EFFECTS AND IMPLICATIONS

To tackle this piece of development work within the everyday business and achieve real speed and accuracy at the above skills has always proved a substantial undertaking. Like all the principles recalled in this work, the concepts have the simplicity of common sense. Intellectually understanding them has always been easy. Delivering them into the routine business has proved quite a different matter. However the effects have always been sustained and far reaching – for the subordinate, for his manager, and for the organisation. Each of these is detailed below:

● **Effects on the subordinate**

Firstly, the above skills fundamentally improve how the subordinate individually operates. Secondly, they significantly improve how he operates within any team. Recounting experience of each of these areas:

<u>Effects on how he individually operates</u>

○ **It's improved the discipline and relevance of his own thinking.**

Previously, subordinates (including myself) have followed convention, and only focused on the content of their ideas and their relevance to the problem in hand. Developing the additional skill of knowing the decision making step the idea belonged to allowed them to check if that was the appropriate step to be considering. Of course if it wasn't, then it alerted them to start considering a different step. It has also indicated steps that they had inadvertently missed out – preventing a potentially significant error.

A typical example has been a manager being instinctively drawn to an idea as to what the practical solution might be, in the very initial stages of a problem. If he had the discipline of knowing which decision making step that idea belonged to, then he stood the chance of preventing a key error. His solution is an example of the step – 'deciding the practical detail' of what will happen: a plan. Realising this may have alerted him to his omission of the step of exploring the relevant knowledge, facts, resources, and experience. Committing to a plan in the absence of exploring the background knowledge step has proved to be extremely risky and an almost certain serious error.

His natural enthusiasm for his initial idea can distract him from identifying which decision making step it is an example of. In contrast, becoming aware of which decision making step one's idea fits into helps to ensure the quality and relevance of the eventual work produced.

○ **It allows an individual to continuously view the overall process by which he is tackling his work**

Previously, subordinates (including myself) have been totally caught up in the convention of finding the solutions to the problem in hand. However, developing the above skill, constantly provides an overall view of the decision making steps he is using. It offers him an ongoing overall picture of the process he is following. This has flagged up occasions when he has judged that his chosen process has become inappropriate. He then has the opportunity to adjust that process, and prevent the potential error emerging in the final business solution.

A typical example is that people have assumed that the challenge facing them did not pose any undue risks. However, having the above discipline ensured their deliberate exploration of the background information to the challenge. On occasions that exploration has disclosed that the commercial risks were far higher than first thought.

They have accordingly altered their pattern of decision making steps to protect themselves against those risks. This has often resulted in them having at least one trial run of their intended operational plan of action. Naturally, a trial run involves a first pass plan, followed by some sort of trial action step, followed by a review of what happened, leading to some amendments to the original plan. Obviously as people's assessment of the risks rose, they have repeated this cycle of – plan, action, review, – plan, action, review,– etc., until they felt able to commit to a final action plan.

- o **It allows the individual to gain experience and skill at choosing the sequence of decision making steps that best tackles the challenge in hand.**

   This is a sophisticated and powerful skill that people work at, towards the later part of their development work on the decision making steps. It first requires all the basic disciplines of instantly knowing what steps they themselves are considering and also knowing what steps colleagues are focussing on. The priority is to practise these basics skills until smooth instinctive accuracy is achieved before embarking on experiments with the pattern(s) of decision making steps.

   An example of its use has been when managers have decided that a particular challenge has wide strategic implications. They have often chosen a pattern of steps that recycles between the aspirations they need to pursue, the knowledge and information they can glean about those aspirations, and the consequent targets and end results. They have recycled through those steps until their successive amendments to each have convinced them that they have satisfactory answers to their strategic concerns. Only then have they gone on to consider the detailed plans for action that they would carry out within the business.

- o **It opens the door to becoming more aware of the nature and meaning of others' contributions.**

   Previously, when others have made contributions to their work, subordinates (including myself) have followed the convention of only considering the content and relevance of those contributions. Developing the additional skill of always knowing which decision making step he is personally thinking of essentially makes him more aware of the exact nature of his own thinking. He then has the chance to become similarly aware of the exact nature of others' contributions to his work. The particular decision making step their thinking fits into becomes clear, and the nature of their help can be better understood.

   A common example has been to realise that colleagues have developed thinking strengths in particular decision making steps. An instance has been someone who is consistently seen to be able to rapidly foresee and identify all the critical activities that will need to be tackled with detailed operational plans. Recognising this highly valuable skill has allowed teams to deliberately deploy it to their significant advantage.

   Becoming increasingly aware of the nature of others' thinking strengths has often acted as a catalyst to discover their other strengths. These operate in many other areas, apart from those concerned with decision making (e.g. see all the areas recalled in the Man Management Section), and so provide much scope for enquiry. One of the chief effects has been to gradually increase the fact content of a person's understanding of how to best work with others. This has helped to moderate any overly emotional responses that he may initially have been distracted by.

- o **It continuously confirms that he is master of the development of his managing habits.**

  All the subordinates (including myself) who have worked at this piece of development have found that it demands sustained mental effort. However, the effect is that the work gives personal control over the pace and direction of how their managing habits on decision making are developed. It offers a chance to be master of one's own progress on this issue. Simultaneously, it illustrates that the same is true for developing skill at any managing habit. It offers the real chance to be master of one's development of all managing habits we choose to work at.

Effects on teams he interacts with

- o **He is better able to help the team remain cohesive as they work through challenges.**

  Previously, he would have concentrated on his own contribution, and its business connections with others' contributions. Becoming aware of the decision making steps that others are considering has enabled him to time his contribution to match the step being discussed.
  A more developed level of this skill is to help guide colleagues' contributions into the appropriate step, when they've offered them at an inappropriate time, i.e. at a time when the group is working at a different step. This has helped retain a missed timed contribution that will nonetheless be helpful in resolving the total problem. The effect has been to help his team remain cohesive in its work and maximise the use of its different ideas.

  An example of this skill has been to work with someone who has honed the habit of instinctively suggesting what targets and end results he thinks should be achieved. That thinking can often be volunteered, regardless of the fact that his team are working at a different step. He has naturally felt his contribution to be of vital importance, and has been very concerned that his team include it in the agreed work. More skilful colleagues have recognised that he is offering potential targets and end results at a time when they are in the middle of trying to resolve other concerns. They have nonetheless supported his contribution into the step where they will consider targets, and use it as a starting point for discussions when they reach that stage. This sounds simple enough when described, but involves developing considerable skill to do accurately at the speed of normal business discussions.

- o **No skill is capable of fixing every difficulty.**

  I hasten to add that powerful though these skills are in helping to competently accomplish work in a way that nourishes sound relationships, they are not a panacea.

  I have worked closely with those who chose to be rigidly fixated on certain decision making steps. In the case of one talented individual, the effect on the work in hand was highly disruptive with serious commercial losses being made in the business concerned. Core difficulties could not be grappled with because appropriate decision making steps were not being considered. Despite agreeing the nature of the difficulty with the person concerned, he chose not to rein in his fixation for certain steps and his avoidance of others.

No level of skill is proof against an individual exercising their prerogative to indulge a direction that damages the business. We had to cease working together. The business subsequently recovered and was highly successful.

- **Effects on the line manager**

It is the personal coaching within the guided partnership of the management line that has been vital to developing the conscious use of the decision making steps. It is this individual work that is the very basis of building effective teamwork across the whole organisation (see Issue 3–2.14 Teamwork: Some Benefits and Implications, – p.192).

The supervising line manager has needed considerable skill and determination to lead and coach this work by his subordinates. There are two powerful factors that strongly motivate managers to accomplish this work:

- o **The first is that they fully realise that it is the only secure way to enable their subordinates to produce sustained, commercially successful results.**

  Only by doing such development work can the manager harness the latent talents in the team working for him. Only then can he deploy their full range of strengths against the business challenges facing him and his team. Not to do so leaves him with the ineffective option of deploying only his own developed skills, and operating a command and control system with his team. It is clear to perceptive managers that it is very much a case of develop your subordinates, or fail to deliver high quality business results.

- o **The second is that they realise that they advance their own development in the skills being coached, as well as exploring the complex skill of coaching itself.**

  Accurately guiding and supporting a subordinate's development of particular skills test the very limits of a manager's own ability in that area. Being able to pin point what has to be done that fits another's different pattern of strengths and weaknesses, so that he can make significant advances, automatically challenges the manager's own skill and understanding. Learning to then support his uniquely different progress is a yet bigger challenge. My own experience is that these two challenges are a worthy test of where one has got to in one's own development path.

  Observant managers will have seen their most able senior colleagues display an ability to coach key managing habits within the delivery of complex pieces of work. They will therefore welcome any opportunity to develop their skills in this key attribute.

- **Effects on the organisation**

  o **A recognised highway code for tackling issues.**

  A common challenge in large organisations has been to mutually understand where a particular decision making process has got to, what are the key things that need to be worked at, and what signs of progress will signal future success. In the most testing of situations, this has been achieved across the different locations and cultures of a multinational's operation by sharing the status of work in the relevant decision making steps.

  o **A practical means of combining very different individual strengths and an effective means of developing teamwork.**

  All organisations face the need to harness very different talents and abilities within the solution of business difficulties. They realise such harnessing gives those solutions a broader basis of ideas and a robustness that would otherwise be absent. Disciplined use of the decision making steps has allowed people with widely different talents and skills to contribute at steps that reflect their abilities. It has consequently provided the basis for developing effective teamwork across the organisation.

  o **A practical aid to leading complex work.**

  Leaders have been able to decide the priority steps they would pay particular attention to. This has been especially useful when faced with large projects, involving a number of teams across different locations and nationalities. It provides a means of planning such work systematically, tracking progress (e.g. through completion of various steps), and anticipating and responding to difficulties.

  o **An aid to interactions between teams.**

  Teams working at different but interactive projects found it useful to have a mutually shared way of working. They could then accurately plan the stages in their work at which to coordinate their efforts, and exactly in what manner that would happen.

  An example has been when teams have agreed that the overall business needs would be best met by their joining together at for instance the target setting stage. They have then agreed certain end results that have interacted with their separate projects. Teams have therefore coordinated their separate work using the common framework of the various stages.

  o **The decision making steps are the fundamental basis with which all other managing skills are interdependent.**

  The development of every man management skill has turned out to be rooted in the decision making steps. They have proved to be the very foundation of that extensive work. This is not an immediately obvious or accepted truth, and it may be helpful at this point to illustrate such an interdependence between the decision making steps and another managing skill commonly treated as being unrelated to them:

EXAMPLE :   **THE 'DECISION MAKING STEPS' AND 'MOTIVATION'**

These two issues are usually the target of separate modular training, and little to no interest is shown in how they interact and interdepend. The reality is that working managers continuously find that particular problems confronting them can inextricably bind these two concerns together. They are interdependent in an analogous way to the different parts of a Rubik's cube. Just one example of that interdependence is:

- **Consistently dealing with the same decision making step raised by another person is one key way of showing respect for their contribution.**

  The skill of being able to consistently match the decision making stage that someone else is thinking at, with one's own contribution, has a fundamental impact on his motivation to be involved in the work. When consistently applied, it has helped foster a feeling of being in tune with each other's thinking, and a confidence that they will be successful together in resolving whatever difficulty faces them. It is one effective way to show respect for what the other person is saying: 'I value what you have to say enough to consistently spend real effort in staying on the same ground that interests you'. Continuously showing others this respect for their thinking has an inevitable and deep impact on their motivation to be involved.

  The reverse is equally true: consistently making contributions that don't match the decision making step others are at has irritated and annoyed them. When done repeatedly, it has convinced them that it is both emotionally unpleasant to work with the person concerned, and highly unlikely to yield effective results. It is one basic way of demonstrating disrespect for what the other has to say: 'I think so little of what you have just said that I shall habitually suggest something that is entirely different'. The net result on the other person's motivation to be involved can easily be imagined.

  Should these positive or negative options be played out within the guided partnership of the management line, then the motivation levels of all involved have been deeply affected one way or the other.

- **The naturally occurring decision making steps promote handling matters via a basis of shared fact and logic**

  These steps have two essential features:

- firstly, they demonstrate a logical, systematic pursuit of any aspiration identified for the challenge in hand

- secondly, they rely on mutually exploring the facts within the background knowledge step describing any aspiration and challenge

The automatic result of habitually using the steps is to help the organisation towards taking its decisions on the basis of shared fact and logic.

This has given teams a pragmatic perspective within which to better manage the range of different personalities within their groups.

I do not mean to imply that shared fact and logic are the only ingredients that are required. Of course, the experience has been that other vital factors are needed. However, this work confirms that shared fact and logic provides a key platform to handle difficult issues in a cooperative and objective fashion.

COMMONLY ENCOUNTERED DIFFICULTIES AND CHALLENGES

There have been two areas of particular difficulty that managers have had to grapple with when working at the above skills and delivering their commercial benefits.

- **People can decide not to consider the nature of their own thinking.**

  The first difficulty comes from the natural tendency for us to be instinctively and fiercely wedded to the worth of our own ideas. We are determined to see them adopted. We will have put in much effort and practice over our careers to ensure that we succeed more often than not at this key ambition. Understandably, it has been challenging for managers to develop the additional skill of always being aware of the decision making step to which their thinking belongs. It has been a further discipline to use that understanding to decide whether to pursue that thinking and offer it to others. Of course, some managers have decided to opt out of such effort and continue with the more conventional habit of being mesmerised by their own ideas at all times. Ironically, they can be amongst the most vocal in mouthing the rhetoric of the need to do the work. The result has been that such managers have become road blocks to rapid and cohesive decision making. They start to cause extra work, effort, and time in the attempts to deliver crucial decisions speedily. The unfortunate track record is that in a significant number of cases such managers have been unwilling to alter their habits. This has been despite them often agreeing the common sense of doing so, and recognising that support is being offered to aid their efforts to change. That has led to much energy and effort in factually looking at the full picture of the individuals' strengths and weaknesses, and taking account of that analysis. Their supervising manager has had to shoulder this unwelcome duty.

- **The prevailing decision making process significantly enhances the focus on the business or on 'politics'.**

The second difficulty has been much larger. It represents a fundamental organisation-wide challenge to the CEO and his senior team. A feature of all organisations that greatly concerns their managers is the level to which 'politics' intrudes, consumes, and distracts effort and attention from the real business issues that need resolving. The method of decision making chosen by the organisation has strongly influenced its balance between 'politicking', and focusing on its business.

- **Intuitive decision making processes accelerate the appetite for 'politics'.**

If the organisation's standard decision making process is intuition led, then the effect on the tendency to 'politic' has been analogous to throwing petrol on to a fire. A much larger fire instantly erupts at a speed impossible to contain and great difficulty is had in ever bringing it under control. So it is with the effect of intuition led decision making. As recalled above, its impact is to strongly focus the issue of personality as the basis for deciding things. In the absence of any logical basis for making decisions, the key question has then become: 'Is that person with me or against me, or doesn't care one way or another?'. It has been this feature of the intuition led decision making process that has testosterone-enhanced any latent inclination towards politicking within the organisation. The impact has been to nurture the well recognised political habits of competitive manoeuvring, the selective disclosure of information, the obscuring of motives, the pursuit of personal power, etc.

- **Clear, unambiguous, sustained support is needed to make the 'fact and logic' based way of decision making become the norm.**

It is the unique responsibility of the CEO and his senior team to be unequivocal about which decision making method the organisation will operate. Much more importantly, it is their obligation to personally lead it there. The worst of both worlds has been to proclaim the fine sounding rhetoric of 'decisions based on shared fact and logic', whilst intermittently operating 'decisions via politics' whenever expediency beckons. The result of this loss of courage has been that all fact and logic inspired decision making ceases. Initiative taking slows to a near stop as confused anxiety and cynicism spread at speed through the organisation.

ISSUE 3 – 2.11   **TAKING INITIATIVES.**

SUMMARY

Initiative taking has been one of the core managing habits that has produced sustained commercial success.

Enterprises have rightly striven to cultivate its growth. It has not proved to be a simple challenge. Sustainable success has come from understanding that it requires four other skills to be embedded:

- creating proposals in the face of difficulties

- supporting those proposals

- continuously reviewing progress

- responding to mistakes of endeavour differently from mistakes of omission.

It is in the interdependence between these four skills that initiative taking has been systematically nourished into sustained growth.

The positive effects of achieving high standards at initiative taking have deeply benefitted the business. They have reached into every corner of the organisation's commercial performance.

These are truly considerable prizes. Inevitably, their price is also high. Tenacity has been needed to habituate the above four skills, and so provide the seedbed for initiative taking. Some have proved willing to pay this price and thence reap the rewards. Others have not. Equally, they have not enjoyed the rewards.

BACKGROUND CONTEXT

Initiative taking has been an accurate indicator of how successful the organisation is.
Cohesive initiative taking has been a highly noticeable feature of effective organisations, and, conversely, is revealingly rare in ineffective ones. One client organisation actually moved from being demonstrably effective in their business over some ten years to being ineffective over the following eighteen months, and then back to its original effective operation. It kept precisely the same people throughout. The level of initiative taking moved back and forth to exactly reflect the way in which the organisation was being run. The switches back and forth were exactly mirrored in the organisation's bottom line.

PRINCIPLE

Initiative taking is nurtured by the management line's daily routine of:

- **coaching subordinates to grow the habit of creating proposals**
  within the tackling of every day difficulties

- **appropriately supporting their efforts** to implement those proposals.
  The principles underpinning this key area of support are detailed in the section on 'Managing Ideas'

- **reviewing the results of their efforts**
  by applying the principle described in the Section 'Responding to Success and Failure'

- **responding appropriately to mistakes of endeavour, as opposed to mistakes of omission**

EXPLANATION

Exploring each element in turn:

- **Coaching subordinates to pursue the habit of creating proposals**
  within the tackling of every day difficulties.

  o **We start from the basis of a groomed habit of competitive debate.**

  The core habit that has underpinned initiative taking is the discipline of making proposals to resolve every day difficulties.

  The sad reality is that throughout every facet of our society, we have nurtured precisely the opposite habit. We groom our best talent to value the destructive, erudite question. An endless stream of questions querying the negative facets of an issue is regarded as proof of a penetrating intellect and much valued 'gravitas'. We value endless articulateness on difficulties as proof of a constructive prudence. These are all habits of competitive debating. I am as guilty as the next person of having practised my ability to do all of these things to an instinctive standard. I allowed myself to be as conditioned as the next person to think that they were the habits needed to 'get on'. *Mea culpa.*

  I see now that all these habits trained me to selectively focus on the negative information surrounding an issue. They discouraged me from moving to the much more challenging step of considering what I could constructively do about the issue. It was easier to stay in the safety of the endless information about what was wrong with matters. It enabled me not to risk sticking my neck out, and suggest anything to improve the situation. After all, if I remained there, I might never do anything, and thence I could never be proved to do anything wrong.

- ○ **Creating effective proposals requires the full information to be processed.**

  However, to take the bull by the horns and make a proposal, I would need a different type of thinking. I would need to closely examine all the information about the issue to find strengths and opportunities around which I could build some proposal. I was very grateful to managers I worked for at this stage in my development – they would patiently yet persistently respond to all discussions of difficulties I raised by saying, 'So, Frank, what do you suggest we/you/they do about that?'. I quickly grew to know that if I brought up any problem, then I absolutely needed to have processed the information about it and arrived at a workable set of proposals. I was certain to be asked for them, and whatever I said would be carefully scrutinised. Off-the-cuff answers would be noted, and definitely would not pass muster at that scrutiny. The absolute certainty was that I would be seen as a shallow and unperceptive thinker: all mouth and no mind.

  It is truly impressive to witness a 'discussion' in the management line between a well trained manager and his subordinate about real operational difficulties. Its hallmarks are a quiet, thoughtful stream of sequential proposals that inexorably close down matters towards the action steps that will happen. It's an exchange that takes no sidetracks, wastes not a word, and is characterised by quite long silences as each man thinks deeply about what has been said. He strives to construct the next proposal to move the discussion one step further forward. Contingencies are carefully probed and key areas to monitor also agreed. The real benefit of coaching these habits within the management line is to embed them within subordinates' normal everyday thinking. They simply become an automatic part of the mental equipment they bring to bear on any matter they deal with, in whatever team they are involved with.

- ● **Appropriately supporting their efforts**
  to implement those proposals.

The principles underpinning this key area of support are detailed in the later section on Managing Ideas. However, to capture the precise connection with initiative taking:

- ○ High quality support is the engine that drives proposals into initiatives.

  One thing I was totally convinced of was that my manager would relentlessly support whatever proposals I had suggested and reviewed with him. I could absolutely rely on his support as I progressed my proposal into an initiative. If that support meant that he needed to risk his reputation at the most senior levels by backing the proposed judgements, then he would not hesitate to do so. This type of high quality support is crucial to growing the subordinate's confidence and nurturing his ability to produce more creative initiatives. It also usefully tempers any temptation to be hasty and unprepared in the framing of those initiatives. The more senior audience will be well able to spot any flaws in the suggestions made.

- **Reviewing the results of their efforts**
  by using the principles described in the section 'Responding to Success and Failure'.

  - o Reviewing initiatives for success and failure is the engine
    that drives sustained initiative taking.

    I was equally certain that, as night followed day, my manager would casually but inexorably review my progress in implementing my proposals. It was entirely inescapable. I was as certain that he would work with me through those reviews in exactly the patterns described in Responding to Success and Failure (Issue 3 – 2.8, p.137). We would emerge with joint views of any successes that had occurred, any errors that had escaped my attention, and any improvement plans I/we would need to operate next time. I would be totally confident that we would end up with precisely the same view of what had happened, and what there was to learn from it. Nurturing a subordinate's capacity to take initiatives crucially depends on his confidence that his efforts will automatically be reviewed in a totally factual fashion, take full account of all that he has done, and encourage him to learn from his work to date. He will not grow his capacity to take initiatives without being confident that these reviews will happen in this fashion. He will correctly regard their absence as the inevitable sword of Damocles, poised above his head, ready to strike at a time and in a fashion that he cannot anticipate. It would be naive to take initiatives in such a situation. If the reviews were to happen, but follow the conventional pattern of a sole focus on analysing error, it would be reasonable for him to prioritise his survival and avoid initiatives altogether.

- **Responding appropriately to mistakes of endeavour, as opposed to mistakes of omission**

  - o <u>Mistakes of endeavour are key to nurturing ambitious growth</u>

    Managers trying to take initiatives in uncharted and challenging areas automatically run the risk of making what can be regarded as mistakes of endeavour.

    This is the basis for experienced and successful business men observing that 'you can't make an omelette without breaking some eggs', or equally 'you never make anything unless you make some mistakes'. It is simply common sense for the growth of any business that whilst these mistakes do need to be reviewed in precisely the same way as any other review, they need to be seen in an appropriate perspective. If managers are to take on the untried challenge, then even with the most competent preparation, errors of endeavour will occasionally occur. These can often be easily seen with the usual 20 X 20 hindsight, but would have been difficult to anticipate under the operational conditions of the time. If we want to grow the appetite to keep on attempting the unusual and ambitious, then managers need the encouragement to keep trying to get better at anticipating these types of difficulties. We grow that encouragement by viewing the improvement planning step of the review as a sign of success, and a cause of deep satisfaction. It marks a significant move forward for both the manager concerned and the organisation. It is a legitimate cause for real celebration.

- ○ <u>Mistakes of omission are a 'yellow card' event.</u>

  Mistakes of omission are entirely a different matter, and deserve a different response. These are errors that people make whilst carrying out familiar, standard tasks, or ones which are new to them, but well within their scope to adequately plan for. They are simply omissions they have made in their thinking, which have got translated into action.

  Once again their work needs to be reviewed in precisely the same way as all work. People need the absolute confidence that the logic and common sense built into how the organisation carries out reviews, will not buckle under the emotional pressure of any mistake. Having said that, the perspective that the mistake needs to be seen in when the improvement planning step is carried out needs to be very far from one of celebration. It needs to be a cause for concern. People need to realise that the alarm bell has just rung loud and clear, and that the organisation has heard the warning. The person concerned will therefore need to grasp the urgency of raising his game.

- ○ <u>Making accurate judgements about these different types of mistakes nurtures growth and sharpens the operation.</u>

  Management lines have the opportunity to make their judgements about the balance between mistakes of endeavour and omission that occur within the work being done. To treat them all as mistakes of omission – which is the usual error – quickly kills off initiative taking in the high value, unusual, ambitious challenges, and significantly damages growth in the business.

  To treat them all as mistakes of endeavour – which is a most unusual error – would quickly lead to reckless initiative taking, and damage the business's existing reputation.

  There is a significant commercial incentive to develop increasing skill at making the above judgements on the different types of mistakes that occur.

SOME BENEFICIAL EFFECTS AND IMPLICATIONS

The above intensive coaching within the management line relationship has had some deep and far reaching effects:

- **Debate decreases. Action increases.**

Nurturing the habit of making proposals as the basis for building the habit of initiative taking has usefully altered the standard exchanges about business matters. Debate has markedly decreased, and the attention and time spent on action increased.

- **Managers see the interdependence between managing skills as a practical business tool.**

It has been revealing for managers to live through the effect of combining the encouragement of proposals, ensuring support for them, reviewing their effects, and separating mistakes of endeavour from ones of omission. They experience that it is in the interdependence between these skills that initiative taking can take root. This interdependence is therefore a practical managing tool that can be deliberately deployed by managers to aid their business. There are numerous other examples of how particular principles interact to provide the basis to grow other effective managing habits.

- **It has put the organisation on the front foot, especially when market pressures have risen.**

It has moved the organisation away from responding to the pressure of events to a position of always moulding its path forwards, ahead of those pressures. The rise in confidence to 'manage' key difficulties has been marked. This has been especially noticeable, for example, when either negative market factors put pressure on businesses or when large regulatory changes are threatened that can radically alter the bottom line.

- **It has given the organisation a commercial advantage that is very difficult to copy.**

Embedding the combination of principles – proposals, support, review, and mistakes of endeavour/omission – within the management lines has always required significant discipline and tenacity. Whilst the logic behind each of these four areas is the merest common sense, it is definitely not a simple, quick fix, 'bolt on goodie' that is in any way easy to copy. The commercial advantage it gives has put significant pressure on competitors. The fact that it cannot be easily copied has increased that pressure. It has consequently helped secure the organisation's growing position in its market place.

COMMONLY ENCOUNTERED DIFFICULTIES AND CHALLENGES

- **People may not be ready to accept the reality of resolving a problem with a number of root causes.**

On a number of occasions senior managers have simultaneously bemoaned the absence of reliable initiative taking, and declined to grapple with the above four conditions that produce it. As has been said, the effort required to embed those four factors is substantial – as are the commercial prizes that come from its achievement. This work does not offer any 'cheap, easy, big wins'. There have been no quick significant victories requiring little effort. Work at fundamental issues using fundamental solutions has demanded appropriate effort to enable the substantial prizes to be captured.

● **The trend is to verbalise eloquently. This distracts from the necessary hard mental work.**

There is a second common difficulty in growing the above principles. It is again a sad reflection of how we run our education and other systems that we condition our best talent to burnish their ability to compete verbally: to debate, intellectualise, speculate about difficulties, theorise, etc. We habituate our talent in focusing on working with the mouth on the basis that that is proof of ability. Instead, the opposite is true. Effective ability has always been based on the capacity to work quickly and accurately with the mind to produce contributions that can move matters forward – such as rigorous proposals. To achieve that, the mind has to take account of all the relevant information and cut through to an actionable solution. That necessarily involves incisive, disciplined, inventive and rapid mental work. People who have habit formed their appetite for rhetoric have found it extremely difficult to cultivate the opposite habit of focused silence so as to engage the mind in that work. It is this habit of focused silence that is the unexpected root of making proposals, and hence the root of initiative taking. It is no accident that one of the most common features of effective teams has been the level of silence within their work. I have personally observed over many years the hard work needed to achieve that quiet, extremely rapid, and steadily focused way of working. One of the most common features of ineffective teams has been the intense level of incessant talking and noise that characterises their work. You invariably hear people complain, 'you just can't get a word in edgeways'. This entire issue, its underlying principles, the benefits that come from their application, and some commonly encountered difficulties are described in the following section on Managing Ideas.

ISSUE 3 – 2.12   **MANAGING IDEAS**

SUMMARY

This issue concerns the challenge of managing people's very different ideas as they work together. Inescapably, it is the area where people most commonly interact. The commercial and emotional impact of how people's ideas are handled has been rapidly and enduringly felt.

Faced with the raw material of people's different ideas in response to a problem, the business has two requirements. It first needs people to find a way of combining their creativity within any solution. Secondly it needs that solution to be consistent with the strategies agreed for the business. The support between ideas, or a synthesis of them, together with the occasional appropriate offering of an alternative has met both requirements. Simultaneously, these habits have significantly affected the levels of trust and confidence within working teams.

The conventional habit of either competitive debate, or the use of hierarchical power, to decide which ideas are progressed, produces poor commercial results and even worse emotional effects. Competitive debate destroys creativity and fosters aggressive defensiveness. The use of hierarchical power on this issue has similarly eliminated creativity and accelerated feudal politics as the means of survival.

People's ideas are the children of their imagination, and the bond between us and our ideas is rightly felt to be a precious one. We do well to tread skilfully when managing this area. Significant effort spent on it has been handsomely rewarded both in the quality of business results and in people's levels of motivation. The support between ideas, or their synthesis, has been a challenging habit to develop, but the rewards in both business results and motivation have been beyond the reach of any competition.

BACKGROUND CONTEXT

The challenge is to find effective ways of handling the many different ideas that people are keen to contribute. People are usually strongly committed to those ideas, and want them to play a key part in the final outcome. The manner in which they are handled needs to harness the maximum amount of that commitment. Equally, the effectively run business demands high quality, consistent decisions that incisively pursue the agreed strategy for the challenges in hand. Most organisations have not been able to solve this apparent conundrum of the need for the maximum range of ideas, as well as the need for high quality, sharply focused decisions.

As one common convention, people have tried to copy political democracy and pursue 'management by consensus'. The consequence has been a partially inconsistent patchwork quilt of ideas and concepts, not bound together by business logic but by the political desire to garner as much commitment from all the interested parties as possible. This option usually fails to meet the quality standards of an optimum business decision. Neither have the levels of commitment gained from the inevitable horse trading built into the compromises involved stood the stern test of real action in the business. Democracy and quality have never been easy bedfellows.

At the other extreme, numerous ways have been tried to artificially constrain the decision making process to produce a more focused decision. A top down edict restricting the decision to certain characteristics has been a common example of this option. This type of constraint more often than not fails to gain the real commitment of affected parties and the result does not contain the depth of imagination that comes from using a wide variety of ideas.

The experience has been that there is nowhere along this continuum that simultaneously produces both quality and commitment.

The solution has proved to lie in another direction.

PRINCIPLE

Managing ideas at speed, producing high quality results, and commanding reliable commitment involves:

A. **Practising the skill of producing proposals**
within the appropriate decision making step.

B. **Finding ways of totally supporting the proposal already suggested.**

C. **Failing that ideal, identifying what is consistent between ideas**
and using that as a basis for amalgamating them into an integrated whole. This needs to meet the business aspirations chosen for the job in hand.

D. **Identifying what is not consistent**
and suggesting a way of handling it, if it supports those aspirations. Disposing of it if the facts say it does not support those aspirations.

Managing ideas by offering alternative proposals is productive only if:

E. **the judgement is consciously made that the additional potential of your idea** would benefit the group by diverting it from its current course.

EXPLANATION

The long experience of working with numerous managers in these areas again says that the following explanations have only ever given a superficial understanding of them. Their intellectual simplicity has always proved misleading.

Only real practice in situations important to the business has disclosed what they actually entail and what their effects are. In the case of these principles the commercial and human effects are fundamental and far beyond what the intellect alone can perceive from their obvious concepts.

Taking each of these areas in turn, and recounting the detail of their use:

A. Practising the skill of producing proposals
within the appropriate decision making step.

- **Unnecessary questions, doubts and alternatives stop and fragment a group's work. Proposals progress that work, and aid cohesion.**

    In their earlier stages of development, people have often found this initial requirement difficult enough. The conventional habit of immediately voicing instinctive questions, doubts, and alternatives about a situation requires very little – if any – mental work. However, the effect of doing so has been to both stop and fragment the working group.

    Colleagues have to stop and consider the many different solutions that might deal with those questions, doubts and alternatives. They instantly fragment as a team, because they are now thinking of different solutions from amongst the many that are available. The statistical chance of everyone simultaneously thinking of the same route forwards, in business situations where no unique solution exists, has not happened once in the many years of this work.

    By contrast, when people have put in the mental work to process their instinctive questions, doubts, and alternatives into a chosen proposal, the effect has been quite different. It has helped the group to progress, and kept it cohesive. It has a chance to progress, because it's just heard a suggestion as to what might be done. It remains cohesive during the time it focuses on the same proposal.

    This is not to say that it has not been useful to pose appropriate questions of clarification. These have proved effective in creating common understanding.

    The fundamental challenge is to become practised in the focused silence of the mind, to do the work of producing proposals at speed. It's simply a habit that has been honed with practice – lots of practice.

- **Supporting or synthesising different proposals within the same decision making step is challenging. It is extraordinarily difficult if they are in different steps.**

The associated requirement for effectively handling different ideas has been that they need to be appropriate examples of the decision making step being worked at. An example would be that the team is practised enough to only contribute targets, if that is the decision making step they have chosen to work at. The experience has been that when teams are skilful at this habit, then supporting or synthesising different ideas within that particular method step becomes a possibility. Bringing ideas together that belong to different decision making steps is considerably more difficult, and often impossible. So, for example, if someone suggests a target to be achieved, and the next person instantly offers an unrelated plan of action, then it becomes much more complex to support or synthesise these two ideas together. It is sometimes possible to find a consistency in these types of situations around which one can build a synthesis. However it has required a very high level of practised skill to achieve at the speeds of a normal business discussion.

B.   Finding ways of totally supporting the proposal already suggested.

Typically, this most effective and direct element of managing ideas receives little to no attention. Worse, it is generally held in low esteem. The convention is for me to automatically see my own ideas as significantly better, simply because they're mine. This blocks my mind from seeing inventive ways of supporting any proposal that has already been made.

The experience, however, has been that habitual, skilful support of others' ideas has some powerful effects.

- o **At a practical level it is the fastest way** of managing ideas.
  It eliminates debate and drives relentlessly towards action.

- o **It has a direct impact on the levels of trust and confidence** between colleagues. People's ideas are very much their creation, and personally dear to them. During the many years of this work involving numerous groups enmeshed in a wide variety of challenges, people have invariably regarded their ideas as inseparable from their identities. Their view has been that their ideas 'are' them.

As a result, the most powerful response amongst all the skills that make up the jigsaw of teamwork is: 'Yes, I agree'.

This has been particularly potent when:

- o the originator knows that the person choosing to support has ideas of his own and is committed to solving the problem in hand

- o the person supporting is more senior

- o the idea offered is in some way novel or unusual

Absolutely no other response has proven as effective at generating trust and confidence in working relationships. When it has consistently been backed up with action by the person supporting, then that trust and confidence is well on its way to becoming a significant long term factor. The experience has been that this is a valuable commercial asset, quite apart from its natural personal benefits.

- o **It is a deep development for the person supporting and it helps safeguard his future.**

This is an entirely neglected benefit of 'support', but has far reaching implications. My experience has been that it has an effect that reverberates for a very long time after the support and its immediate work results have long passed.

For me to give another's idea real support, especially when I have an idea of my own – and I generally do – I am forced to mentally go through these questions:

- ▪ What are the comparative strengths and weaknesses of his idea and mine?

- ▪ Given there are countless alternatives to any idea in the business setting, will the balance of strengths and difficulties in his idea be at least as effective for the business as mine?

- ▪ Can I think of a way of supporting his idea so that the group gets the most out of it, and the end result is at least as good as, or better than mine?

My 'yes' to another's idea will probably involve me in its implementation. The above thinking has been needed to safeguard the success of what I may end up doing. It is enlightened self interest, as well as business sense.

The deeper effect has been that it forces me to work rapidly and rigorously in silence, considering wider aspects of what I have heard before saying 'yes'. That mental practice has helped me survive later and different challenges requiring similar thinking effort. I make no apologies for repeating that these managing habits do not remain at a static level of skill – they decay with non application or improve with practice. My survival as a solver of problems depends on such practice, and 'support' can demand I practise my very best creative thinking at speeds at which the business is transacted.

It is a fundamental and basic part of my own continuous development. So it is for others.

I notice with sadness that the convention is for managers to have a complacent disregard for the skill and effects of 'support'. They make the cardinal mistake of dismissing it as something that people do who have nothing else to offer – it's for the 'losers', the 'guys who can't cut it when the going gets tough'. The inescapable result is that their practice at the rapid and careful mental work described above decays and eventually atrophies. They render themselves vulnerable to failure when faced with future challenges requiring just such mental speed, accuracy and agility – an inevitable result of being unaware of, or disregarding, one's own developmental needs.

C. Identifying what is consistent between them
and using that as a basis for amalgamating them into an integrated whole.
This needs to meet the business aspirations chosen for the job.

Should I decide not to support the entirety of another's idea, then I am left with the challenge of what to do with his idea and my own.

Every one (including myself) becomes habit formed over many years to first rapidly spot the part of another's idea that they think is incorrect/unwise, etc. It's the whole basis of competitive debate, by which we are led to believe we establish our identity, and, even more perversely, establish others' abilities. So ingrained has this habit become, that along with countless others, I am easily capable of working out several reasons why a part of another's idea is ineffective, well before the speaker has finished. Like many others, I have even worked out the most logical and irrefutable way of feeding that back. The speaker has hardly had chance to draw breath when I mount my attack. One response has been that the other person thinks I'm correct, backs off, and is understandably reluctant to surface with any more ideas for some time. I have succeeded in eliminating one of my team's resources. The other more common response is to start a defensive debate. These never end. Now I have succeeded in derailing the whole job.

The reverse habit can equally be practised and groomed to the same standards, if that is what I choose to do. Instead, I can hunt for the section of the idea I'm hearing that is consistent with either my own idea, or the fundamental directions we have agreed to pursue, or the background knowledge that we have shared about those directions. I can then find a way of integrating my idea with as much of the other that I can to produce a synthesis in the form of a proposal that can move us forward.

The choice is always entirely mine as to which path I choose to follow within my mind in response to another's idea. Competitive debate or synthesis is always my choice to make.

D. Identifying what is not consistent and suggesting a way of handling it,
if it supports the agreed aspirations being pursued.
Disposing of it if the facts say that it does not support those aspirations.

If I've got the further horsepower, I can look at any part of the idea I think is unworkable and devise a further suggestion to help with its difficulties. In the worst case, should it not be consistent with the aspirations we're pursuing or the information we have to date, then I may have to check that the speaker agrees that is the case. That checking can of course reveal a flaw in my own reasoning, or a misunderstanding I have of what he has said. If indeed parts of his idea turn out to be entirely inconsistent with the aspirations we've agreed or the information we have shared, then the suggestion to drop them is one of fact and logic, not one based on personal preference.

Managing ideas by offering alternative proposals is productive only if:

> **E. the judgement is consciously made that the additional potential of your alternative** would benefit the group by diverting it from its current course.

It is common for alternative ideas to rapidly come to mind:

> 'On the other hand we could ...'
>
> 'Instead, why don't we ...?'
>
> 'Or we can ...'

and it is equally common to hear them instinctively and immediately offered.

Instead, if I am practised enough, I can first think through the possible implications of my alternative and take a judgement as to its extra potential to the business in hand. I can then decide that it is worth halting the work and ask that the team spend the extra time and energy to consider my alternative and its potential. Should I prove to be correct, I will have aided my team and our business. Should my decision prove to be an error, I will have hindered my team and done the business no favours. I will have to learn from the instance and try and improve the way I make similar judgements in the future.

The steps recalled in **A), B),** and **C)** are of course some of the mental steps of listening, supporting another's idea or developing it in some way with one's own. They clearly represent mental work that can only be done in silence. It is not the silence of inactivity. Indeed, on many occasions, rapid and difficult mental work needs to be done to find an appropriate contribution that advances the dialogue. Seen in this perspective, it is inevitable that the best teams are amongst the quietest. They've discovered that they have to be, as they strive to quickly accomplish that mental work so that they can move their business along. The most ineffective teams are invariably the noisiest, as they persistently ignore the need to do that work and obsessively verbalise their own individual ideas.

SOME BENEFICIAL EFFECTS AND IMPLICATIONS

- **The speed and quality of decision making significantly improve**

    Everyone who's experienced this way of working observes that:

    o <u>Despite the effort required – maybe, more accurately, because of it – the speed of decision making is far higher.</u>

    Times taken for decisions have been halved, and have sometimes taken considerably less time dependent on the skill levels that people have at the above practices. The very nature of the interchanges within working groups changes from being discursive to being entirely decision and action focused. No unnecessary side tracks are raised, or taken. Much more silence automatically occurs, as colleagues strive to do the required mental thinking that is the core basis of this way of managing ideas.

- The quality of decisions, represents the accumulated worth of all ideas in the group.

  It is the exact opposite of the 'survival of the fittest' principle underpinning a competitive debate, which by definition strives to end with just one idea (yours, you hope). Consequently, the synthesis of ideas represents the combined creativity within the group. The results have inevitably been of far higher business quality than the 'survival of the fittest' debate can ever produce.

- Synthesising ideas in this fashion very often geometrically increases quality.

  It is the detailed procedure of how to produce the oft quoted '1 plus 1 equals 3' effect.

- **The support and synthesis of ideas are every day managing practices
that directly affect levels of trust and confidence within working teams**

  - 'My idea is the child of my imagination.'

    It is certainly true for me, and for every single person I've worked with over the years, and who I've observed working. If my idea is challenged, my instinct is to defend it with every ounce of my intellectual and verbal ability. My attachment to it is closely analogous to what I feel for my children. I notice I am far from being alone in these tendencies. As a result, if I can consistently rely on my colleagues to search for what is sound and usable in my ideas, then the analogous situation is that created between two sets of parents, who can rely on each other to care for their children when that need arises. The essence of that relationship is trust and confidence.

    These two qualities have not proved easy to reliably and consistently develop within the work scene. The deliberate habit of supporting or synthesising another's idea with one's own is a practice that directly affects the level of trust and confidence between people. Affecting these two characteristics by practising skills focussed primarily on competence is a quite different way of fostering sound relationships. They are attributes that are as inaccessible as they are valuable. I have heard senior managers refer to them as 'managerial gold dust'. They are correct. The common observation is that those groups with high levels of trust and confidence in them are successful. Conversely, it is those groups with low levels of trust and confidence in them that are ineffective.

- **Cooperation is Effectiveness**

In essence, the support or synthesis of ideas is the co-operation of ideas. I will find some way of pursuing your idea or harnessing it with my own, to implement our jointly held aspirations for the job.

The experience has been that it is the regular habit of supporting or synthesising ideas, mixed with conscious judgements on offering alternatives, that offers an optimum way of managing ideas. The key difficulty is overcoming our long and intensive conditioning that competitive debate with its central mantra of 'the survival of the fittest' is the effective way of handling ideas.

The firm conventional belief is that:

Competition (between ideas) = Effectiveness.

Working exposure to this different way of managing ideas confirms instead that to satisfy the business criteria of speed, quality and commitment, the truth of the matter is:

Cooperation (between ideas) = Effectiveness

- **It strikingly demonstrates a core characteristic of this development work and the challenge it poses**.

Of course, the skills to support or synthesise different ideas – as described in A), B), C), and D) – have required determined mental work and considerable practice. The good news is that it turns out to be no more inherently onerous than the ingrained habit of negatively focused, competitive debate – it's just that initially we're totally unused to doing it.

Early attempts at trying it have always been tortuously slow, and necessarily filled with strained effort. Our mental muscles are just not used to this new activity. The analogous development of new and sophisticated physical skills in a complex sport follows precisely the same pattern. Consequently the experience has been that if the practice is persevered with, then it has been possible to retrain the mind to acquire the new skill of rapidly synthesising different ideas. The reader will discover that the development of every skill recalled throughout this work follows this pattern. It takes little ability to understand the concepts being explained. They are simple common sense. There are two key challenges.

The first is to recognise the ineffectiveness of conventional management practice in most of the areas covered by this work and have the courage and determination to turn aside from them.

The second is the considerable practice involved in developing real speed and accuracy at applying these different principles to the business problems at hand. Only then, as performance levels improve well beyond conventional levels, will a deeper, operational understanding form of these skills and their implications.

COMMONLY ENCOUNTERED DIFFICULTIES AND CHALLENGES

- **We come habit formed to compete with our ideas**

As recalled above, the conventional habit of instantly selecting the weak points of another's idea, and both attacking them whilst simultaneously highlighting the merits of one's own, has been very deeply ingrained by most of us (including myself).

'**YES**,... (by which I mean all the things in your idea that I may agree with, but which I am now dismissing with this single word),

BUT ...' (by which I mean all the incorrect/illogical/irrelevant facets of your idea that I am now going to explain to you in a tightly reasoned, exhaustively complete, and factually undeniable fashion).

Of course, ' **Yes, but** ...', is the socially acceptable way of saying, '**No**'.

This is the competition of ideas. I will use my intellect and compete with the child of your imagination to prove that mine is better. I will prove that your intellect does not belong in the same league as mine. The result has either been the ignition of endless defensive debates, or the 'defeat of another's idea' and hence the elimination of people's creativity. Competition between people has not resulted in better business results. 'The survival of the fittest' competitive debate has proved to be the very best way of eliminating talent, and absolutely narrowing the quality base on which decisions can be made. It has also guaranteed sustained and or repressed antagonistic defensiveness with a dramatic deterioration in levels of trust and confidence.

- **There will always be an alternative. Mine is not unique.**
  It will not automatically move things ahead simply because it's mine.

A common difficulty is the belief that it is helpful to respond to others' ideas or the ones the team is already progressing, by knee jerking the offering of alternative ideas.

The rationale can be that 'the child of my imagination simply has to be uniquely better than yours, which the group has already invested valuable time in listening to'. The harsh reality in the commercial world is that there are a multitude of perfectly valid alternatives to any idea. My idea is not guaranteed to be uniquely better simply because it's mine. There are many, many more from where that one came from. The other fantasy is that by stopping the group to make it invest yet more time to listen to my alternative idea, I have automatically moved it forward – simply because it's heard my idea. The truth is that the team has just spent extra time listening to my idea, and consequently stayed at precisely the same place.

There can be significant resistance to facing up to the challenge of becoming skilful at making the conscious judgements about offering alternatives explained above in item **E,** p.180.

ISSUE 3 – 2.13   **MANAGEMENT OF TIME**

SUMMARY

All the managing processes affect the capacity to manage time.

At the organisation level, the competence with which the principles in the structural, procedural, and man management areas are pursued critically affects everyone's capacity to manage time. An example is the omission of not involving all levels in the organisation in forming its strategy. Managing time has then been a common casualty of pursuing unclear or inconsistent priorities across those levels. Similar shortcomings in the procedural and man management areas have significantly affected people's capacity to organise time.

At a personal level, the need has been to identify the particular processes that an individual is using in his work that especially impact his handling of time. An example has turned out to be his competence at ensuring all his decisions are led by the aspirations he is pursuing and the business information associated with them. Poor skill at this discipline has produced confused, slow or inappropriate work, with a consequent poor management of time. Having identified these problem processes he can be supported to improve them, and simultaneously coached to implement the elements of time management.

Those elements are time planning, time monitoring, and time effective practices. The first two are conventionally well understood. The third is the most influential in its effects and has received no attention. For example, the practice of being able to sustain focus on a given decision making step within individual and team work is one of the two most influential practices that affect the use of time. The yet more influential practice is the skill of synthesising different ideas throughout the course of any piece of work. Improving performance at such time effective practices has had dramatic effects on an individual's capacity to organise his time.

BACKGROUND CONTEXT

Difficulties with time management very often surface as the first symptom/complaint that people feel pressure about within an organisation. In the minimum case they see it as a key issue to resolve. In the most extreme situation, they can feel very concerned about their ability to complete or organise their duties, and vulnerable in their job security. Common comments are: 'too many meetings overcrowd the day', 'too many discussions overrun all time constraints', 'too many competing priorities clamour to be met', 'too many unexpected shifts in direction in the organisation need to be adjusted to', 'too many 'fire fighting' demands must be dealt with', 'too many sudden unforeseen demands from other levels in the organisation 'must' be dealt with urgently and ahead of any planned priorities', etc.

Disentangling these difficulties has revealed:

- **All the key decisions the organisation makes in the structural, procedural, and man management factors impact sharply on how time is managed across the outfit.**

  Examples of such decisions in each of these factors are:

  Structurally:

  The very first structural choice described in this chapter – the move away from the conventional functional departments, towards business units – has a dramatic effect on managing time. The organisation has effectively streamlined the levels of management involved in operational decision making, and focused it down to the single one of the Business Unit Head. This elimination of previous decision making hurdles has fundamentally changed how time is managed.

  Procedurally:

  The principle of ensuring that those who action procedures have worked through the guiding aspirations they are pursuing has significantly improved how time has been used when operational difficulties have arisen. They have been able to quickly resolve them at the point they have occurred. Those who haven't done this work, have had to recycle through loops of communication and levels of management to attempt to cope with such difficulties. Managing time has consequently been fraught with much frustration and delay.

  Man Management:

  The man management habit of probing for assumptions amongst the information background describing a challenge has significantly benefitted the management of time. The unknowing inclusion of any assumption within the information base of an operational plan has caused real difficulty. Significant time and effort has then been spent in discovering such an error, and further time has had to be spent in going back to research the factual basis for that assumption. Serious problems have consequently arisen in managing time for the work.

- **All the management processes a person uses significantly affect how he manages time**

  As an example, the skill with which he uses the naturally occurring decision making steps has had a key effect. In the worst cases the person can be only dimly aware of them and have developed little skill at knowing at which step his own thinking fits. His work progress has been unnecessarily slow and his capacity to manage time significantly affected.

The management and consumption of time turns out to be much like a crossroads, at which all the managing processes used by the organisation as a whole, and those used by the individual, inevitably meet and have their effect.

The unavoidable implication of this reality is that making useful and sustainable improvements to a person's management of time needs two factors to be carefully analysed.

     o   Firstly, how does the organisation manage its structural, procedural, and man management factors, and what impact does that have on everyone's capacity to manage time?

     o   Secondly, what processes does that person use in his work, that particularly affect his management of time?

No fixed formulaic procedure for 'time management' – no matter how fervently marketed – will achieve this. Indeed, where these have been used the focus has unhelpfully shifted to the mechanics of the procedure. That has distracted attention from, and obscured the real underlying causes for the person's poor management of time.

PRINCIPLES

- **The principles detailed for the structural, procedural, and man management areas create a working situation that enables individuals to effectively manage their time.**

- **The particular interaction between the key managing processes being used in the person's work and his management of time needs to be precisely understood.**
  Changes to those processes can then be made to both improve business results and his management of time.

- **Simultaneously, the person concerned needs to embed the three elements of managing time within his work.**
  Those elements are time planning, time monitoring, and time effective practices.

EXPLANATION

All three of these principles need to be applied to enable a person to reliably manage his time. Taking each in turn, and recounting some of the operational detail that explains them more fully:

- **The principles detailed for the structural, procedural, and man management areas create ...**

  Examples have already been given in the above 'Background' of how elements within each of the three key organisation factors inescapably affect the capacity to manage time.

- **The particular interaction between the key managing processes being used in the person's work and his management of time needs to be ...**

  A detailed example may help at this stage.

**EXAMPLE   UNDERSTANDING ONE CHEMICAL ENGINEER'S WAY OF TAKING DECISIONS
CHANGED HIS MANAGEMENT OF TIME**

Michael (not his real name) was an extremely energetic, enthusiastic chemical engineer who found great difficulty in managing his time to solve his quota of problems in a particular oil refining business. He was diligent in his efforts to plan his time, and produced schedules that appeared to specify all that he had to do. However, whatever time deadlines he agreed to meet generally weren't met, and those he managed to meet caused him to work very long hours. The quality of the eventual work usually meant he had to repeat a lot of it, and the eventual results did not match the amount of effort he put in.

Getting him to analyse the key process he spent his time on – problem solving/decision making – revealed a basic difficulty: his enthusiasm and drive to find answers repeatedly tempted him to unthinkingly follow a fixed pattern of problem solving steps. He would intuitively choose what he felt was the cause for a problem from what he already knew of its background, then instantly implement plans based on that intuition. These plans had a low rate of success, and he would then return to what he knew about the problem and intuitively choose another suspected cause as the basis for his next plan of action. He put in considerable effort at this work without being aware at any time of which problem solving step he was using. He would repeat this unconscious cycle of – selected cause/ plan of action/ action/ failure – next selected cause/ plan of action/.. , etc, until he struck on a solution that would vary from being barely reasonable to unacceptable. His reputation amongst operational managers trying to rely on his work was poor.

He had the intelligence, desire and open mindedness to take account of the analysis of how he worked. He spent three weeks diligently working at becoming increasingly aware of the problem solving /decision making steps that he was using within his daily work. Simultaneously, he practised hard at the three elements of managing time. The results were spectacular. He was credited by his peers and senior management with successfully tackling a serious problem capable of shutting down the entire refining operation. His solution was so creative and effective that it stands to this day as unique in its field. The solution became known as 'the wooden wall' – because that was precisely what it was. As far as I am aware no such solution has ever been devised. It solved the problem precisely. It was conceived, tested and installed exactly on time, to the shortest time schedule witnessed for the particular piece of refining equipment involved. His track record of problem solving, and hence his management of time was sustained at his now high level, and his career deservedly took off.

- **Simultaneously, the person concerned needs to embed the three elements of managing time within his work.**
Those elements are time planning, time monitoring, and time effective practices.

Time planning and time monitoring have been well worked through

The first two elements of time planning and time monitoring are immediately obvious, and are competently handled using well tried and tested methods. I don't intend spending much time describing them.

Critical path planning, bar chart scheduling, etc., are examples of well known, effective means of planning time. They have provided proven ways of scheduling work in various time frames within complex jobs. Simultaneously, they provide the framework for monitoring progress and the passage of time. Re-planning the remaining time in the light of any unforeseen event has also been routinely done within these methods.

Time monitoring has long been a well worked through discipline and no further time is spent exploring it here.

<u>Time effective practices are a critical element, and have escaped attention</u>

The third element of time effective practices has proved to be far and away the largest and most influential factor in affecting the control and use of time. Used skilfully, these practices enable rapid and systematic progress. Conversely, if not used, or used unskilfully, progress has been significantly slowed and confused. The consumption of time then becomes a major concern, and has placed those involved under great pressure. Over the many years of working at this particular element of managing time, it has consistently escaped any recognition and attention. Yet its effect is so significant that a skilful performance in it removes pressure on the planning and monitoring of time to the point where they cease to be a major concern. Of all the managing practices, the synthesis of ideas and the habit of being able to stay within a chosen decision making step have the largest impact on the speed of progress. I am of course not suggesting that the sound disciplines that need to be in place for time planning, and monitoring should in any way be sidelined. They need to be vigorously implemented as well.

SOME BENEFICIAL EFFECTS AND IMPLICATIONS

● **The managing of time and its interdependence on all the natural decision making steps.**

The above example of Michael's improvement of his management of time clearly illustrates its connection with his individual skill pattern in using particular decision making steps. The same principle applies to all the decision making steps and their interaction with managing time. An example involving one of those steps is detailed below.

<u>One connection between handling the fundamental aspiration selected for a job, and time management</u>

One common difficulty with time management has stemmed from differing assumptions made by those working to deliver the aspirations step of a particular decision. This has led to blurred or inconsistent views of priorities and a consequent problem with meeting deadlines. The correction has been to ensure the discussions on aspirations and priorities are explicit and commonly shared.

- **It has focussed a need to rebalance the attention to detail versus clarifying fundamental business aspirations.**

However, on occasions the root of the difficulty with 'time' has been deeper. Managers have often habit formed the handling of large amounts of detail as their means of controlling what is happening. They have understandably grooved the instinct to focus on copious detail rather than the more intangible issues of clarifying business aspirations and priorities. This has on occasions led to the above difficulty on priorities and missed deadlines. In such instances the manager concerned first needed to clearly grasp the implications of his proven and useful skill at handling detail. He has then needed to start the personal development work of rebalancing his focus towards a greater emphasis on the broader aspects of the business. It has always needed substantial effort to achieve this change.

COMMONLY ENCOUNTERED DIFFICULTIES AND CHALLENGES

There have been two main difficulties in encouraging managers to tackle time management in the above fashion. They are:

- **A belief in the technology inspired view of learning in modules.**

  o <u>Modular learning/training is appropriate for technologies.</u>

  I am a technologist, and am well aware from my own discipline of chemical engineering of the usefulness of using modular training as a method of imparting knowledge and information. It depends on a significant level of independence and separateness between modules. It is useful in that instance to segregate different sets of information about various topics so that they can then be more readily focused, studied and absorbed. It's interesting to note, however, that recent advances in most technologies have trended towards discovering increasing overlaps between previously self-contained 'modules' of such information. The assimilation of information and the gaining of knowledge on essentially independent focuses have proved appropriate areas for modular learning/ training.

  o <u>It is inappropriate for skill development.</u>

  In contrast, the development of any management skill amongst a set of such skills where each interacts and is interdependent on the others is a challenge of an entirely different nature.

  Firstly, the very nature of skill development is opposite in nature to acquiring information and knowledge. The close analogy of developing skill in a complex sport illustrates that it depends primarily on the capacity for continuous practice and observation, based on retaining an open and enquiring mind as to what is happening during that practice. The process of acquiring knowledge and information is solely a one-off intellectual pursuit with its own disciplines of understanding, collating, probing for meaning, cross-checking relevance, etc. It does not depend for its advance on continuous repetition and practice within the same area of information.

Secondly, where the subject matter is intertwined and interactive – as in the case of the issues underpinning management – its analysis needs to prioritise, probe for, and accurately take account of those interactions. The same is clearly true in the analogous case of developing performance at a complex sport, where similarly close interactions are built into the component skills within that sport.

Separated, essentially self-contained modular training is appropriate for the information transfer needed in, for instance, technological training. Its use for skill development in the management area does not reflect the realities of that quite different challenge. Time management has attracted more than its fair share of merchandising based on the simplistic marketed idea that it is a 'module'. It is not. Similarly, every other management issue is not a module. Reality continuously confronts ordinary line managers with problems whose component management issues intimately interact to produce the core characteristics of the particular problem. Successful sustainable solutions are obliged to accurately reflect those interactions. Modular training by its very nature does not set out to recognise, prioritise, examine or explain those interactions.

○ <u>The persistent pursuit of modular management training is an error of omission.</u>

The cynic in me – and most of us line managers have a healthy dose of cynicism to inoculate us against dispensers of bull manure – is tempted to suspect that the financial returns from marketing a seemingly endless list of modules have been too much to resist. If on the other hand, this is an error of endeavour the cynic in me apologises, and I applaud the efforts made. I fear, however, that this is an obvious and simplistic error of omission that continues to obscure the depth and scope of the challenges facing line managers and their businesses.

● **Appearing endlessly active and under pressure has its attractions.**

When I have supported a person to look more closely at his apparent poor performance on managing his time, deeper issues have sometimes emerged as root causes. A typical example has been the person's view of his value to the organisation. Commonly, such a view prioritises continuous activity under apparent pressure, as a key basis for his importance and usefulness to the business. It has often been the case that the person concerned has other, useful, proven strengths. Intense drive, tenacity, capacity to handle large amounts of detail, and strong commitment to the business and organisation are all typical qualities that have emerged. Such skills are valuable, and it is worth while making strenuous efforts to help him forwards on his development path to retain those skills, yet master the challenge of managing time. In these cases, the manager concerned has to be supported to first absorb in his own way, the effects of his activity focused work on those around him and the business. His supervising line manager has to help him to reach his own conclusions about its strengths and weaknesses, versus the potential performance he could offer the organisation. He then needs support and encouragement to improve the impact of his work rather than simply depend on its quantity. Simultaneously he has had to commence work in the three areas of time management listed above. Inevitably, each manager's route forwards through those areas has been uniquely different, as it necessarily reflected his particular pattern of strengths and difficulties. The prime obligation of his line manager has been to support and guide his particular development path using his strengths to cope with his difficulties.

Issue 3 – 2.14   **TEAMWORK**

SUMMARY

This is the management band wagon of the moment. Of all the 'management skills', this is the one that convention most quotes, and is most in vogue. Its band wagon status has inevitably encouraged fervour, but not detailed factual scrutiny. Ironically, the truth is that it is not a skill in itself. Instead, it is just one end effect – albeit a critically important end effect – of practising the seven fundamental skills detailed in the previous sections (Responding to Success and Failure; Creating, understanding and using Strategy; Decision Making; Taking Initiatives; Managing Ideas; Managing Time), and in the following section (i.e. Leadership).

The commercial effect of developing these seven core skills within the management lines of an organisation has been to equip it with a standard of teamwork unmatched by its competition. It has allowed the organisation to tackle its challenges as a cohesive unit, have consistent views about the key issues facing it at any time, and rapidly take complex decisions that commanded firm commitment across the enterprise.

Such teamwork has grown secure levels of trust and confidence within working relationships. These have stood people in good stead in times of difficulty.

BACKGROUND CONTEXT

Organisations have urgently sought to understand the operational practices that produce effective 'teamwork'. They realise that identifying those practices and having a clear idea of how to grow people's skill at using them have significant commercial incentives. They also know that whilst 'teamwork' remains an unspecified blanket generalisation, it can mean an infinite number of different things to different people. It is then not possible to systematically develop it to benefit the business.

At one extreme, people are seen as irrevocably belonging to various 'behavioural types' as defined by psychological theory. Teamwork is then seen as the gathering of the right sorts of people, fitting the desired models/types, to tackle the job in hand.

At the other extreme is a view that teamwork contains a collection of learnable skills that anyone can work to develop to varying degrees. The decisions they continuously make on their developmental path then control their growth – or otherwise – of these skills. Each person's progress in this issue has therefore been totally unique.

The organisation's choice between these two alternative views has determined how it has developed teamwork. It has defined its chances of reliably gaining the commercial advantages that go with it. There are significant vested interests and consequent merchandising associated with the view marketing the psychological models option.

PRINCIPLES

1. Teamwork has proved to be an interactive, interdependent set of learnable skills

2. Those learnable skills were described in the previous sections within 'Man Management', together with those detailed in the following section on Leadership.

3. The choices people have made on their development path to date, and their willingness to develop the mental habits of the above skills, have defined their capacity for teamwork.

4. The organisation's level of ability in this area has depended on two things:

   - firstly, the extent to which the management lines deploy those skills within their tackling of the everyday business problems.

   - secondly, the quality of the example set by the CEO, with the senior team in operating those skills.

EXPLANATION

Exploring the detail of the above four principles in turn:

1. **Teamwork has proved to be an interactive, interdependent set of learnable skills.**

2. **Those learnable skills were described in the previous sections within 'Man Management' (relisted immediately below), together with those detailed in the following section on Leadership.**

   The seven core skills that produce a variety of effects one of which is teamwork are:

   o   Responding to Success and Failure

   o   Understanding, Creating, and using Strategy

   o   Decision Making

   o   Taking Initiatives

   o   Managing Ideas

   o   Managing Time

   o   Leadership (covered in the following section)

Work within the management lines to grow people's skill at these areas has equipped the organisation with effective teamwork across whatever groupings it has chosen to use. It has been plainly evident that given each person's unique starting point, their performance level at these areas has been controlled by the amount of practice they have been prepared to diligently apply.

Detailed examples have already been worked through that illustrate the interdependence between the above seven core skill areas. The section on initiatives (Issue 3 – 2.11, p.167) described how that habit is rooted in the interdependence of making proposals, support (both part of 'Managing Ideas'), responding to success and failure, and distinguishing mistakes of endeavour from those of omission.

Similarly each of the above skill areas and their interdependence cause the numerous symptoms we grapple with in work problems – some of which display themselves as 'teamwork issues'. The line manager's continuous challenge is to accurately observe those symptoms confronting him and understand the particular skill areas from the above basic seven that he needs to attend to. That analysis has both helped his own development and his leadership of his subordinates' progress.

3. **The choices people have made on their development path to date,
    and their willingness to develop the mental habits of the above skills,
    have defined their capacity for teamwork.**

    Unavoidably, the unique nature of the development path a person has so far chosen to follow has controlled the ease with which they have tackled this work.

    At one extreme, if they have chosen a path that has led to a closed and highly dogmatic frame of mind, then only a road to Damascus experience has allowed them to see the opportunities open to them. These 'bolts of lightning' have occasionally occurred, and whilst this work does not set out to contrive them, people have been encouraged to review that experience carefully. Significant personal benefits have always followed.

    At the other extreme, if the chosen path has led the mind to be open and interested, then the potential for developing improvements in the above skill areas has been significant. One of the genuine pleasures of this work has been to witness the startling developments in skill that managers have achieved who originally were firmly categorised as limited performers in this area, or people having no potential at all.

4. **The organisation's level of skill in this area has depended on two things:**

    ● **firstly, the extent to which the management lines deploy those skills
      within their tackling of the everyday business problems.**

    ● **secondly, the quality of the example set by the CEO with the senior team
      in operating those skills.**

This issue is a cornerstone of the organisation's performance and culture. Having said that, it has proved important to avoid being carried away with the messianic fervour that leads lots of people to hype up and dramatise the cultural aspect. This has over excited them to drown the organisation in endless fine sounding rhetoric – instantly recognised by ordinary managers as bull manure.

Instead, the emphasis needs to be on delivering these skills as the daily practiced, hard-nosed, common sense ways of doing business that are so ingrained as to hardly need mentioning. To indulge in rhetoric on the subject needs to raise suspicions that the person concerned doesn't practise these skills intensively enough in the heat of the daily commercial battle. Those who do, do not prioritise talking about it that much. They have no liking for the bull manure – they just want to do it and get results.

The CEO's personal example and leadership of the senior team in using these skills have controlled the whole organisation's performance and attitude to this area. In some instances CEOs and senior teams have talked eloquently about their commitment to these skills, but have done little to grapple with the continuous hard work of rigorously applying them. This has not fooled their more junior colleagues for one moment. They have been careful to echo the fine sounding rhetoric, and equally careful not to explore the skill areas either. The organisation's performance at this issue has been predictably strong on bull manure and weak on delivery.

In contrast when the CEO and senior team have not concerned themselves with their eloquence on this matter, but have concentrated on delivering it into the business, the beneficial effects have been clear to see.

SOME BENEFICIAL EFFECTS AND IMPLICATIONS

● **A practical way of ensuring cohesion across the work of all teams, and the organisation as a whole**.

The set of managing practices in the seven core issues has:

- o **consistently produced effective teamwork**, as evidenced by the commercial results of the teams, and their joint commitment to the work when it has come under pressure.

- o **developed managers' ability to operate in teams in a consistent fashion**. It enabled detailed fact based assessments of managers' abilities in these skills to be formed in a systematic fashion. Plans to improve performance could then be agreed in an objective fashion.

- o **enabled a factual analysis of the strengths within a team's operation** to be agreed, and an equally clear picture to be formed of necessary improvements.

- o **enabled the forming of commonly agreed detailed plans to bring about those developments**.

The operational effects of the CEO and the senior team using those skills within the everyday running of the business cannot be overstated:

- ○ **Initiative taking has significantly improved.**

  A key effect has been that pivotal decisions have been taken with the whole senior team acting as a cohesive and committed unit. The rest of the organisation has been similarly affected. Initiative taking at all levels rises as people become confident that their efforts will be backed by a senior team un distracted by politics.

- ○ **The whole organisation becomes clear about its direction.**

  The direction the CEO and senior team have taken on particular issues has become transparently clear to other levels. This has affected the quality and extent of initiative taking.

- ○ **Desired standards of performance become commonly understood.**

  It has made it clear that these skills are the template the whole organisation will use to do business with. It has simultaneously set visible and understandable standards for applying that template across the full width of the organisation's concerns.

The commercial impact of these effects has proved truly significant. Competitors have been outperformed in the most testing of markets, i.e. in ones that were falling, or in ones where pressures have occurred that were regarded as unmanageable (e.g. regulatory changes).

- ● **The impact on relationships has been deeply felt.**

Implementing practices that are primarily focused on business competence, and which have the effect of producing teamwork, has had an enduring impact on the quality of relationships involved. It is not an accident that people who can come to rely on their colleagues to consistently and skilfully come to their aid in each of the areas listed above (Responding to Success and Failure, etc.), come to occupy a special place of trust and confidence. It's a place whose reliability has been proven again and again, as the appropriate skills are diligently practised, to achieve effective business results, e.g.

- ○ the skill of reviewing the comprehensive range of effective things a colleague has done ahead of any attention to errors that might have occurred

- ○ the skill to cut through to a proposal to help cope with a difficulty that besets a colleague's work

- ○ the skill to synthesise his quite different idea with that of another colleague, so that the team can go forward with the worth of both within its solutions

- ○ the skill to find aspirations for the key issues that jointly concern colleagues

These skills, and many, many more within the listed areas, are first and foremost concerned with delivering business results. However, they simultaneously speak clearly and unmistakably of a person's reliable and skilful support for his colleagues. The effect on the quality of relationships has been inevitable. The sense of security, trust and confidence within teams practising these skills has been palpable and enduring.

● **A consistency in tackling challenges and difficulties. A secure way of synergising talents**.

A common challenge in organisations is to find a means of harnessing the varied talents of people involved in tackling difficult work. Managers are aware that this diversity of skills is an immense source of potential strength. They are as aware that without an effective answer to the issue of teamwork, then that diversity becomes an equally powerful stumbling block.

The above pattern of seven skill areas has provided a complete set of interlocking, interdependent habits that delivers teamwork across the organisation. Its effects are:

○ **It allows effective team members to be drawn from anywhere in the organisation** to tackle particular challenges .
No restrictions exist on 'personality type', or indeed any other sort of categorising. The focus has been entirely on what knowledge and expertise individuals bring to the work in hand. The resulting teamwork has allowed the chosen groups to produce appropriate solutions at speed.

○ **Those solutions have carried the firm commitment** of all levels in the organisation.
The essence of the above set of skills is delivering the full set of ambitions that the team itself created for its work. It will have taken account of the needs and views of other relevant parts of the organisation in setting out those ambitions. That has produced firm commitment across the enterprise for the ensuing results.

○ **A confidence has grown that the processes on which teamwork is built are reliable and powerful enough to produce effective solutions that were not originally envisaged.**
People learned that it was perfectly possible to commence work without any idea of a solution. Scrupulous and skilful application of the processes could be trusted to unearth an effective solution, if one was to be found. This is of course one of the foundation stones of the principle of leadership via guiding the processes involved in work (described later in the Leadership Section).

○ **It has grown a conviction that the unique pattern of strengths that each person has developed is of practical value to the business.**
Teams that skilfully use the natural decision making steps are able to encourage each person's contribution to be made in whatever steps it appropriately fits. This has enabled the unique pattern of strengths that each person has developed to be reliably deployed within the work. The impact on personal confidence has been profound. It is an acceptance of individuals at a deep level. It is an acceptance within the tackling of the risky and unknown, where both success and failure are equal possibilities. It incontrovertibly says, 'when the chips are down, we value and will rely on the pattern of skills you have '. Not unsurprisingly, relationships that pass through these particular valleys emerge as ones that people have learned to trust and have real confidence in.

COMMONLY ENCOUNTERED DIFFICULTIES AND CHALLENGES

- **Teamwork and its associated terms suffer from being very much in vogue: lots of rhetoric, and little useable understanding.**

It was the norm within the organisations who undertook this work for people to start with lots of the rhetoric about 'team work'. Certainly its current vogue status encouraged some to talk about it with messianic fervour. However their actual experience and thinking had given them no picture of the practical detailed meaning of their rhetoric. They had no view of exactly how one would go about "walking the walk" in the actual heat of the business. When supported into exploring what it was like to actually 'live' those terms, it was rewarding to see those who decided to take it on board within their development paths. There were those who exercised their prerogative not to engage in the hard work of developing skill at living the rhetoric. I noticed however, that they invariably kept their appetite for "talking the talk" about teamwork. The strange irony has also been that they very often sang the praises of doing the work – but never did it.

Currently there is a strong fashion to take terms associated with teamwork and use them as a means of judging people's suitability for particular roles . Hence claims that someone is a 'team player' – or not – are used as a universal yardstick of acceptability. The current conventional view of teamwork neither covers the width of issues defined by the above seven core skills, nor grasps the depth of detail of the practices that underpin them. Inevitably such terms as 'team player' then carry an entirely incomplete and inadequate description that does not portray its real significance in the actual work scene. Without an accurate, detailed and complete grasp of what such a term means, it becomes impossible to collect data about it from the person's track record to reach factual and balanced judgements. The door becomes wide open to speculation, opinion and prejudice. It is inequitable to both the person being evaluated and our businesses to run such risks.

- **The focus on offsite teamwork training has ironically detracted from developing teamwork within the business.**

The key focus of the ingenuity and creativity of management teamwork training has been, and is currently, on what happens offsite during that training. The centre of gravity of such work is firmly within the offsite training. I know from some forty three years personal experience of developing such training that considerable and successful effort has gone into raising the quality and relevance of the work.

However, the line manager within the business can only deliver sustainable teamwork when it is a seamless fit within a strategy to work at all the other managing issues facing him. Otherwise it merely becomes a non business focused 'bee he has in his bonnet'. Instead, he needs a clear picture of how teamwork will specifically support the organisation's work on the wider issues: Structure, Procedures, and Man Management. Without that bigger picture, it is not possible to fit the line manager's work on teamwork into any business strategy. He can then only 'try things in the dark' to encourage interest in the issue. I have personally experienced just such stumbling around in the dark. It is not a competent way of doing business. People have said, 'If you work for Frank – you have to get interested in teamwork – because that's simply how he is'. This means that teamwork cannot be developed within the organisation in a systematic, business focused fashion. It gets marooned on the islands of people's personal preference, and isolated from the business mainland.

Hence we produce the irony that our key focus on the offsite element of teamwork training has obscured the much more important and complex challenge of how to develop teamwork within our organisations.

ISSUE 3 – 2.15   LEADERSHIP

BACKGROUND CONTEXT

People see leadership as an issue of identity and survival

I have reserved this most emotive of issues to the last, so that it can be viewed in the light of all the other issues and principles.

It is also a skill area that is highly interdependent and interactive with all the previous principles, and is best explored at this point. Equally, it has proved an intricate and difficult issue to work at. The *quid pro quo* has been that when that work has been successfully progressed, the commercial and human benefits have been highly significant.

The principle that has most helped client organisations at times of great crisis has been to have the discipline and courage to 'take a step back' to view such crises in the widest perspective. They can then view a full width of information on which to base plans to handle that crisis. This is of course very easy to say, but has always proved extraordinarily difficult to do. The instinctive emotional reactions to a crisis have been so strong, that the overwhelming temptation has been to get sucked into the vortex of simply responding. It has been extremely difficult to 'hold the emotions steady', take a step back, and view a wider perspective. However, the experience has always proved that practice at this habit has both radically improved decisions and confidence levels at times of crisis. So it is with the issue of leadership.

It also instinctively raises intense emotions and brings into play the most vivid parts of a manager's formative experience. It has usually touched an emotional nerve spot in most people. Similarly, the temptation can be to get sucked into simply responding to these emotions and the intense history that has usually been associated with them. People are then inclined to take up a 'position' too quickly – and thence close their minds to anything different. In the same way as responding to a crisis it has proved helpful to take a step back to see the issue of leadership in the widest perspective we can. We can then take on board the full width of operational information associated with it. We stand the best chance of seeing it in the round, and being able to take our best balanced judgements as to what it may mean – and what may be best to do.

The emotional whirlpools that we have to navigate past to reach those judgements are intense. Two in particular have claimed a lot of people attempting this journey:

Identity

The first one entwines the issue of leadership in people's minds with personal identity, self-worth, and respect. It has always proved a sensitive and difficult subject to fully discuss. Emotions can run high, and cool objectivity be in short supply.

Survival

The second one associates leadership in people's minds with advancement, acceptance in the organisation, and security – seemingly the very core of survival. Intimations that one doesn't, or can't, cut the mustard have never ever been taken lightly. The utmost seriousness has always greeted any comments on this issue. Survival is at stake.

As stated above, this issue is also highly interactive and interdependent with all the other principles. Patience and accuracy have always been needed to grasp the way in which all the other issues are an integral part of leadership, and vice versa. The reward is to catch sight of the extensive continuum of its different forms, their differing effects, and the choices to be made.

Though unconventional, a particular set of choices has proved highly effective for the business, the organisation, and the people within it. They are described in the following principles:

PRINCIPLES

1. **A key focus is guiding the processes of people's thinking and interactions that produce sustainable results.**

2. **Each person's style is a legitimate gift and privilege bequeathed to them by their particular background. It can be effectively used in guiding the processes needed to deliver results.**

3. **Leading one's own development, the development of subordinates, and the development of the whole organisation's managing habits, is one and the same integrated challenge.**

    The root of success at that challenge is the pursuit of one's own development.

    That success has to be validated by tangible benefits for the business.

4. **The CEO leads this integrated approach to leadership.**

    His particular contribution is to:

    - **lead the processes that will deliver the business strategy**

    - **monitor the leadership across the organisation to ensure its consistency with the principles he is implementing**

5. **An equally key focus for any leader is to share and support the efforts of other leaders with whom his management line regularly interacts.**

Each principle is detailed below using the following format:

- summary

- explanation

- benefits and implications

- encountered difficulties

PRINCIPLE 1

A key focus is guiding the processes of people's thinking and interactions that produce sustainable results.

SUMMARY

Leaders throughout the organisation have inevitably needed to personally take certain key business decisions. Typically, these will set out such things as fundamental aspirations for the core business concerns at their level. Though few in number, these decisions have provided a framework for other levels to grapple with the challenges facing them.

With that framework in position, leaders have primarily focused on guiding the processes that enable subordinates to effectively tackle their work. That guiding has consisted of three elements:

- firstly, to support people's application of the principles involved in those processes

- secondly, to help them to see for themselves how redirections of their efforts would improve their business performance

- thirdly, to monitor the effects on the work concerned, and respond appropriately

A full range of successes has consequently resulted. The number, quality, and speed of decisions together with their associated commitment have laid the basis for success.

The fundamental and longer term benefit to the business has been the sustained and detailed attention to the underlying processes that produce effective results. This has continuously improved the quality and consistency of resulting work.

The key benefit to the organisation has been the rapid deepening of the guided partnerships within the management lines. It has nurtured a robustness that has been able to better weather subsequent difficulties and strains.

The key benefit to both leaders and subordinates has been to significantly increase the scope and complexity of what they directly control. This has inevitably accelerated their development and commitment to the work in hand.

In contrast, as leaders follow the more conventional route of taking an increasing number of decisions themselves, the narrower that range of possible successes has become. At a point not too far down that steep and slippery slope, they inevitably constrain their subordinates into a feudal relationship. This demands loyalty and conformity to 'the leader's decisions' as the price for survival. Each one of the above benefits has then rapidly disappeared.

The choice has always been continuously open to leaders as to which of these two directions they pursue.

EXPLANATION

● **Choosing a deliberate balance between focusing on 'what is happening' and 'the way it is happening'.**

Leaders have the opportunity to strike whatever balance they choose between concentrating on the business content of the work they are leading and the way that work is being handled.

As a general guideline, this work has encouraged leaders to pay priority attention to the processes by which the work is being tackled. This has resulted in creating the maximum space for their subordinates to contribute to the content of the work.

Of course, matters have never been as simple as to allow anyone the luxury of only one guideline – particularly when it comes to an issue as complex as leadership. Another guideline among a number to take account of has been the nature of the work being tackled and its influence on the balance between processes and content.

As an example, emergencies and situations of very high risk have understandably called for a leader to step much closer towards directly controlling the precise content of what happens. Even so, my abiding memory of the best handled emergencies still saw the leader skilfully masterminding how the processes of managing that event were coordinated. He obviously made sure he simultaneously had a closer grip of the operational detail of what was occurring. In the most skilful of instances, I saw leaders still take every opportunity to maximise the delegation of operational detail to their subordinates. They pursued this guideline not out of 'principle', but simply because they knew it produced the best results.

- **A key step has been to identify and prioritise the processes that the work requires.**

The manager has become clear about the key issues to focus and selected aspirations to pursue for each of them.

With that as a basis he has thoroughly analysed the work challenge facing him to identify which processes are particularly important for success. The range of such processes has been indicated in this chapter. In this form of leadership, much depends on the accuracy of this analysis and choice of processes to prioritise. The required standards for that analysis have only been reached by managers who themselves regularly practise their own skills at these same processes. Those who have made the mistake of not grappling with that challenge have found that their mere intellectual understanding of the processes cannot produce a competent and useful analysis. They have been reduced to intuition, guesswork or prejudice.

Being clear which processes will unlock success, the manager has then looked carefully at both the exact situation facing him and the people involved in the work. He has made his judgements about how he will lead those processes to reflect that information.

In summary, the leader will have decided:

- **the key issues of concern** that he wants to prioritise

- **the aspirations** that he wants to pursue for those issues

- **the processes he anticipates** will need to be grappled with to deliver those aspirations, and the priorities between them that he judges are appropriate

- **how he intends to guide those processes** to take account of the particular people involved in the work, and the specific situation surrounding it

- **some outline preliminary targets** that he judges will indicate progress with the total piece of work and its aspirations

This preparation has aided effective leadership of what subsequently happens.

Guiding subsequent work: Supporting, modifying and monitoring.

Supporting

Having identified and briefed his team on the processes facing them, the leader has then been careful to support individuals in their particular way of working. His need is that they take initiatives in their own personal style – not his own. His support will therefore reinforce their own key strengths in what they do, and encourage them to probe areas they see as needing improvement. He will want to support their own planning to respond to those problems – not insist on how he would deal with these matters.

Modifying

This has been a critical part of this form of leadership. The reviews to modify work – however informal they may be – have followed the principles described in Issue 3 – 2.8: 'Responding to Success and Failure', p. 137. Conventional practices in this area have been unhelpful. Indeed, for the reasons detailed in that section they have proved to be the absolute kiss of death.

<u>Monitoring</u>

As has been described in Chapter Two, Business Challenge Three ('Growing the Line Management Discipline of... p. 45), the management line depends on its regular one-to-one dialogues to monitor work. It has only been in that searching mutual exploration that both people can reach a common view of matters. They can then understand how each can help the other with the difficulties facing them. Some monitoring can usefully be done within a group setting. The guideline has been to only use a group to check highly interactive issues. Even then, it has been restricted to the sharing of information. Subsequent follow up on a one-to-one basis has been critical to pick up the inevitable individual responsibilities. Only this discipline has given a clear accountability about contentious and involved matters. Continuous monitoring via groups has both prevented this happening and rapidly led to manoeuvring, blurred accountability, unresolved conflicting beliefs, with favoured 'in groups' and denigrated 'out groups'. This has proved to be an inevitable fast track to management by politics and feudalism.

SOME KEY BENEFITS AND IMPLICATIONS

- **The business benefits from focusing on the processes for success.**
  This maximises the operational information used in them.

  The leader's focus on these processes automatically creates the maximum space for their subordinates to apply their more detailed operational information to the work. This has helped business decisions and actions to better reflect the practical reality 'on the ground'. Untoward assumptions are minimised.

  The levels of commitment nurtured in both leader and subordinate stem from the different talents they can each bring to the business. The leader's talents for strategically thinking through and guiding the processes needed for success – and the subordinate's talents for applying the depth of his more detailed operational information to those processes. The core obligation of the leader is to create and lead this mutually beneficial partnership of talents.

- **It continuously clarifies the organisation's view of accountability.**

  Each leader's accountabilities have included:

  - o   how key issues are tackled at that level and what results flow from that work

  - o   how his subordinates are developed within those efforts

In essence this direction requires leaders to primarily focus on the width and depth with which issues are grappled with. It is the antithesis of the pursuit of personally focused power.

- **It positions observation as the key basis for leadership**

The conventional views of leadership would not see the skill of observation as its basis. It seems an unlikely choice. Reality says otherwise.

The capacity to observe in detail what is occurring in evidenced factual examples is a formidable ability – much more so if the leader has reached the level of skill where he can observe at speed what is happening around him whilst in action himself. It places him in a powerful position. He can immediately access the pattern of strengths and weaknesses being operated around him. He can accurately support particular strengths to increase the chances of success. He can pin point weaknesses to minimise the chances of failure. Detailed observation accesses the operational information that enables the leader to lead.

It simultaneously opens the door to identifying what is occurring within any of the processes the leader is guiding. This allows his continued personal exploration of the processes, the information to thence sustain his own development, and the capacity to support others' development.

Convention is obsessed with the outer trappings of leadership: what he sounds and looks like, the style in which that happens, etc. The reality is that effective leadership first depends on the capacity of the mind to rapidly and accurately observe what is occurring in front of it. Without competent skill in this area, all subsequent abilities are rudderless.

COMMONLY ENCOUNTERED DIFFICULTIES

- **The convention of leading solely by one's view of what should happen.**

'Are you a man or a mouse? You just tell them what you think, and what you want – and if they don't like it, then they know what the alternative is. If they don't understand it, just keep saying it louder. They'll get it eventually. You're the boss!'

Whilst this may sound like an exaggerated parody, it is perilously close to an extremely common view of leadership. It is built on two premises:

  o the leader's right is to personally take all, or most of, the key decisions in his area.

  o the bases for those decisions come only from his own thinking. Consequently, his subordinates have been in a variety of different positions to his own. He therefore commonly tells them what he wants to happen, in the absolute belief that one can command commitment.

The conviction that the essence of seniority is a greater personal power to decide more and bigger decisions is very widely held. 'What else do you have experienced, successful managers for, if not to take the burden of the majority of decisions, as well as all the big ones?' is the common refrain. 'They get the big bucks for sticking their necks out and saying how it should be' is the other. When the leader decides to follow that convention, an automatic spiral has swiftly and inexorably swung into position:

- o his teams spend their time practising every political trick in the book to second-guess his decision. They then try and pose the pretence that they were already there – or at the very least, 'close by' – waiting to agree with his decision. The teams see this sterile conformist behaviour as simply necessary to survive.

- o the leader will feel that his authority and reputation rests on his decision 'carrying all before it'. He will therefore canvas support for it and work to undermine any opposition he comes across.

- o those of his teams who decide to be seen as 'loyal', or decide it is politically prudent to do so, will engage in the same canvassing and undermining.

- o his teams will automatically self-select only those ideas and initiatives that they judge are going to be consistent with their leader's decisions. Again, they will naturally see this restrictive conformity as a means of surviving.

The detail of how this spiral of effects happens shows a deeper inevitability.

The convention of having a leader habitually take the majority of the decisions throughout his patch – or all of them – has created management by politics. It has instantly enshrined the pursuit of personal power and influence. It has installed loyalty and conformity as the means of survival. The habit of trying to drive the business via one's own thinking alone has unfailingly had these effects.

This is in essence eliminating the diversity of talent via politics. In contrast, the essence of leadership via guiding the processes needed by the business is to nurture and harness the diverse talents of others together with one's own. This produces a cooperative of talents, in contrast to a politically driven elimination of them.

- **The other difficulty lies in the sheer amount of work and determination needed to become skilful at leadership via focusing on processes.**

The prizes described above for this form of leadership are truly significant. The effects on numerical indices have often proved to beyond normally accepted possibilities. Genuinely harnessing people's diversity can produce those types of results. Common sense says that such prizes cannot come cheap. The price is a particular attitude, wedded to much hard work.

The attitude
is one of increasing open mindedness to the variation, subtleties, depths, and interdependence of the processes involved. It is an attitude of decreasing certainty that 'one knows it all, and has it cracked'. It is an attitude of interested, continuous, and curious exploration. The conventional attitude to increasing seniority has none of these characteristics.

Sustained hard work

is needed to become progressively more skilful at these processes.

Only then can one discover how to support/encourage others to securely experiment with them. The shallow understanding that comes from just an intellectual grasp of the processes has never given that ability. This has misled people to wax eloquently about these matters and present a facade of ability – a symptom instantly recognised by capable good track record managers as a liking for bull manure. Deeper understanding that is capable of guiding operations has only come from persistent personal practice at the processes. That knowledge has only come from hard won experience. The analogy of coaching a complex sport from the position of an armchair expert versus one of achievement is a very close one.

The conventional view is that seniority excuses one from the rigours of such continuous hard work.

Usefully, some senior managers have decided that they would take on board both the attitude and the hard work (see the example of 'John', detailed below). Others have exercised their prerogative not to explore either challenge. That is their right. Equally, neither have the significant prizes been theirs to have. The impact of their free choice on those working for and around them then becomes a matter for their supervising line manager to grapple with.

PRINCIPLE 2

- **Each person's style is a legitimate gift and privilege bequeathed to them by their particular background**

- **It can be effectively used in guiding the processes needed to deliver results**

SUMMARY

Each of us has a unique style. Many influences on our particular developmental paths, and the decisions we made along its way will have helped to shape it. It is a deep reflection of our individuality and personal chemistry. It is a unique attribute, and much will have happened to evolve it.

Asking leaders to accept and value their particular style, and use it just as it is to guide appropriate processes, has had particular effects. Most importantly, the prime reward is that the business results have been of high standard. Additionally, the organisation has:

- **improved its understanding of the real skills at its disposal**, and stopped being limited/misled by judgements concerned solely with people's style

- **identified those skills that can improve its performance in a fundamental fashion** – not merely in an incremental fashion. Step changes in performance become a possibility

- **shifted the focus of its decisions towards detailed operational facts**, and not have them obscured by only concentrating on issues of style

- **deeply affected how people feel valued**, and thence accelerated initiative taking beyond any standard that competitors were capable of matching

These are significant rewards to capture and have put considerable monies onto the bottom line of client organisations. However, it has always required much more effort to penetrate to the detail of what a person is doing, as opposed to the immediately visible nature of his style. The good news is that as line managers, the choice as to which focus we pursue – content or style – is always ours to make on a minute-by-minute basis.

EXPLANATION

There is a very common and strong conviction that the source of success or failure in leadership has been the personal style of the leaders concerned. Complimentary comments such as 'a sense of presence', 'charisma', 'a sense of command', and 'he's a big man with a big presence' appear to carry the finality of a shrewd and pondered judgement. Negative versions such as 'he lacks an aura of authority', ' he gives no sense of dynamism', ' he simply can't present confidently', ' he lacks total conviction', etc., have invariably been regarded as the absolute kiss of death from which there can be no recovery or reprieve. Positive or negative, such statements about style are generally accepted as the core bases for explaining why someone is an effective or an ineffective leader. They are taken as final – particularly the negative ones – and the distillation of careful and penetrative perception.

Whilst this view of leadership is a widely held one, it is at best very incomplete. In most cases, it has caused – and continues to cause – significant damage to organisations, their businesses, and individual managers. It mistakes the 'packaging' a person's talents come in, for the actual 'contents'. It promotes interest in the 'packaging' whilst actively obscuring the nature of the 'contents'.

Perhaps an example will help to illustrate this vital issue.

> **EXAMPLE   A FAILING CEO COMMENCES AN UNEXPECTED TURNAROUND**
>
> o <u>An inexperienced CEO realised that he had created an ineffective organisation</u>
>
> John (not his real name) had become the CEO of a large organisation for the first time in his career. When I was introduced to him, his own judgement was that he was doing so badly as a CEO that absolutely any change had to be better than what was happening. A mutual colleague had seen the effects of this development work and suggested that John describe his difficulties to me. It was

desperation that brought him to my door. Indeed, when I checked out what was occurring, he had in fact committed every mistake I had ever come across within all the other six organisations I had worked in – not once, but many times. It was a Gordian knot of mistakes, added to a business analysis that predicted a significant loss over the next two years. An embarrassing eight figure number would appear in red. In addition, just prior to John's arrival, key customers had legitimately and publically voiced a strong distrust of the organisation.

- He was written off because his 'leadership style' was not acceptable.
  However, he had one last card to play, and it was an ace.

John was seen by his chairman and others as a technically competent 'nice man', but 'without a leadership bone in his body', he 'simply can't present confidently', and 'his style lacks the necessary conviction'. What was apparent was that John was totally unclear what the unique obligation of a CEO actually was. What was he supposed to be doing that no one else could do? Inevitably, he was unclear what his job actually was and how to go about doing it.

However, he had one vital set of habits, which would turn out to be the ones he needed to commence a famous and spectacular turnaround. He would painstakingly write down the detail of our regular reviews about the issues confronting him. He would always think them through overnight, and return the next morning with an internalised version written in his own terms. He would then diligently carry out action plans that he'd created to tackle the issues discussed. He used to say, 'I may not be any good at this, but I'm a good learner'. I hasten to add that I am not saying that these particular practices of John's are the complete answer to the meaning of management life. They were very much his own way of doing things, but the principles of which they were an expression were to prove vital to the solution of the challenges facing him. It is important to recall that we paid not the slightest attention to any of the 'shortcomings' in leadership style that so exercised his chairman – and everyone else – and for which John was so roundly condemned.

- He produced measurable performance improvements that showed he had turned the tide – keeping the same discredited 'leadership style'.

Over some twelve months, he cut through the vast majority of the Gordian knot of mistakes that he had previously created. He worked hard to install appropriate managing habits – starting with himself. The overall effect was that his organisation started to fundamentally deal with its key challenges. The enterprise received objective, nationally recognised written assessments that categorically confirmed he was truly making significant progress. He turned the eight figure projected loss into a result that ranged from a break even to a positive six figure number dependent on certain eventualities. This was regarded as a remarkable feat that his chairman and board had judged to be impossible. He worked with his key customers to the point where they voiced their confidence that a 'new dawn was breaking' in creating a constructive and trustworthy relationship with the organisation.

It is a matter of great sadness that prudent reasons then led him to decide to leave the organisation for a different position, before the full flowering of his spectacular recovery could be brought to completion and duly savoured. Nonetheless, the facts and the record of what he achieved in a very short, but extremely intense period of activity, stand to his permanent credit. It left him a different man, the organisation a better place and its people reinvigorated. He recalled that the pivotal realisation that drove this remarkable event was when he became clear about the CEO's key obligation as a leader. 'I realised that I was the person in charge of the processes that made things happen, and not the person that made things happen'. What is critical to highlight is that John retained his original personal style throughout this tour de force. It was precisely the same style for which he had been branded as beyond hope.

- o _The actual detail of John's skills showed he had what it took to be effective._

  Observing the factual detail of what John actually did disclosed him to be naturally self-effacing, disinterested in the limelight of the set piece presentations/PR events, totally sincere and honest in his portrayal of what was happening, totally committed to his business, intensely hard working, deeply respectful of other people, naturally collaborative with others whilst seeking to take no advantage of their weaknesses, and never seeking any overt recognition. These qualities, when viewed through the prism of the 'style packaging' that convention uses to recognise what it thinks is 'a leader', had led to the resounding condemnations listed above. If that assessment had been allowed to stand – as it would in most organisations, given the seniority of the people voicing it – then John would not have been given the chance to prove it to be both irrelevant and incorrect. Once he started to take initiatives in all the processes that guided how things happened in his organisation, people saw those very same qualities in a totally different light. Managers and customers now saw him to have an unusual and trustworthy integrity, a dependable honesty that could be relied upon amidst a sea of uncertainty and rumour, and a person who would always try and quietly help when the going got tough. This quite different view was being seen against a background of all the appropriate processes being grappled with.

- **The style 'packaging' in which a manager's skills comes wrapped in does not necessarily indicate what the skills content of the package is**

- **We need to be patient in discovering the real contents – and set aside the packaging**

Seen through the lens of conventional stereotypes for leadership, the 'packaging' in which John's skills came in looked uncharismatic, pedestrian and distinctly uninspiring. It ticked none of the 'style boxes' so beloved by those who live by such convictions. However, the real content of John's skills actually had the necessary ingredients for success. An obsessive focussing on arbitrary stylistic concerns – which are in essence gifts of individual chemistry – has proved capable of totally obscuring whether a leader has the practical skills needed for success.

I have seen many examples of senior men being drawn to the bright lights of a person's chemical gifts of 'presence', 'command', 'presentational style', 'charisma', and be totally convinced that 'this was the leader for the job'. In these instances little to no attention was being paid to the fundamental managing skills needed to lead the processes that underpin real business success. The fact that they might have been substantially absent was always a late and reluctant discovery. Revealingly, that discovery sometimes never came, despite there being copious evidence to prove it. It is a measure of our attachment to the instantly visible issue of a person's style and our fascination with management 'packaging'.

Indeed the logic of the situation would lead anyone to ask whether there is any common sense connection between the two – style, and process skill. A person's God given gift of a believable and strong presence, a powerful sense of command, and a charismatic presentational ability are all valuable attributes of his style. However, these cannot imply that he has put in the many hours of painstaking work that is the sole route to developing the managing skills to guide the processes needed to get things done competently. My experience has been that the two areas are evidence of entirely different, and opposite, attributes.

The presence of one cannot imply, and never has implied, the presence of the other.

SOME BENEFICIAL EFFECTS AND IMPLICATIONS

- **Being free of a concern for stylistic stereotypes has allowed us to see, value, develop, and deploy an individual's talents**

Accepting another's style just as it is has helped their real skills to be more accurately perceived. Their significance and use became clearer.

Valuing the person just as they are, without being conditioned by whether they conform to this or that 'type of style', has given a much more accurate picture of two vitally important things.

   - Firstly, it gave a much fuller, sharper and more balanced picture of the current pattern of strengths and weaknesses that the person was operating. Seeing that information accurately has always been a significant challenge. Starting with an acceptance of his particular style has greatly helped in seeing the detailed truth of the matter.

   - Secondly, it gave a clearer indication of what the person might achieve in the next few steps of his particular developmental path. It was only an indication, and had to be carefully checked out with the person. After all, only he could make them happen.

It created the best mutual basis for developing/deploying those talents.

This careful process of gathering detailed information about the person, and checking it with him, is an open way of valuing where he's got to and how he got there.

That valuing is the basis for supporting the particular way he will choose to develop his pattern of strengths and difficulties.

- **The message of individual acceptability to the organisation has inevitable effects on initiative taking**

<u>The level of initiative taking is the commercial cutting edge of the business.</u>

Businesses naturally depend heavily on the level of initiative taking throughout the organisation. Senior managers have correctly been very concerned as to how to improve it when low levels of it threaten their commercial performance. It can often appear as one of those nebulous qualities that seems difficult to grasp in a practical fashion, yet any line manager will have experienced how sharp-edged the commercial reality can be when people don't take appropriate initiatives. Issues such as delivery, quality, and other aspects of customer service, can visibly and rapidly deteriorate. Initiative taking is a vital commercial asset, which any organisation wants to thoroughly understand how to nurture in very practical terms. It will, at the very least, certainly want to be clear about which things to avoid which deteriorate initiative taking.

<u>Each person's style is a worthy servant to 'leadership by guiding the relevant processes'.</u>
<u>It has never been a substitute for that leadership.</u>

John's style, – which remained constant throughout the above recalled piece of work – was a unique gift of his personal chemistry. It proved to be a highly effective tool in the service of his newly developed managing skills. Those skills centred around paying rigorous attention to guiding all the processes within his organisation, which are detailed throughout this work. The experience has been that the unique gift of any person's style has always proved to be an effective servant to that rigorous guiding of processes. The business and human results have invariably been resoundingly successful. Equally, the experience has been that leadership with the most charismatic, magnetic, and attractive style, without that rigorous guiding of processes, has been commercially ineffective. Style has not proved to be a substitute for that underpinning process guidance.

<u>The organisation's consequent acceptance of each person's style is a powerful message of respect.</u>
<u>Initiative taking is inescapably affected.</u>

One essence of this form of leadership is its absolute acceptance of whatever style a person's chemistry bequeaths to him. Experience says it is an entirely effective basis for success. The organisation has consequently advanced and promoted whatever range of styles it has available. It has not sought to groom them in any way. It has not pursued the habit of most large organisations – the conventional and vacuous obsession with a conformity of style as proof of organisational / cultural identity.

Instead, the unmistakable message of individual acceptance has deeply nurtured personal confidence. It has directly affected the appetite for taking initiatives that all businesses look for. Other factors needed for growing the capacity for initiative taking have previously been detailed in Issue 3 – 2.11, p.167, and obviously remain necessary.

The effective organisation does not pursue a uniformity of style
as a sign of cultural identity.

It nurtures a diversity of styles to implement a uniformity of processes.

A key basis for commercial success is laid.

COMMONLY ENCOUNTERED DIFFICULTIES

- **We see the speed of reaching a final 'judgement' of where people are as a proof of perceptual and intellectual horsepower.**

There is a pervasive belief that the quicker one can come to such judgements, the greater must be the perceptual and intellectual horsepower being deployed. The judgement is held to be 'incisive', and is regarded as accurate. This has helped to drive the use of stereotypes and 'models' against which individuals can be rapidly and summarily 'boxed' and type cast.

The first difficulty is the concern for speed. This has inevitably invited shortcuts. Taking shortcuts in understanding something as complex and changing as individuals has proved to be an extremely risky and disrespectful habit. The very long operational history of this work has never discovered the individual that is not unique. That uniqueness has always, without one exception in forty years of intense onsite work, had to be patiently and carefully understood. Accurate deployment has not been possible without it. Shortcuts and stereotypes encourage us not to put in that work. They deny the business the operational, individual detail on skills and weaknesses needed to optimise its running. Much worse, it is a statement of profound disrespect for the individuality of the person concerned. My experience of those who condescend and patronise in this manner is that they are never forgotten, and rarely forgiven. Certainly, having personally experienced its crudity, I was left with an indelible memory of its wild inaccuracies and closed minded certainty. This was the bigotry that underpins racial prejudice – the mechanism is precisely the same. I have experienced that too. There is no difference in the processes being used in both instances.

The second core difficulty is the pursuit of a fixed judgement. This entirely misunderstands the reality of each person's individual developmental path. This work has encouraged sufficiently accurate analyses by an individual of their own strengths and difficulties to enable them to bring about significant developments in that pattern. These have been sufficient to allow them to produce sustained differences in numerically measured performances. At no time in this process is a fixed judgement/categorisation being made. There is nothing that is a 'fixed' view of the person. In fact, it is the very reality that there isn't a 'fixed' judgement to form that powers the individual's capacity to move forwards. The pursuit of a fixed judgement/categorisation is a council of despair. It closes doors, and locks them. It is the very antithesis of this development work. This has opened doors, and invites the untried. Only the individual has the right to shut that door.

- **We are strongly tempted to focus on the visible and easily accessible issue of style.**

We can become 'addicted' to a short cut that doesn't work.

The activity of continuously observing accurate, exampled, information on people's pattern of strengths and difficulties has always been painstaking work. The temptation can be to bypass that altogether, and substitute that detailed data gathering, with facile comments about people's style. This requires very little, if any, mental work and encourages people to quickly sit in judgement and make pronouncements with apparent authority. The further temptation can then be to use those judgements around stereo types of style as the means of deciding whether someone can do a particular job or not. The above example of how 'John' was initially viewed showed that judgement was held with 100% conviction. The fact that it turned out to be 100% wrong did not cause the smallest rethinking about how the original judgements based on his 'style' were made. That is one example of many of our ability to remain committed to a proven way of making failed judgements. Having crashed the car whilst driving blindfolded, we see no reason not to habitually use the blindfold whilst driving.

- **Focussing on style deteriorates the rigor of the organisation's key decision making about people**

The example of 'John' – one of numerous encountered over the many years of this work – is typical. The key decision making discussions about how to allocate responsibilities across an organisation are downgraded at unnerving speed. They become political exchanges of firmly held opinion with little attention to the facts of the matter and a determined disinclination to examine them.

- **Persisting with that focus has prioritised the superficial – rhetoric, presentations, etc., – and discouraged concern for diligent application.**

Judgements by style have affected an organisation's competence in deeply negative ways. It rapidly shifts people's focus to the superficial. People have been encouraged to concentrate on 'first impressions', things that are easy to see, fine sounding rhetoric, become 'presentation obsessed', and are drawn to any similar opportunity to display 'their style'. This has slipped quickly into 'taking the eye off the ball' – the central issue of delivering end results. It has discouraged the unglamorous habit of diligent application and hard work.

Style has proved to be a truly valuable servant,

but a truly dangerous master.

PRINCIPLE 3

- **Leading one's own development, the development of subordinates, and the development of the whole organisation's managing habits is one and the same integrated leadership challenge**

- **The root of success at that challenge is the pursuit of one's own development**

- **That success has to be validated by tangible benefits for the business**

SUMMARY

The challenge of leadership has been best met by a unified process that integrates the efforts of leaders at all levels in the organisation.

Three core components have made up that challenge:

- the continuous individual development of each leader's managing habits

- the guiding of subordinates' managing habits in their tackling of everyday business

- the development of the management habits of the organisation as a unit

They require a fundamental solution to produce sustainable business results.

The following interactions illustrate how the first of these components forms the key basis for the remaining two.

- o Each leader continuously improves his own understanding and skill at the processes that drive his and others' work. These are described throughout this chapter.

- o He necessarily uses that understanding and skill to lead his subordinates' handling of the same processes that underpin their daily business. It has been through the application of those processes that the subordinates' managing habits are guided and developed.

- o This development of habits within each management line is the seedbed for creating the organisations' managing habits as a unit.

Using this process across the whole organisation integrates the efforts of each leader in delivering the above three core components. The practical focus of that delivery is always the quality of the routine business being transacted in each day. The proof of its competence is always the visible tangible effects in the business.

Experience says that the key player in leading this unified process is the CEO. Only when he has exampled the process by applying it at his level has that energised and motivated other leaders to implement the same process. The detail of exactly how the CEO has led the whole organisation to securely follow the process is described in Principle Four.

EXPLANATION

Exploring the operational detail of each of the three elements of Principle Three:

- **Leading one's own development, the development of subordinates, and the development of the whole organisation's managing habits is one and the same integrated leadership challenge**

What happens in any one of these three areas has had automatic effects in the other two. These three activities are inextricably intertwined and interdependent. Success at all three requires a consistent and integrated approach. Looking more closely at each element to see more clearly how they interdepend:

Leadership of one's own development
is the continuous exploring of the principles described throughout this chapter.

It is the persistent trial and success/error of attempts to apply the principles of this work when tackling actual business difficulties. You deliberately explore ways of optimising your use of the principles in order to produce the results the business requires. You repeatedly retest those ways on similar difficulties in different problems to gain a better rounded skill and understanding of their use.

One example is the attempt to gradually improve one's skill at the process of reviewing successes and failures. Each leader treads a unique path in this quest which reflects his individual pattern of strengths and difficulties. However, all such paths unavoidably explore such issues as:

- how does the balance between analysing successes and failures relate to the stage of development of the person being reviewed?

- how does that balance relate to the type of relationship between the leader and the person being reviewed?

- how does that balance relate to the type and importance of the job to the organisation?

   etc.

This learning takes time and considerable effort. However, keeping the mind open and reviewing one's efforts using the principles described in 'Responding to Success and Failure' brings gradual progress.One key effect is that you become intimately aware of every aspect of your 'current understandings' of the principles you have applied. That view is experience based – not theory based – and puts you in the best position to help subordinates meet the same challenge.

Leading the development of subordinates
is the journey of improving their use of the above principles within the tackling of their everyday business.

Managers best support their subordinates on that journey if they themselves continue to face the same rigours. Only then can they speak with the absolute conviction of first-hand experience. Only then can they speak of intimately knowing the resting spots, retreats, sources of strength and succour, pitfalls, inviting but ineffectual short cuts, the siren voices that tempt you to stop, and the false dawns that lie along that journey. You cannot discover these land marks other than by experience. No theory can illuminate them. Those of us in pursuit of actually delivering performance and supporting others to aspire to the same ambition are obliged to travel that journey. Subordinates need the strength and support of experienced and hardened travellers. Leadership by example has been the only basis to provide that support.

Leading the development of the whole organisation's managing habits.

This has depended on each line manager striving at the above two areas of work. The effect is to create a consistent development of managing habits across the organisation.

Inevitably the CEO has been the appropriate line manager to lead this concerted effort by applying the same process to his work and that of the senior team. He will inevitably continuously review their individual efforts to lead each of their management lines in exactly the same endeavour.

- **The root of success at that challenge is the pursuit of one's own development.**

The engine that drives both the development of subordinates and the total organisation is the effort each line manager spends to progress his own development path. Without that pursuit at every level, led by the example of the CEO, an effective response to this challenge cannot be mounted. With those 'pursuits' in position, success becomes possible.

When all is said and done, the lofty and grand aspiration of organisation wide development of managing habits reduces to something of elegant simplicity:

- **can each line manager be inspired to set forth on his own path of developing his own managing habits?**

- **can the CEO lead that to happen?**

Simple in concept though this is, the prizes are so significant that it seems only reasonable that implementing it should be challenging. The blunt truth has been that the minority of people find it in their hearts to set forth on that inward journey. Each of us has to make our choice. The only certainty is this is the only route that reflects the real nature of the challenges facing us in the work place. Any other route has proved to be a misunderstanding or an evasion of that reality.

- **Success at each of the three has to produce tangible benefits for the business.**

  The only acceptable proof that all this hard mental and emotional work isn't so much delusional psycho babble is that each of the three parts of this integrated challenge has to yield concrete benefits for the business. These have to be sustained into the long term. Without that demonstrated proof, pursuing this route or not becomes a matter of mere intellectual debate having no relevance to the real business world.

  Managers who set out on this journey need always to seek the touchstone of: 'Is this step capable of helping me produce sustainable, tangible benefits for the business? At the very least, is it a key stage en route to being able to achieve that?' If the answer is yes, then the action is worth considering. If the answer is no, then whatever the attractions the action offers, pass it by.

  The effect of testing all conceptual thinking against this hard and unyielding yardstick is that it demands continuous attention to the facts of the situation facing managers. It is this rigorous attention to facts that so benefits the manager's journey. It stops it being an indulgent self-administered hallucinogen.

SOME BENEFICIAL EFFECTS AND IMPLICATIONS

One could continue expanding the undoubted effects of the above principle. However, enough has already been said to clearly indicate its merits.

COMMONLY ENCOUNTERED DIFFICULTIES

- **Vested interests pursue separated solutions.**

  Not only is the market flooded with self contained modular training, but a whole industry has grown up around splitting up 'leadership' into self contained packages for this or that level of management, or this or that 'style', etc.

  The ease of marketing and the attractions of 'selling more and different products' seem irresistible. The separated, modular approach certainly has an appealing simplicity, and the unwary manager can be lulled by it to 'follow the crowd' and buy his quota. He will certainly not be blamed by his superiors for taking that route – even if it fails. When I asked one senior manager why he had bought what he knew was some ill thought out, naive and simplistic modular training for his men, the reply was, 'No one ever got fired from this company for investing in training – any training. At least I get the brownie points for trying'. Realpolitik.

  The reader will be in no doubt by this stage what my experience has taught me about this approach. I will bore him no further by repeating the factual realities that inexorably bar this approach from producing real and sustainable business success.

- **The excuses and rationalisations for not engaging in the hard work of personal development have been legion.**

They always will be legion.

People have been endlessly inventive in providing themselves with rationalisations for not facing this work. It is their prerogative. It is their future. It has to be their choice. Of course, their line manager has then been faced with resolving the situation. He has a business to run. He is obliged to explore every avenue he can, of coaching and supporting a reluctant subordinate to engage with his own development. Sometimes this has been successful – but never, I note, without considerable effort from the manager and his colleagues. Sometimes, the subordinate has been unwilling to piece together/come to terms with the common sense of doing the work. A more senior manager may then be needed to stiffen the resolve of the supervising line manager, to face the inevitable and not 'fudge' the issue. In the best case, that support has not been needed. However it happens, the norm has been to seek a redeployment that plays to the existing strengths of the subordinate, or face the unpleasantness of a parting of the ways. As has been already said, this is not a Walt Disney movie. Happy endings are not guaranteed. The *quid pro quo* for a management that develops its staff to achieve a competently run business must be the risk of departure for particular individuals. They will have chosen not to join that mutual effort to improve the business.

- **Endless attempts are made to verbalise/intellectualise a pretence of doing the development work.**

This development work is not rocket science. It is easy to understand. At its most complicated, it is just common sense. Anyone can intellectually understand it – that is not where its challenge lies. This ease of understanding has misled countless people to feel a warm glow that they can quickly grasp enough of it to enable them to talk knowledgeably about it. The irony is that they can easily do that – because there isn't a lot to know about it that the intellect alone can tell you. They have then assumed that, if you intellectually understand something enough to talk about it, then de facto, you must have cracked it. A less charitably rationale has been that they have used the verbal window dressing as a pretence that they are doing the work. Again, it is their prerogative to make that choice. Again, it is the unwelcome job of their line manager to deal with the situation in precisely the same fashion as above. Effective line managers do not tend to have plentiful room for those who choose to be eloquent non performers. 'S..t, or get off the pot', has been the elemental and inescapable guideline.

PRINCIPLE 4

- **The CEO leads this integrated approach to leadership.**

  His particular contribution is to:

  - **lead the processes that will deliver the business strategy**

  - **monitor the leadership across the organisation
    to ensure its consistency with the principles he is implementing**

SUMMARY

The above form of leadership has only come to life within the organisation if unambiguously led by the CEO. His particular obligation is to apply the above process to delivering the business strategy.

Other leaders need the example of the CEO using his own development path to judge which processes to prioritise at his level to deliver his section of the strategy. They need his example of leading the senior team to replicate that thinking down each management line. They need to feel the intensity of the CEO's insistence that each leader use his own development to judge which processes he will concentrate on to deliver his section of the strategy.

Finally, they need to feel the CEO's absolute priority of applying this thinking to improve the tackling of the routine daily business.

The effect is to create a management team that is cohesive in its application of a unified process of leadership. Nonetheless, it simultaneously nurtures intense individuality in demanding that each leader exercise his own judgement as to the processes he will prioritise to deliver his section of the business strategy. Finally, it asks each leader to translate those judgements into guiding his subordinates' daily business habits to achieve that obligation.

Only tenacious leadership by the CEO via this process produces this combination of cohesiveness, diverse individuality and an absolute focus on better meeting the practicalities of the daily business.

EXPLANATION

Taking each element of Principle Four in turn:

- **The CEO leads this integrated approach to leadership.**

  The above principle of leadership via one's own development only takes root if the CEO personally demonstrates its daily use in the business. Plenty of examples exist where the CEO has decided – for whatever reasons – not to engage with that challenge. There has never been any logical rationale offered for not doing so – because there isn't one. The reasons supporting it are simple, comprehensive and irrefutable. The reasons for opting out are other than logic and the needs of the business. Such a decision obviously has to remain a matter of personal judgement and choice.

Assuming the case that the CEO sees and pursues the simple logic that ganders are only interested in whatever the geese are getting, he will meticulously plan his efforts in this matter. He will know that all CEOs live in a gold fish bowl. Every single thing they do is inspected for its meaning and inference – nothing is missed. The advantage is that it is much simpler than most CEOs believe to lead their organisations. They just have to walk the walk, and everyone immediately picks up the message. The slightest deviation into pretence and facades has been instantly recognised for what it is. The inexorable result has been skilful conformity. The loser has been the business. In contrast, the CEO's determination to improve his own skill levels at these processes has enthused and driven those that have the ability and inclination to emulate his example. The business gains from quality initiatives taken at all levels in the organisation.

His particular contribution is to:

- **lead the processes that will deliver the business strategy**

- **monitor the leadership across the organisation to ensure its consistency with the principles he is implementing**

Taking each element in turn:

- **Lead the processes that will deliver the business strategy.**

  <u>The CEO has demonstrated that such leadership must first serve the business.</u>

  He will first want to study the business strategy (developed in the way described in the Section 3 – 2.9: 'Understanding, Creating, and Using Strategy', p.144) and the full range of issues it is aimed at. From his understanding of the processes and their interdependence, he will judge which ones he and the senior team should especially focus on that will help deliver the strategy.

  Having prioritised these processes, he will brief his senior team and iterate that thinking until they are all of one mind. He will want to think through how he supports each of the team to repeat this process throughout their different management lines.

  The net result is that each leader has used his own development to help him judge which processes he should guide his subordinates through to deliver their section of the business strategy. He has then coached their development of whatever managing habits are needed in their daily business to ensure success at this obligation.

This is an integrated process of leadership that involves every level in the enterprise facing their own strategic challenges in a consistent fashion.

- **Monitor the leadership across the organisation
to ensure its consistency with the principles he is implementing.**

The CEO will be aware that in facing this challenge he is playing for the highest personal and business stakes. He is pursuing an integrated form of leadership initiated by his example at processes he has chosen, which he judges will deliver the business strategy. There are no higher stakes. Success will be very publicly and directly attributable to his judgement and skill. Failure will have the same characteristics. He will want to check progress with great care, and rapidly respond to any unexpected difficulty.

The standard one-to-one dialogues with his senior managers have therefore become key to his monitoring of the activity. Ensuring the same discipline is being implemented down each management line has become equally critical. He has repeatedly spot checked further down the organisation in unannounced fashion to check that what he is hearing is in fact the truth of the matter. His senior team have been sure to do the same. No precaution will be too onerous or too small to neglect.

SOME BENEFICIAL EFFECTS AND IMPLICATIONS

- **A powerful unifying force, focused solely on the business**

This represents a unified way of leading all the central matters of the business.
The consequent effects have been that:

- o   all business concerns throughout the organisation are tackled in a consistent fashion

- o   all levels can observe those above and below them facing similar judgements that they all have to make, and consequently working to deliver sound business results.

- **A powerful release of individual talent and potential – 'one size does not fit all'.**

It is a message of fundamental individual acceptance by the organisation of each leader: it asks not that he copy anyone else, or any 'created model' – only that he rigorously explores his own managing habits.

Whilst clear unity exists across the organisation on the process of leadership, the same process nourishes the diversity of each leader taking his own judgements about how best to serve the business needs in his area.

- **An enduring and growing sense of confidence and cohesion.**

It is the above individual acceptance that generates a particular type of confidence. It is not the confidence that comes from a network of influential relationships or an achievement. It is instead a feeling that comes from seeing one's individuality built into the common sense of an embedded process aimed at business competence. The process will continue to make business sense, despite whatever tides might wash through various relationships. This is the nurturing of confidence and cohesion based on pursuing hard-nosed competence. Experience says that it is a very stable and enduring way to build sound relationships.

The uniformity of process gives the organisation great cohesion.

The diversity of judgements that underpins the process simultaneously grows robust individuality throughout the organisation.

COMMONLY ENCOUNTERED DIFFICULTIES

Superman rules.

A surprisingly common view of leadership is that the CEO flies around the universe of his organisation at better than the speed of light. He has the big 'S' on the underpants, inexplicably worn over his tights. Single-handedly, he effortlessly accomplishes absolutely everything that's important, to the mystified admiration of us ordinary mortals.

Improbable though it sounds, there is a strong feeling that if you can't perform this 'man of steel' feat, then you are simply not a real leader. In fact you're not a 'real man' at all – goes the script. I witness the same fantasy being played out at lower levels in organisations.

The key challenge is that the previously described integrated approach to leadership demands a CEO committed to lead matters through the sets of teams around him. He believes in the power of harnessing others' talents and commitment. He believes that the consequent cooperative of talents is more effective than the display of 'the best single set of talents in the business' – no matter how good that set is. The real problem is that too many people still believe their worth is only proved by the Superman display. Could be that they simply like wearing their underpants over their tights. Whatever. Definitely cannon fodder for some aspiring Freudian psychoanalyst.

At this level, there are no easy wins.

I have heard the argument that 'This sounds like too much hard work'. When I've probed for the bases for this reservation, I hear a selection of views, e.g.

- 'I didn't get to where I got to today by jumping through all these new hoops. I've just stayed myself and did what came naturally. Now I've made it, I'll continue just as before.'

- 'I decide, and then I make them think it was their idea. It's worked so far. I'm simply going to continue.'

- 'This stuff makes sense – for others to do – I'll agree with everyone else doing it.'

The simple inescapable truth is that the higher up the organisation one goes, the more complex and intangible are the issues that confront the line manager. There simply are no easy wins involving little personal work or risk. The prizes are far too large to involve such insignificant payment. This work has no 'tricks', quick fixes and 'smart short cuts' to offer in gaining the big prizes and paying the cheap prices.

The long experience of this work has been that paying the appropriate prices has gained access to the big prizes. Those unwilling to pay these prices need to look elsewhere. Those willing to pay them are assured of potential success, but the road to be travelled is appropriately demanding.

PRINCIPLE 5

- **An equally key focus for any leader is to share and support the efforts of other leaders with whom his management line interacts.**

SUMMARY

Better business results have been more reliably produced when line managers have actively supported one another across the interfaces they share. Whilst this is the merest common sense, it is not the norm. The section detailing structural principles has already described that managed teams need to be set up at those interfaces to ensure the business delivers an integrated operation (see Issue 3 – 2.3, p.107).

However there is a deeper reason why that support between leaders of different management lines needs to be deliberately encouraged and coached. The business has been powerfully affected by the width of vision and concern at the most senior level. The experience has been that an ingrained narrowly based view at this level is almost impossible to reverse (refer Business Challenge Three, Chapter Two, p.40 – Operations Director, Bill, for the exceptional example). Success therefore heavily depends on people reaching that level with the managing habit of being committed to the wider horizons of business obligation. Additionally, they need to be comfortable with working towards meeting them. That habit is most commonly grown at earlier stages of development by habitually joining with colleague managers to resolve the issues at the interfaces between their management lines. Parochialism may serve short term promotional needs, but it ultimately does serious damage to the much more important habit of growing wider perspectives at the senior levels.

EXPLANATION

Effective line managers routinely check work that interacts between their management lines and other lines. Typically, issues at those interfaces have effects on quality and customer service matters. These concerns have been a central focus in the regular reviews with his colleague line managers with whom he shares those interfaces. Each will want to ensure close support between them on the core operational factors of structure, procedures and man management. They understand that competence in these three factors guarantees their delivery of issues such as quality and customer service. Accordingly, they have regularly reviewed the operation of the teams and leaders working at their interfaces. It is certain that their senior managers will regularly seek reassurance that the wider needs of the business are met in these teams, and that no parochialism interferes with that priority.

Line managers have first learned to master the operation of their own management lines. One important sign of their further potential has been their work at the interfaces with other management lines. They need to prove that they can help the business operate in a consistent, integrated fashion. Repeated success at this challenge has been one of the key signals that they are ready for promotion to handle more complex parts of the organisation, and tackle the less tangible issues involved.

SOME BENEFICIAL EFFECTS AND IMPLICATIONS

● **The effective manager needs to develop the skills to manage without direct line authority.**

The supervising manager has made sure his subordinate attaches a high priority to how his line interacts with those of his colleagues. Not having direct line authority over those interactions has naturally required him to grow a more developed range of skills than he will have honed in managing his own line. His supervising manager has encouraged him to grapple with that next phase of his development. He will need to become skilful at delivering the same quality at those interfaces as he can deliver within his own line. Clearly the capacity of the whole business to perform as a unit in the eyes of customers critically depends on those interfaces operating in a seamlessly competent fashion.

● **The above widening of obligations is key to the development of managers at all levels – but particularly the senior one.**

The first part of this chapter listed the three requirements needed at the senior level to lay the basis for improving managing habits across the organisation (see Section One, p. 85.). If managers reach that level with a commitment to explore more effective ways of grappling with the wider issues, then this development work is within their grasp. Business managing habits can be systematically improved. However, if at the other extreme they have grown a closed minded view of matters and a main concern for sustaining their power base, then such improvement has not been possible. Business performance levels have had to take their chances on the tides of fortune. The precise manner in which managers have been developed has therefore heavily influenced their chosen position on the continuum between these two views.

The discipline of encouraging managers to meet wider business priorities, in addition to the management of their own lines, has proved useful in nurturing that habit in future senior managers. This has helped to lay the basis for the senior teams' ability to improve managing habits across the organisation.

COMMONLY ENCOUNTERED DIFFICULTIES

The 'devil take the hindmost' competitive belief is a much simpler, more tangible, and more common guideline.

A conventional motivation is to see the business solely as a vehicle for personal success, and a means of engineering the most rapid advance that one can. Examples abound of young (and sometimes not so young), energetic, totally focused, talented, driven managers who can be easily spotted obsessively looking after 'number one'. On the positive side, they will put Herculean effort into those pieces of work that they judge will directly reflect on them personally. That will always be done at the drop of anyone's hat. However, the manager has often not used the same energy and intense focus on interface issues that involve other management lines, but they can usually verbalise the rhetoric of needing to do so with the best of them. They are keen not to be seen as uncommitted to the business.

The observed reality has always been different. They are invariably highly ambitious. Their supervising manager has ensured that they realise the need for unambiguous delivery of such interface issues. Some have responded well to that redirection; some have not. Whilst one can get someone to agree the common sense of altering their habits, at times they have simply not been ready to drop their attachment to them. Their habits have been too deeply ingrained for their current stage of development to deal with the problem. That choice always has to remain a personal prerogative. However, the supervising manager has a business to run. A non common sense/non business focused response from his subordinate has forced unpleasant truths to be faced. At the very least, a redeployment into much less interactive responsibilities has resulted – if indeed it exists. One issue has been inescapable: the senior manager responsible for the area will want to make sure that the supervising manager realises that a vital principle is at stake. He will want the supervising manager to see it as a test of his personal ability to accurately deal with such a matter where it arises. He will also be acutely aware of the track record of such issues causing escalated trouble if 'fudged' and consequently allowed to later reappear.

CHAPTER FOUR

APPLYING THIS WORK

SECTION ONE

PROVEN WAYS OF USING THIS WORK TO DEVELOP ONE'S OWN MANAGING HABITS

SUMMARY

The good news: the majority of people have found the principles uncovered by this development work relatively easy to absorb. It has been simple to grasp their relevance to commonly encountered work challenges. As said on a number of occasions, this thinking is merely distilled common sense. Having said that, I continuously experience this to be the most stringent criterion that a line manager has to meet.

The bad news: a minority of people successfully master the real and much harder challenge of working out their own ways of applying these principles. The key question is: can the person fire up and then sustain the engine of their own development?

The even worse news: there is no fixed formula that can guide how this question is answered. In common with every other aspect of this work, there is no formulaic solution for success. Reality is simply not built that way. Each person has had to continuously explore ways of applying this work that suit his strengths and weaknesses at a particular time, and also take account of the situation around him. It turns out to be an ongoing process of trial and success/error. I'm still trying. With good fortune, I hope I will always have the chance to keep on trying. Having said that, clear guidelines have evolved from much practice that can help people make their judgements along whatever path they choose.

Those guidelines are concerned with the practical means of sustaining the habit of improving habits.

They come from distilled practice – not any artificially created theory – as indeed does all of this work. Every single part of them has been tested numerous times, and proven in the sternest of work challenges. However, I have seen – and continue to see – many people who choose to ignore and discount them. That must always remain their prerogative. Perversely, their reason has often been that they have judged them to be intellectually simple and obvious – which they are. The inescapable result has been their failure to deliver the performance improvements that were sought. Those that did take account of them would be the first to admit that the journey to 'live' them has not been easy or short. They would equally claim that the rewards to the business and themselves have been of an exceptional standard, fundamental, and enduring.

BACKGROUND CONTEXT

Over the many years of this work, people have tried numerous ways of applying it. Equally, they have approached that application with a wide range of attitudes. Both the particular way of applying the work and the chosen attitude towards it have proved important ingredients in its success or failure.

Various ways of applying this work have ranged from attempting to simultaneously use all of the principles described in Chapter Three to trying out various selections of them. People have applied the principles to selected pieces of work (e.g. self-contained projects), or to specific situations (e.g. meetings). They have focused on applying them for chosen time periods, or all the time. Numerous combinations have been attempted.

Attitudes to this application have also varied enormously. There have been those who believed this work to be the answer to life and the universe, and whose missionary zeal knew no bounds – or common sense. Nothing could stop them setting out to 'convert' everyone, and change everything instantly – to the intense annoyance of everyone concerned.

Yet others in senior positions have proved that Pontius Pilate still has his acolytes. When the work necessarily grappled with the unpopular correcting of previous management mistakes, they chose to wash their hands of what had to be done. They distanced themselves from the efforts of colleagues who helped them in the darkest hours, for fear of 'mud that might stick' to their image. A clean political score sheet was apparently more important than supporting those who were actually helping them. As has been said, this work has never promised to be a Walt Disney movie.

Others' attitudes have solely focused on applying this work to just their individual issues. They have only been concerned with bringing what they saw as order to their own world, and have not wanted to deal with the interaction with others.

The number of attitudes chosen by people to approach this work has been as many as the number of people applying it.

Described below is a principle and guidelines recalled from people's successful applications of this work, which may help you in making your own judgements for your path.

PRINCIPLE

- **This work is concerned with developing what you habitually do.
  It needs:**

    o **an effort of the mind to observe**

    o **an effort of the will to explore**

- **The guidelines for success are those for forming different habits.**

EXPLANATION :

Exploring each part of the principle in turn:

- **This work is concerned with developing what you habitually do ….**

  <u>The journey is long ; the challenge is fundamental ; there are no quick fixes</u>

  The essence is to choose a way of applying this work that fits you and others, and that will last the distance.

  Each person has a unique pattern of strengths and difficulties, and will need to find ways of working at these fundamental habits that specifically suit their pattern. As it then changes, so those ways must change.

  This work is dependent on gaining others' cooperation and the chosen ways of working also have to fit with others' needs. This is not a case of 'one size fits all'.

  The journey to develop better managing habits unavoidably touches all the core centres of how a person works at any issue. It necessarily reaches into every feature of how he interacts with others. These fundamentals have never been advanced quickly with little effort. This is a triathlon; it is not a sprint. However you choose to do this work has to be able to last the pace of a very long journey. This development work has absolutely no element of the quick, superficially attractive, catchy sound bite, easily marketable management trinket that one can quickly acquire in a short time, display, and say 'job done'. If that is being sought, then this work has nothing to offer– there are no 'quick fixes' available here.

  <u>Each person's journey is unique ; the principles remain the same; the challenge is searching observation</u>

  Every person I have worked with or observed has inexorably followed a path unique to his changing pattern of strengths and difficulties. Necessarily, no two people have travelled the same journey. The principles they have been forced to explore to deliver sustainable successes, remain immovably the same. They are inbuilt into the nature of work itself. They are those described throughout Chapter Three.

  One skill above all others is the traveller's searchlight that can guide his footsteps accurately on his unique path. It is his capacity to observe the processes that he is involved with – accurately, at speed, under pressure, and without fear or favour. Specifically:

  > **'Accurately'** has meant the capacity to observe in exampled operational detail, without any unsubstantiated generalised opinion that can hide an assumption or a prejudice.

  > **'At speed'** has meant the capacity to register those observations at the pace at which the business is being transacted.

  > **'Under pressure'** has meant the capacity to see and accept the detailed facts of the matter regardless of the implications that may flow from those facts.

  > **'Without fear or favour'** has meant the capacity to delve relentlessly to the core of what is occurring without regard for position or reputation.

Only in persistently working at the skill of observation to these standards does the manager grow the ability to continuously achieve two things:

- to see accurately where he has got to in his performance at the principles

- to take account of that assessment, and pinpoint where and how he needs to make his next set of improvements/developments

● **It has ultimately been a question of 'will' – a question of 'heart'**

The manager's ability to summon the energy and tenacity to carry out his 'next set of improvements/developments' has been a question of 'will' – a question of 'heart'. It is a continuous cycle of factual observation, analysis, improvement planning, and the 'will' to try out what is different. The essence of the developmental path lies in the quality of observation, and having the 'heart' to explore.

● **The guidelines for success are those for forming different habits.**

While each person's particular way of working will be different, the experience is that it will be consistent with certain guidelines in order to deliver practical business results. These are:

- **An immediate start.**
  A gradual and persistent progress

  - **Start immediately with the work that is to hand.**

    Those who have realised that this work is about developing new habits have grasped the need to commence straight away. They understand their need to groove a different way of viewing and thinking about work.
    Any delay has only served to reinforce old habits that need to be altered or improved. Delay has made the job of retraining the mind yet harder. It has served to bolster the emotional resistance to start at all.
    This has led people to commence their practice on work that they have immediately to hand.

  - **Start with tangible work that has short term deadlines.**

    Everyone has needed the early confidence of seeing how things can work differently for them, and getting better practical results than before.
    They have therefore chosen work with tangible end results. It has then been easier for them to objectively assess how their new habits are working out.

    It has also been helpful if the work had a short term dead line. They then got early confirmation whether the direction they had chosen was appropriate and quickly adjusted their approach if that was needed.

It has been prudent for people to start first with the smallest scale work. Understandably, whilst managers have been clear about the common sense logic behind the new habits, they have wanted the reassurance that no unforeseen dangers awaited them. They have therefore often started with work that just involved themselves alone.

- ○ <u>**Take regular stock with meticulous discipline**</u>

  - ▪ **The engine that drives this developmental work is the habit of reviewing**.

    This work is about trying to be more effective at learning from experience. The increasing capacity to observe is the very core of growing that learning. Practising it in regular reviewing is the habit that drives that growth. This is the heart of development. Grappling persistently with this challenge ensures progress.

    The experience unambiguously says that whilst managers may be very talented, ignoring the habit of regular reviewing has ensured their failure to systematically develop their managing habits. Their business performance has then become vulnerable.

  - ▪ **Regular reviewing enables ordered, proactive changes, and the opportunity to develop awareness**.

    Disciplined reviewing has yielded two practical benefits :
    - It helps to minimise mistakes and build on whatever successes you have
    - It enables you to alter direction in an ordered, considered fashion

    More fundamentally it grows the habit of improving awareness and helps progress towards a key attribute of the most effective managers. That is the capacity to remain in continuous review. Very few achieve it. It is the ability to sustain acute awareness in the midst of focused activity, and thence take account of what is happening around him. It is that combination of intense focus and wide ranging, acute awareness that distinguishes the very best. It is very evident at the highest levels of any complex sport. It was plainly obvious in my previous obsession with the sport of fencing. Most competent fencers can sustain intense focus. Only the best learn to combine it with acute wide angle awareness. So it is with managing.

- <u>Translate the principles into others' language and procedures</u>

  - **Translation is cooperation.**
    Jargon/imposing your chosen way of doing things is manipulative exclusion.

    Managing effectively is about nurturing the same picture in another's mind that exists in yours. Only then can another's commitment to the matter in hand have a chance to grow. Necessarily, therefore, you are best to translate the principles you have chosen for the work into the language and terms used by others. In the extreme, this language and their terms may be inconsistent with yours. That does not matter at all. It only matters that you try your utmost to join them on their territory. It has always proved a vital step to earning their commitment.

    The convention of inventing jargon and 'particular ways of doing things' that are then imposed on people is entirely counterproductive. There are many well respected vested interests that encourage such behaviour. However, at the superficial level, it is deeply discourteous and disrespectful of the worth of others' work experience. At the deeper level, it can speak of a way of excluding people, and attempting to manipulate how things are done without their understanding. It has laid the basis in others of cynical conformity and the total absence of their genuine commitment.

    Having said this, I am a technologist and I understand the appropriateness for commonly agreed technical jargon as a shorthand way of referring to complex technical issues. That legitimate process is founded on the joint universal understanding and acceptance of the terms concerned. In contrast, the above use of jargon and fixed procedures on management matters is not similarly motivated or justified.

  - **It improves real understanding and grows skill in applying the principles.**

    The capacity to use others' language and terms to accurately describe using a principle that is new to them, usefully tests whether you deeply understand the core of what you are suggesting. I have often been alerted to the uncomfortable reality that I don't understand deeply enough what I'm suggesting, because I can't find a way of accurately describing it in another's terms. I have had to go back, rethink, and improve my own understanding before trying again.

    When you can easily translate a principle into another's thinking, you have one key indication that you understand it deeply enough to apply it more effectively yourself. Accurately translating a principle into another's terms is an important part of my own development. It is enlightened self interest.

○ **Connect any principle being used to the naturally occurring decision making steps.**

    ■ **All management principles are rooted in the decision making steps.**

Each of the principles is based on the application of some combination of the naturally occurring decision making steps. For example, reference back to the section on Understanding, Creating and Using Strategy (p. 144) will show that each manager has the opportunity to do two things. He can choose the information that he judges he should grapple with, and he can choose the aspirations he wants to pursue for that information. The principles in formulating strategy involve him in dealing with two decision making steps: the information and setting aspirations steps.

Consequently, before applying any principle, check that what you intend doing is in fact centred on some combination of the decision making steps. If it is, then you will automatically be pursuing a key feature of those steps i.e. being lead by the facts and business logic of the situation facing you. If it is not, the chances are very high that you will be pursuing 'belief', and/or 'cultural change' for their own sake, or any of the multitude of other '-isms' that the market place clamours to sell to you. Whilst you may choose to do that, you will not be pursuing this development work.

    ■ **It helps to ensure all work is common sense based, and thence effective.**

The experience is that these principles are inconsistent with most of conventional management practice, and have produced what are regarded as radical solutions. They only appear radical because our management norms prioritise the status quo/convention and not common sense. The accurate application of the principles will therefore inexorably lead you to do what others regard as radical. It is then even more important that what you do is indeed common sense based. That is your guarantee of its commercial effectiveness. You can afford to stand accused of being radical only if your key defence is that the work has brought sustainable success to the business.

○ **Tackle each management challenge 'in the round'.**

    Each challenge offers a number of issues to work at.

It is extremely rare to come across a management challenge that has just one issue and one principle at its core. The vast majority of challenges have proved to have a number of such issues and principles that need to be accurately understood. They need to be tackled fundamentally to resolve the matter in hand. It is therefore prudent to carefully check the information about the challenge to ensure it is being looked at 'in the round', and that all the related issues are in focus.

o **<u>Continuously check that you are forming an increasingly interconnected and interdependent picture of the principles.</u>**

Work challenges inevitably present different issues that intertwine and interdepend. Uncovering that reality also discloses that the principles needed to tackle them interact in the same fashion. As a result self contained compartments of 'motivation', 'leadership', 'teamwork', 'strategy', 'time management', 'decision making', etc. simply do not exist within the problems that confront line managers. Solutions built on that misconception have proved both superficial and unsustainable. Check that as you explore the combination of principles that best apply to a particular challenge, you are learning something new/different about this aspect. You are learning more about how each and every one of those principles interdepends and interacts with the others.

They are in fact one entity within which each component principle is indivisibly bound up with all the rest.

The interconnections are many and varied, and careful scrutiny of their visible effects will gradually start to disclose them. As you start to accumulate a growing grasp of these numerous interconnections, your appreciation of the actual scope of a particular challenge will deepen. Your analysis as to what to appropriately tackle will quicken, and improve in its accuracy and relevance.

o **<u>Check that the journey continues to reveal new things, and challenges your existing 'current understanding'.</u>**

Developing better levels of skill at applying the principles is a continuous process.

The sporting analogy is accurate. Once a fencer's exploratory practice stops and he feels he has nothing more to learn and no further level of skill to develop, then he has already lost to the next challenging opponent. He will continue losing, and his standards will deteriorate until he reverses his view of matters. Standards of skill have never stood still – they have either improved with practice or deteriorated with complacency. He needs to return to being open minded, curious about how better to perform, avid to explore what no one else has tried, determined to continuously practice, and thence sustain a 'sharp edge' in the mind. So it is with this work.

This is the development of skills in the most complex interactive activity in our societies, involving a bewildering range of factors, all of which can vary at a moment's notice. It is a challenge worthy of sustained effort, and it is arrogance for me to believe that my level of current skill cannot and need not be improved. Such arrogance opens the door to my failure at the next difficult challenge. Reversing my view of matters to regain an open mind best secures the possibility of success at the next difficult hurdle.

SECTION TWO

PROVEN WAYS OF USING THIS WORK TO DEVELOP THE ORGANISATION AS A WHOLE

SUMMARY

The organisation's performance as a total unit can be systematically developed.

Initiatives to improve its three basic factors – its structure, procedures, and man management – can be deliberately coordinated to ensure its progress through them is secure and sustainable. This has supported individual line managers in their efforts to develop their performance and that of their teams.

The underlying progress of the organisation through these three factors has had to be linear, and in the above order. This implies that over the medium and long term the organisation has focused largely on structural matters, then procedural concerns, then man management issues. However, at any one time, conscious judgements were taken to recycle between these three factors. These have taken account of the commercial priorities at the time and the stage in development the organisation had reached. This has ensured successful overall linear progress over the longer time frame.

Unavoidably, precisely the same principle of systematic development applies to every group within the organisation. Every leader will want to have a factual view of where his group(s) have reached in their development of their structural, procedural and man management issues. He can then take his considered judgement as to his next developmental improvement. The result is that the overall enterprise has a high degree of consistency in how its various groups develop. It also affords managers at every level in the outfit the chance to practise the challenging skills of operating this principle.

The core skill that this principle critically relies on is the ability to observe what is happening across a broad range of activities in factual detail.

Without that ability, it is impossible to form an informed judgement as to where progress in the three basic organisation factors has reached. The only option then becomes the standard game of chance, guesswork, and politics. The paucity of observation has proved to be one of the key contributors to generating management via politics. The link is not immediately obvious. It has, however, proved inexorable.

The CEO and senior team will therefore want to encourage the development of that skill throughout the outfit.

BACKGROUND CONTEXT

The question is:

'Is there a way of systematically developing the operation of the organisation as a whole?'

Inevitably, the previous guidelines capturing what individuals can do to nurture their own development interact and interdepend closely with the answers to this question. The two are not separated concerns. The answers to one intertwine with and closely affect the answers to the other.

However, the focus of this question is somewhat different. On the largest scale, the CEO has to be clear as to the pattern of developmental steps he is leading the organisation through as a unit. He has to be certain that:

- there is a fundamental logic to that pattern that will deliver the commercial results he is looking for

- his decisions on this issue guide and support the efforts his men pursue to develop their own performances and those of their teams – as described in Section One

- his skill at penetrating to the appropriate sequence of developmental steps and implementing them is a key example that all other levels can be inspired to follow within the same judgements they have to make in their teams.

This ensures that the entire organisation is cohesive in how it develops.

PRINCIPLE

- **The organisational factors – Structure, Procedures, and Man Management – are areas that can be systematically developed**

- **The underlying pattern of development is linear: Structural development, then Procedural, then Man Management**

- **The day-to-day handling of these three factors recycles between them, and makes choices to take account of**

  - **the commercial priorities**

  - **stage of development people are at**

- **Detailed, factual observation is the key skill that guides the judgements needed for such choices**

EXPLANATION

Exploring each of the four elements in turn:

- **The organisational factors – Structure, Procedures, and Man Management – are areas that can be systematically developed.**

  The organisation's performance in these three fundamental factors has ultimately controlled whether it achieves its business aspirations.

  The experience has been that all the enterprise's operational needs are catered for by work in these three factors. The extensive and complex challenges successfully resolved in the various organisations (detailed in Chapter Two) are some of the business illustrations of that reality.

  A key to those successes has been to consciously pursue overall plans that continuously took account of all three factors.

- **The underlying pattern of development is linear: structural development, then procedural, then man management.**

  The unyielding overall logic imposed by operating any business has been:

  - first decide who is accountable for what (i.e. STRUCTURAL)

  - then decide how to do the regular activities (i.e. PROCEDURES)

  - then agree how ongoing decisions will be made (i.e. MAN MANAGEMENT)

Unfortunately, the common practice is to respond directly to a perceived difficulty in the organisation: e.g. 'poor teamwork' is a typical problem in the Man Management area that has often been singled out. The temptation has then been to knee jerk a response to spend investment/effort to correct that problem.

A diligent analysis of the organisation's performance in its three fundamental factors – structure, procedures, and man management – will show if an appropriate basis exists to work directly on such matters as teamwork. The experience of this work sadly says that such an analysis is extremely rare. Too often it has emerged too late in the day that 'poor teamwork' was merely a symptom. Instead, the organisation had a root difficulty that was typically in one or more of the other two fundamental factors: structure and or procedures. In the case of one organisation their difficulty in teamwork was largely caused by unresolved difficulties in the issue of accountability: a structural matter. Resolving this issue first, created a sound basis on which to improve teamwork. I have witnessed such a realisation never dawning on the senior managers of an organisation. The result was the robotic procedure of sheep dipping hundreds of managers through management team training. It merely became a rite of passage, and the vast majority of 'treated' line managers resignedly recognised that it had no rigorous commercial return.

The key is to have an overall view at all times as to where the organisation 'is' in its development of those three fundamental factors. It is then possible to form a considered judgement as to which initiatives can produce sustainable results.

- **The day-to-day handling of these three factors recycles between them, and makes choices to take account of**

    o **the commercial priorities**

    o **the stage of development people are at**

Having said that the underlying pattern of progress through the three basic factors is linear, that is not usually what appears on the ground at any moment in time. Would that reality's needs were so simple. The above two pressures of priorities and developmental status have often dictated that a manager cycle between the relevant factors to produce the results he is looking for. Taking appropriate judgements about those recycles has also enabled him to secure the longer term linear progress through those factors.

For instance, he has on occasions judged that to improve his team's procedural efficiency, they needed first to improve their skill at creating statements of aspiration, which all effective procedures need. Only when his team had reached the appropriate standard in the man management area of stating 'aspirations' did he return them to focus on 'procedures'. He then knew that they could create appropriate aspirations for those procedures, and thence improve their reproducibility. He has therefore cycled appropriately between the 'procedures' and 'man management' areas to achieve the business results he was seeking.

The CEO's job is to constantly repeat the same skill and process on the larger scale of the entire enterprise.

- **Detailed, factual observation is the key skill that guides the judgements needed for those choices.**

Choosing patterns and sequences for appropriate initiatives to develop the whole organisation has always proved a challenging decision. It is probably the most intangible and opaque task that faces senior managers. Fortunately it faces managers at all levels and the opportunity exists to practise it and gain experience in its difficulties and effects. The business rewards for developing skill at making appropriate judgements have been considerable. Knee jerk ones, or those driven by politics, have led to poor commercial results and confused cynicism.

The manager's skill of factually observing where his team is in their development within the three fundamental factors has been the key to his success in this challenge. Without the capacity to observe in detail how his team performs in the everyday heat and toil of the business, he cannot come to an informed decision on this matter. He cannot factually choose a pattern of work at the three basic factors which takes account of exactly where his team have reached in their progress to date. He will be obliged to play a game of blind man's bluff as to what initiatives he takes and what pattern he takes them in. A diligent pursuit of his skill of observation opens the door to conscious judgements and the chance to deliberately improve performance.

CONCLUSION

- **THIS IS THE MEMORY OF AN INCOMPLETE BUT VIVID JOURNEY.**

- **MY CURRENT UNDERSTANDING IS UNDOUBTEDLY INCOMPLETE, AND NEEDS FURTHER WORK.**

- **IT IS ALL I HAVE TO OFFER TO ENCOURAGE YOU ON YOUR OWN JOURNEY.**

I am certain that I have yet to discover more effective and more skilful ways of applying the principles described above. I am equally certain that many further principles that are new to me await to be understood.

My journey so far and my attempts to learn from it have only taken me this small, but exciting, distance forwards. I offer it with all its short comings, in the hope that it may inspire others to pursue their own journeys and form their own continuously changing 'current understandings'.

The more of us who set out on the journey the better, and the more competent our work places will be. My suspicion is that we are also better people for stepping out on that path. We can then contribute more effectively to the quality of the lives of people who work with us.

I WISH YOU AN ADVENTUROUS JOURNEY.

I WISH YOU PERSONAL DEVELOPMENTS THAT ARE PROFOUND AND DEEPLY REWARDING.

I WISH YOU EVERY CONSEQUENT SUCCESS ON YOUR JOURNEY.

FRANK GOH

2015.

www.businessdevelopmentmanual.com

APPENDIX ONE

ADDITIONAL INFORMATION ON BUSINESS CHALLENGE FOUR, CHAPTER TWO

TWO ADDITIONAL EXAMPLES OF STRUCTURAL DEVELOPMENTS

1. DETAILED ACCOUNTABILITIES

● **Accountability became an individual responsibility**

The business unit structure described above accurately clarified the accountabilities of the Business Unit Heads, business unit team members, and the Functional Heads. Each business decision became the sole responsibility of one person. Each technical/operational issue within those business decisions became the sole accountability of one person. There was never any suggestion of seeking decisions by consensus. The above recall of the essential differences that characterise the business unit structure obviously infers the key accountabilities at each level. However, it is worth focusing them in full at this point:

o A Business Unit Head was solely accountable for all decisions within his business.

As previously mentioned, the Business Unit Head had total responsibility for the operational and financial implications of decisions within his unit. Most of those decisions inevitably involved a number of inter related technical/operational issues. The priorities between these issues, and the nature of how they should interact, were naturally decisions that the Business Unit Head saw as his personal duty to make.

o Business unit members were solely accountable for their decisions on relevant constituent technical/operational issues.

Individual team members saw it as their sole responsibility to offer decisions about their area of expertise. It was entirely their obligation to ensure that those decisions had the support of the relevant Functional Head. They would equally see it as their responsibility to appropriately input their decisions into the total business decision(s) their Business Unit Head was dealing with.

o Functional Heads were solely accountable for their decisions on technical standards, and technical strategy.

Each Functional Head was individually responsible for their choice of the standards to which all the business units would operate their particular expertise. Similarly, he had sole accountability for creating and delivering all the strategies that the total organisation would pursue in their expertise area.

This network of individual accountabilities catered for all decisions and clarified exactly who was responsible for which decisions. It also made clear who was dealing with constituent parts of those decisions, and indeed any associated ones. This clarity had a major impact on the speed of decision taking. It simultaneously affected people's levels of commitment and ownership for what happened in the business.

The essence of the above habits for responsibility was that every decision and every relevant constituent part of a decision was the accountability of just one person. The principle was: 'One decision, one man'. The aspiration at all times was pin point accurate accountability. At no level in the organisation, and on no decision, was any sort of consensus ever sought throughout the history of the enterprise.

- **Accurate teamwork needed to support individual accountability**

It became important for managers to understand how they needed to use teamwork to support individual accountability. Indeed, they had to be convinced that the significant benefits that came from such sharp accountability could not be achieved without that teamwork. The two issues are different sides of the same coin.

All the processes that lead up to a decision being taken by an individual manager or team member involved a number of functional experts. Their effective teamwork became a key ingredient in laying the basis for high quality decisions to be subsequently taken by the appropriate person. This has led to firm commitment amongst those affected by the decision, particularly if pressures have later risen as a result of that decision. This is an unconventional view of both accountability and teamwork. It has nonetheless proved highly effective and perhaps needs to be illustrated here by a specific example.

EXAMPLE   **DECIDING THE MARKETING BUDGET WITHIN A BUSINESS UNIT**

This is a highly interactive decision, and illustrates the above principles in action.

The business unit team member accountable for marketing had done some initial preparatory work in mapping out the major aspirations, information and activities that he foresaw for the period ahead.

He circulated this work to members of his Business Unit – all of whom would automatically be affected – and worked through a number of sessions with them to finalise their joint thinking.

His budget therefore contained all the effects from the latest thinking on every aspect of product development, manufacturing, distribution, technical support, etc. This simultaneously enabled his colleagues to understand and be fully committed to the direction that would be taken in their market place. They would also grasp the parts of the budget that called for critical action from their own expertise areas.

Only effective teamwork within this group would give a meeting of minds over these key operational and business issues.

He then presented the finalised budget to his Business Unit Head as a decision he would be individually accountable for.

The Business Unit Head checked most carefully through the details of the work. He knew that to include this budget within his total budget for the business meant that he would have to be totally confident of two factors. He first needed to be assured of the quality of his marketer's thinking. He secondly needed to be convinced of the quality of the teamwork from the rest of the business unit members in their support of the processes that led to his marketer's proposal.

The combination of individual accountability for every decision, integrated with close teamwork by all the people who interacted with that decision, had a fundamental effect on how the business was run. The quality, speed, and cohesiveness of decisions were markedly affected.

2. THE ORGANISATION REGAINS CONTROL OF ITS ENGINEERING MAINTENANCE FUNCTION.

● **The business's writ did not run within the Engineering Maintenance function.**

The Maintenance activity was heavily unionised. Manning levels bore no relation to the work undertaken. All trades had to be physically accompanied on all work by non functional 'mates' who were handsomely paid – for doing nothing. Overtime was out of control. The men organised their work so that it maximised the times they were 'called in' on overtime to complete it. All communications went through the union structures, and hence happened at the pace controlled by the shop stewards. It bore no relation to the needs of the business. Any attempt to discuss change was met with firm responses of having an all-out strike, which would include the production operatives and hence totally close down all operations. This 'mantra' was endlessly repeated by the previous management teams as their rationale for not tackling the situation. The expense benefits on matters such as travel and phone charges were totally out of control and ran at levels which were hard to comprehend. They were fiercely defended as central job benefits.

The quality and speed of the actual maintenance work completed left a lot to be desired, and thence generated its full share of overtime for the maintenance crews. Restrictive practices and lack of flexibility were very much the order of the day, and were honed to the level of an art form.

No part of this operation was run for the benefit of the business or the organisation. It was like an island state whose borders were fiercely defended, and where a totally different writ ran that indulged and protected the whims of those within it.

- **The maintenance operation was reclaimed by installing managed teams working in partnerships with the organisation.**

  A clear strategy was followed to retrieve this situation:

  - <u>Managed teams were set up.</u>

  Strengths amongst the maintenance crews were identified who had the appetite to lead their own teams to complete quality work to ambitious standards. Like any managed team within the new organisation they would be closely supported and monitored.

  - <u>Accountability with reward was built into a partnership with the organisation.</u>

  A long term and mutually supportive partnership was agreed between the leaders of those teams and their supervising managers. Those leaders were rewarded with a regular lump sum payment for supplying the required service to a given area. They chose men from a stable team of men approved of by the organisation, to provide that service. How they divided that lump sum reward depended on the manning levels they operated. The organisation ensured that the potential rewards could significantly exceed what they currently earned. This assumed that they started with a 'clean sheet' of work practices, ignored all previous restrictive practices and maximised flexibility at all times.

  - <u>Discussions were led by the management line on a one-to-one basis.</u>

  The above proposal was discussed in detail with the selected strengths, and any reservations they had about their involvement diligently taken account of and worked through till they were happy to be committed to trying it out. Only when these dialogues were complete were those who were regarded as 'marginal' and 'weaknesses' also talked with on a one-to-one basis.

  - <u>Union meetings happened after management line discussions were completed.</u>

  When all one-to-one dialogues had concluded between the managers involved and their men, the management team knew:

  - exactly who would operate the new scheme, how they would be rewarded, and that they were fully committed to the new operation

  - exactly who would not be involved in the new scheme, what their agreed route out of the organisation was, and the costs involved

  Only at this point was there a meeting called with union officials. The management team then shared information as to what was going to happen.

The effects

- A trouble free start, with old restrictive practices instantly and permanently discarded.
  The new maintenance operation commenced smoothly with no industrial action.

- The quality and speed of work instantly made a step change up to levels that were better than industry best.
  There were no 'repeat repairs', no 'emergency call outs', no use of 'mates', no weekend working, and the necessity for overtime type work disappeared overnight. It now simply did not pay to do any of these conventional, non business focused practices. Instead, work was completed once, to appropriate standards, by the minimum men, working within normal business hours.

- New business focused practices automatically emerged.
  Flexibility instantly became the norm. It now simply didn't pay to have any demarcation. The men and their leaders realised that their take home portion of the lump sum would be severely affected by any lack of flexibility or any artificially restrictive work practices.

- Security now came from delivering results that benefited the business and consequently secured the payment for the service provided. It did not come from defending the boundaries of a particular 'patch'. Men automatically saw it as in their interests to communicate closely with their colleagues in the manufacturing area to optimise the way work was scheduled and organised. Such sensible cooperation was unheard of even as a possibility within either the old structure or during any of the previous negotiations.

- Rewards, costs, self respect, and control significantly changed.
  The level of rewards that the men achieved for themselves comfortably exceeded their previous situation. Much more importantly, they confirmed their earlier estimation that the basis for this achievement would remain within their control. They were confident of their ability to sustain a sharp grasp of running a high quality, tightly manned, highly flexible, minimum expense operation.

The resultant effect on lowering the cost of the maintenance operation and simultaneously improving its quality was one of the most dramatic changes achieved in the first phase of the company's turnaround.

Most important of all to the organisation was the new found self respect of the leaders and their teams. They knew they provided a high quality, value for money service that simultaneously rewarded them well for their diligence. Job security now lay in the real mutual benefits they generated for themselves and the business. They also knew that no union based arrangement could hope to match the rewards they equitably earned.

www.ingramcontent.com/pod-product-compliance
Lightning Source LLC
Chambersburg PA
CBHW051342200326
41521CB00015B/2585